Carlos Slim

Carlos Slim

*The Power, Money, and
Morality of One of the
World's Richest Men*

Diego Enrique Osorno

VERSO
London • New York

This English-language edition published by Verso 2019
Originally published in Spanish as *Slim: Retrato del hombre más rico del mundo*
© Diego Osorno 2016, 2019
Translation © Juana Adcock 2019
Foreword © Jon Lee Anderson 2019

1 3 5 7 9 10 8 6 4 2

Verso
UK: 6 Meard Street, London W1F 0EG
US: 20 Jay Street, Suite 1010, Brooklyn, NY 11201
versobooks.com

Verso is the imprint of New Left Books

ISBN-13: 978-1-78663-437-5
ISBN-13: 978-1-78663-435-1 (UK EBK)
ISBN-13: 978-1-78663-436-8 (US EBK)

British Library Cataloguing in Publication Data
A catalogue record for this book is available from the British Library

Library of Congress Cataloging-in-Publication Data
Names: Osorno, Diego Enrique, 1980- author.
Title: Carlos Slim : The Power, Money, and Morality of One of the World's
Richest Men / Diego Enrique Osorno ;
  translated by Juana Adcock.
Other titles: Slim. English
Description: Brooklyn, NY : Verso, [2019] | "Originally published in Spanish
  as Slim: Retrato del hombre mas rico del mundo."
Identifiers: LCCN 2019017201 | ISBN 9781786634375 (hardback : alk. paper) |
  ISBN 9781786634368 (US ebk)
Subjects: LCSH: Slim, Carlos, 1940- | Telefonos de Mexico—History. |
  Businessmen—Mexico—Biography.
Classification: LCC HC132.5.S55 O85313 2019 | DDC 384.6092 [B] –dc23
LC record available at https://lccn.loc.gov/2019017201

Typeset in Sabon by MJ & N Gavan, Truro, Cornwall
Printed and bound by CPI Group (UK) Ltd, Croydon CR0 4YY

To Daniel Gershenson, Cuauhtémoc Ruiz and Andrés Ramírez

In memory of Conrado Osorno

All power is a permanent conspiracy.
Balzac

Contents

CONTENTS

Foreword

Since the beginning of his reporting career, Diego Enrique Osorno has dedicated himself to some of Mexico's thorniest issues, covering everything from the Zapatista insurgency and narcotrafficking to the migrant traumas along the northern border with the United States. For the past fifteen years, his books, articles and documentaries have positioned him at the forefront of his generation and earned him wide public recognition and the respect of his peers. That's because Diego always delves deeply into the issues he tackles, and he reports them firsthand. He is brave. If you are a Mexican journalist, it's dangerous to write about drug cartels and police corruption, and Diego's investigations into the Sinaloa and Los Zetas cartels, among other stories, are evidence of his determination to push the boundaries.

Diego Enrique Osorno was born in the northern Mexican city of Monterrey in 1980. When I first met him, more than a dozen years ago, he was still in his mid-twenties, and had just come out of a dramatic experience in Oaxaca, in southern Mexico, where months of protests by teachers had turned bloody as the authorities had responded with a brutal crackdown. Diego said that he felt as if he had been living in a war zone, and when he told me what he had lived through and witnessed, I agreed with him. More than twenty activists had been killed during the time he was there; others had been detained, tortured and some of them forcibly disappeared. Diego had also been an eyewitness to the shooting deaths of several men, including a Mexican mechanic named José Jiménez

Colmenares and an American cameraman named Brad Will, and he had been left shaken and indignant from the experience.

What came next was a profound learning experience for Diego. As he followed up on the abuses he had discovered in Oaxaca, seeking justice, Diego did not find it. Instead, as is so often the case for those seeking redress for political crimes in Mexico, he encountered official obfuscation and impunity. Diego did not let go, however, but dug in deeper and eventually wrote his first book, *Oaxaca Besieged*, about the episode. Over the years since then, Diego has reported on a wide range of other issues, with the topic of injustice foremost in his concerns. In one of his most wrenching inquiries into a case of impunity, Diego probed the suspicious lack of official intervention during a horrific month-long massacre carried out in 2011 by Los Zetas *sicarios* in the town of Allende in the state of Coahuila, just across the border with Texas, that had killed over three hundred people.

———

Diego Enrique Osorno is a *norteño* of a casual and friendly appearance. Tall, bearded, usually clad in jeans, cowboy boots and checked shirts, the only thing missing to complete his wrangler look is a Stetson, and maybe a pistol.

A couple of years ago, during a visit I made to Monterrey, Diego showed me around. The way a Parisian might show off the Moulin Rouge and the Eiffel Tower, Diego showed me how his hometown had become a city governed by criminals. One day, he introduced me to a local soldier for Los Zetas, who spent three hours explaining the ins and outs of his organization. He told us how and why Los Zetas killed certain people and how, in their terrifying "kitchens," they disposed of the bodies by dismembering them and incinerating them with diesel fuel in oil drums. At the time, his organization was the dominant power in much of northern Mexico, and by talking to this man it became apparent that, to him, the bosses of Los Zetas and those of rival cartels were authorities of equal importance as any state governor, police commander, or army general. Intriguingly, he made no moral distinctions between such figures. Instead, he spoke of them as sharing something in common. That something, to him, was power, pure and simple, and it was clear that from his perspective, power was a force that needed neither definition nor justification, but existed in a realm all its own, far beyond equations of good or evil.

The power dynamic between Mexico's citizens and those who exercise control over their destinies—whether Los Zetas killers or elected officials—has become a matter of increasing importance to Diego in his ongoing quest to unravel, and to expose, some of the chronic injustices of his homeland. If Los Zetas understood power as an absolute, a *thing* that transcended moral considerations, it was also true that most Mexicans could point to one man, and one man alone, as their country's king of kings. That man was not the Mexican president, who holds the office for a single six-year term, called a *sexenio*, but Carlos Slim. Impelled by what he has called "a sense of indignation" at the fact that the world's richest man could have accumulated his fortune in a nation where fifty two million citizens lived in dire poverty, Diego proposed to write a political biography of the Mexican magnate. (On the lists of the world's wealthiest people, Slim was number one when Diego began his research a decade ago; over the years since, others have replaced him. As of early 2019, Jeff Bezos was the world's richest man, and Slim was the fifth, with an estimated worth of sixty-four billion dollars.)

In this book, which was originally published in Spanish in 2015, Diego examines this modern-day *pasha*, a symbol at once of twenty-first-century capitalism and of Mexico, a giant among Lilliputians in a country with a long tradition of *caciques*, or strongmen. The surreal dimensions of Slim's economic power lead Diego to openly ask—indeed, it is the guiding question of this book—whether a man as rich as Slim can also be a good person. In *Carlos Slim*, Diego, sets out to find the answer to this question.

What Diego proposes, of course, is a major challenge. As someone who has also written portraits of powerful men, including of the late Chilean dictator Augusto Pinochet and the former King Juan Carlos of Spain, I know that one of the most essential steps in the process is to establish an intuitive understanding of the characters, as well as to gain access to information that sheds new light on their lives. It is always a very difficult thing to approach powerful figures, who tend to avoid journalists and who often retain advisors whose very purpose is to either keep such people at bay or else to ensure that their bosses are portrayed in a positive light.

In a testament to his journalistic mettle, as well as his amiable personality, Diego managed to circumvent the roadblocks around Slim, and to secure several meetings with him. In their meetings, Diego was able to ask him some of the questions he had been seeking answers for, and to converse on a range of different topics. Coming on top of his research that had taken place over several years, including archival documentation and numerous interviews with Slim's friends and foes, his encounters with the man have given his book a human touch and helped make it an invaluable contribution to modern history. In a memorable meeting they had in Slim's personal library, for instance, Slim reveals himself to be an avid and eclectic reader, of everything from poetry by Khalil Gibran to the diaries of Ernesto "Che" Guevara in Bolivia— although books about wealth, business and power dominated. As they walked around, inspecting his books, Slim confessed to Diego that business titans like Baruch, Rockefeller and Getty had been role models. He showed him a good sense of humor, telling Diego he was willing to answer *all* his questions, and the only thing he asked in return was that he not put "too many lies" in his book. He also gave him his copy of Malcolm Gladwell's *Outliers*, and told him to take it, that he simply *had* to read it.

The library scene is just a teaser. There is, of course, much more to *Carlos Slim*. Diego set out to tell the life story of one of the world's greatest capitalists at a time of great inequality in their shared birthplace of Mexico, and he has certainly done that and more in this highly original, fascinating account of the life of Carlos Slim.

Jon Lee Anderson

Preface

The biography of Carlos Slim, one of the richest people of all time, is not just the tale of the first man from a developing country to ever reach the top of the *Forbes* list of billionaires. It's also the story of a businessman who, at crucial moments, supported the PRI—the Institutional Revolutionary Party that governed Mexico for seventy-two uninterrupted years, until 2000—and capitalized on the country's mass privatization of national services and banks, promoted since the 1980s by the United States and other world powers through the Washington Consensus, which consolidated neoliberalism in Latin America.

Slim has been immersed in the world of business since early childhood, thanks to his father, Julián Slim Haddad, a Lebanese émigré who made his fortune as a merchant in Mexico and whose political ideas were aligned with those of Al Kataeb—the Lebanese Phalange Party, an organization created by the Gemayel family, taking inspiration from Primo de Rivera, founder of the fascist Spanish Phalanx.

After studying civil engineering at the National Autonomous University of Mexico (UNAM)—and standing as a personable student who, as well as being a math lecturer and catcher on the college baseball team, championed the use of the then-cutting-edge electronic calculator—Slim married Soumaya Domit Gemayel. She was a niece of Bachir Gemayel, the Lebanese president who ordered the Sabra and Shatila massacres, in which the Phalangists killed over 2,000 people, many of them Palestinian refugees from the war with Israel. The priest who celebrated their wedding was Marcial Maciel, founder of the Legion of Christ, a conservative Catholic order whose scandals surrounding child abuse and corruption led the Vatican to intervene. On his wedding day, Slim was accompanied to the altar by his mother, Linda, and his elder brother, Julián, an active commander of the Federal Security Directorate (DFS), the political police of the PRI regime, which, in the context of the Cold War, killed, tortured and forcibly disappeared those in opposition.

After the wedding, Slim combined letters from his own and his wife's name to found Carso, the group whose operations have resulted in a net worth of over $80 billion, which has on occasion surpassed the fortunes of Bill Gates, Warren Buffet, Amancio Ortega, George Soros, Mark Zuckerberg and other famous billionaires. His wife Soumaya did not live to see the family empire consolidated at a global level, as she died of chronic kidney disease in 1999. Two years earlier, Slim had also been at death's door after he underwent heart surgery in Houston, Texas—an event that caused his companies' shares to plummet in the New York Stock Exchange and elicited rumors of his possible retirement from the world of business.

But by 2015, Slim had recovered from these difficulties—and from some of his most controversial relationships. He is no longer suspected of being a front man for ex-president Carlos Salinas de Gortari, currently considered one of his adversaries in Mexico, along with Televisa, the most important Spanish-speaking television network in the world. Now, Slim's name is associated more closely with those of other former presidents around the world, such as the democrat Bill Clinton, the socialist Felipe González and even Fidel Castro. During Mexico's electoral crisis in 2006, according to associates of ex-president Felipe Calderón, Slim quietly intervened to support left-wing presidential candidate Andrés Manuel López Obrador in his mission to annul the questioned elections.

In terms of philanthropy, Slim says he does not like playing Santa Claus, and although he has donated money to altruistic causes through his foundations, his efforts may appear pretty miserly compared to other members of the global ultrarich elite. Instead, his presence as a benefactor has focused on strategically exerting power in politics and further afield.

Drawing from interviews with his friends and enemies, as well as extensive research into historical and confidential archives obtained from intelligence agencies, and from Slim's own testimony through a series of interviews conceded especially for this book, this biography builds a profile of the richest Mexican in the world, going beyond the cold, hard numbers and clichéd business success stories. With the advantages and disadvantages this entails, he is seen from the distance of a journalistic catwalk, such as the one in Washington, DC, in 2010, where a Getty agency photograph shows Slim striding across a hall, dressed in a tuxedo and wearing the lanyard of a White House special guest, with a painting of ex-president Grover Cleveland in the background.

This book is not financial reportage or an economic view on his empire; rather, it is a portrait of Slim's social influence and the way in which he builds political relationships, and how his actions or omissions affect public life in Mexico and the eighteen countries of Latin America where he has investments. At the same time, I hope it is a journey through key moments in Mexican history, such as the years after the Revolution, the Tlatelolco student massacre in '68, the dirty war, the financial crises of the '80s, the wave of privatization under Salinas, the government turnover of the year 2000, the post-electoral conflict of 2006, the so-called War on Drugs and the return of the PRI to power with the government of Enrique Peña Nieto.

Journalism in Latin America tends to come from the top and address those at the bottom. It represents a way in which power tells its truth to the people, not necessarily one in which the people tell the truth to power. In 2007, when I first started to do journalistic research on Slim, the idea was to provide a portrait of my country from a different angle. At the time I had just covered the teachers' uprising in Oaxaca, one of Mexico's poorest states, and the stories I wrote about elsewhere in the country were always linked to marginalized communities. How, then, to report on power? What would I find if I started to look into the richest man in the world with the same passion with which I followed a popular uprising or visited a hunger-stricken community? What would that point of view reveal about Mexico?

When I started writing this book, my political mindset was very agitated. In addition to the Oaxacan revolt, where I witnessed the extrajudicial execution of several protesters, I had been involved in the Other Campaign, launched by the Zapatista Army of National Liberation (EZLN), the initiative led by Subcomandante Marcos under the guidelines of an anticapitalist manifesto known as the Sixth Declaration of the Lacandon Jungle, which I signed as an adherent. But writing a book like this one with that particular political mindset would prove impossible. As a journalist, I needed other traits, which I had to learn over the years the way we learn the most important things in life: by doing them. Aiming to improve the way in which we view the lives of the powerful and famous within their own environments, I followed and wrote extensive profiles on Mexican actor Gabriel García Bernal, Puerto Rican reggaeton duo Calle 13, Cuban blogger Yoani Sánchez and writer Juan Villoro. In addition, I codirected a documentary about Mauricio Fernández Garza, one of the most extravagant businessmen in Mexico, and another entitled *El poder de la silla* (*The Power of the Saddle*), about the ex-governor of the northern state of Nuevo León. Although these figures differ greatly from Slim, each one of these portraits trained me to develop the patience required for Slim's project, and to look deeply into the contradictions that we all tend to live by.

In 2008, a year after *Forbes*' announcement that a Mexican had topped their list of the ultrarich, I learned that Slim's brother, Julián, had been subdirector of the Federal Security Directorate during its most infamous era, and that he had been a PGR (Office of the Attorney General) commander during the 1980s. For several weeks I thought Slim's brother was an apocryphal character, that his life represented an unfortunate coincidence for the owner of Telmex. However, as I researched more I confirmed that the brothers were extremely close, as I detail in one of the chapters of this book. This was the first surprising fact that I encountered in my research, and in a way it was what stoked my interest in exploring the figure of Carlos Slim. It was not easy to officially prove the trajectory of Julián Slim as first commander of the PGR. His former colleagues were reluctant to talk about him due to his brother's notoriety. I had to turn to the Federal Institute for Access to Public Information and make several appeals against the federal authorities who refused to provide me with their files, but in the end I succeeded. Someone who also helped me fundamentally in this kind of work was María de los Ángeles Magdaleno C., who carried out historical research in different sections of the National Archives, the historical archive of Mexico City, and the archives at El Colegio Nacional and the national newspaper archive.

Although my main project for eight years was to research and write about Slim, I was committed to many other stories: that's why I also researched and wrote about the fire that killed forty-nine children in a nursery in Sonora and the intricate web of corruption behind it; about the political manipulation behind the War on Drugs launched by president Calderón; and about the social collapse caused by the drug cartel Los Zetas in the northern states of Tamaulipas, Nuevo León and Coahuila.

Over the years I was working on this book, I was warned by many of my interviewees that it would not be easy to publish it, and that all the publishing houses would be fearful of the effect it might have on their commercial relationship with Sanborns, the biggest chain of bookshops in Mexico—owned, of course, by Slim himself. These kinds of comments did not shake my determination as much as other warnings around the book being potentially ignored by the media (owned, again, by Slim) or even the risk of being legally annihilated by his lawyers. One of the people who warned me of that possibility was the editor of one of Mexico's most influential magazines, which Slim sued through five different agencies of the public ministry simultaneously on the same morning, over a mild criticism. His case, as that of other activists and critics who have condemned Slim, never became public knowledge.

I traveled to New York, Beirut, Rio de Janeiro and several other cities to research Slim; I was near him during some of his public appearances and private functions, such as the inauguration party of Saks in Mexico. As the ribbon was being cut on the first Mexican branch of the New York store, I ended up standing two meters away from him, which later led some of the guests at the exclusive drinks reception to believe that I was someone close to the richest man in the world, and to treat me extremely kindly, though they soon turned the other way when they found out that, although I knew many things about Slim, at that time the man and I had never exchanged words.

With the aim of providing a view of Slim from several different angles, I formally interviewed over a hundred people, from mere associates to the magnate's most senior business friends or foes, such as Bernardo Gómez and Alfonso de Angoitia, two of the three executives who steer Televisa along with Emilio Azcárraga. In Mexico, the prevailing perception is that this company, the most important Spanish-speaking television broadcaster in the world, aggressively intervenes in public power by grossly manipulating information. Other important members of the political and economic class also gave interviews but have refused to be cited explicitly. That was not the case for Jacques Rogozinski, the official operator of the privatization of Telmex and other state-run companies, who gave me an extensive interview with permission to quote him.

Before having the first of three long conversations with the magnate, in which I heard his version of his story for this unofficial biography, I looked at many of the interviews that Slim had given in the past. Perhaps some of the most revealing ones were those with the American journalist Larry King, who became his business partner and who, some speculate, will author Slim's official biography, although the tycoon assured me he would write it himself. They have both been part of interesting conversations at business congresses in the United States. At the 2013 Milken Institute Global Conference, in a session available on YouTube, King introduces Slim this way:

About two and a half years ago, Carlos Slim has this big conference in Mexico City in which he gives out scholarships, and they called and asked me to be the keynote speaker. And I went down and they said I was limited to twenty minutes, which to me is like phoning it in. So they extended my time and we became friends, he came to my house, we had dinner, we did my show, and then finally we formed Ora TV which is now on the Internet, we're distributed by

Hulu, we started in July, we've done over 170 interviews already, increasing every week; so, he is my partner. He was poor, he needed help [smiling]. He is an incredible man.

Slim already has a short official biography published on his website. This book gleans some information from there, but crucially it adds political angles that have been scarcely explored. It also contradicts or contextualizes, based on testimonies and documents, other aspects of Slim's (auto)biographic narrative. As is necessary in the kind of journalism I value, there is never an intention to lynch him, nor is the aim to glorify him.

Other journalist colleagues have already written about Slim's life. The most extensive piece was by José Martínez, the generous author of a text added to this book, but my purpose was to create something that did not exist: a biography that also examined the influences and political relationships around the richest Mexican in the world. In this sense, this book is not financial reportage or an economic analysis of his empire, but a portrait of Slim's social influence, as well as his political relationships, and his actions or omissions and the way these affect public life. At the same time, I hope it is an overview of key moments in the history of Mexico, such as the years after the Revolution, the Tlatelolco massacre in '68, the "dirty war," the economic crises of the 1980s, Salinas' privatizations, the change of power in 2000, the postelection conflict of 2006, the so-called War on Drugs and the return of the PRI to power with the government of Enrique Peña Nieto.

After I carried out the research, I tried out several ways of writing this biography: using the literary device of a letter to the richest Mexican in the world, or the polyphonic techniques masterfully demonstrated by Ryszard Kapuściński in *Imperium* and Hans Magnus Enzensberger in *Anarchy's Brief Summer*. In the end, looking at my subject's character traits and the information gathered, I opted for a more streamlined register as the best way to tell Slim's story. So my research about him is interwoven with his own point of view.

I should mention that despite my difficult questions in my interviews, Slim always maintained an attitude of respect. If anything, when asked about controversial issues he chose to respond only briefly. I should thank him for the more than seven hours he conceded me for this book, which, as I mentioned, I started working on eight years ago. During our meetings, he showed me photographs of his visits to the dentist, we listened to songs by Chamín Correa, we chatted while he got his hair cut before an event with the president, he gave me the autobiography of his friend Sophia Loren and a biographical essay about Genghis Khan, and he shared with me his process of preparing for a conference that was held in September 2015 with the interns at Fundación Telmex about the evolution of societies over the history of humanity. At some point the tycoon, half reprimanding and half joking, said to me: "You made me say a lot of things I've never said before."

Although this biography may have special force because it includes the direct voice, rarely heard, of its main character, I hope above all that it posits the challenge of getting to know and understand one of the most important figures in the world today, based on information and questions. Questions such as whether he has truly helped combat poverty and whether one can live for money alone, with the belief that the economy is not connected to social and political issues. Whether the richest man in the world can be a good person was one of the guiding questions during the immersive research for this book, although in the end I decided not to openly address it in the text, to give the readers the freedom to consider for themselves this or any other question during their reading. An intelligent friend reminded me of what Javier Cercas says in *The Impostor*: in order to tell someone's story, we first need to understand it, and that understanding tends to bring us closer to them. Therefore, the exercise of narrating in a way reduces any distances that may exist—in this case, imposed by money—and provides readers with a more accurate perspective.

It's not easy to analyze a millionaire beyond the good or bad stereotypes that exist about them. The French psychoanalyst Jacques-Alain Miller, a disciple of Lacan, even believes it's an impossible task when it comes to the ultrarich. In an interview for the weekly magazine *Marianne*, he said that in 2008 he saw a millionaire patient who told him how in those days he earned or lost a million dollars speculating until he was ruined by the financial crisis that year. "If you are truly rich, you are un-analyzable, because you are not in a position to pay—that is, to give up anything meaningful: analysis slides like water off a duck's back," explains Miller, who believes "money is a signifier without the signified, that kills all meaning. When one is devoted to money, truth stops making sense."

This specialist, who studied alongside Jean-Paul Sartre, believes that there are usually three motivations for the great accumulators of capital. The first has to do directly with death and is reflected in the fear of illness and the desire to perpetuate in their offspring. The second is linked to pleasure and is reflected in immediate consumption and extravagant spending. Neither of these two seemed to fit with Slim's motivations. Perhaps Miller's third classification would apply: that of having money for money's sake, for the pure pleasure of owning in itself and the drive to keep earning more.

But this book may say other things about Slim, depending on each reader. It may be the story of a Lebanese immigrant who added his mathematical abilities to his entrepreneurial vision to create a global empire; or it could be the record of economic inequality that is present throughout the world, especially in Mexico, where the wealth of millionaires—with Slim at the top—grew 32 percent between 2007 and 2012, despite the rest of the world's falling by 0.3 percent according to the Global Wealth Report 2014.

Others may find here instead the story of a character who represents the neoliberal mentality of our times, which mistrusts politicians, believes that the market is the most efficient mechanism for everything, even to combat corruption, and sees philanthropy as a social investment and businesses as an aspect of collective wealth.

What is clear to me is that domination and resistance are two concepts that have marked me, sometimes unconsciously, when reporting and writing this and all my other books. My most important journalistic questions reside in that dispute between any kind of established power and the opposition that organizes to combat it. I agree with Bolivian philosopher Raúl Prada in that Marx's theory of social struggle is not akin to a catalogue of plant species, as many dogmatic Marxists seem to believe. Instead, there is an aspect of performativity to it, "through the drama of conflict between two historical protagonists: the proletariat and the bourgeoisie. It is not just a critical but also a dynamic theory of class struggle."

It has fallen to me to witness and tell the story, from different perspectives, of the existence of that class struggle. My first book, *Oaxaca sitiada* (*Oaxaca Under Siege*), tells of the first insurrection in Mexico in the twenty-first century, in a state that had long been poor and subjugated. It tells of the conflict from the barricades, although I also interviewed the questioned the governor and members of the political class in power at the time, including the police chiefs who lead the repression.

In contrast, what I tried to do in this book was to tell the life of one of capitalism's greatest figures; class struggle propels my stories and those of many other narrators living through this dynamic era riddled with inequality.

To refuse to see the class struggle behind an insurrection of the people or behind the life of the richest man in the world would be delusional. It is around that drama that history revolves.

Diego Enrique Osorno
Oaxaca de Juárez, Oaxaca,
October 2015

1

Negotiating

A few years ago, at a public charity event, a man approached Carlos Slim to make a business proposition: to produce a coffee table book about Mexico City for the tycoon to give away to clients as a Christmas gift. Slim accepted the offer. He asked them to prepare a print run of 1,000 copies to give away to his special clients at Inbursa, the bank he owns, and at his dozens of businesses across twenty countries, which include the largest telecom in Latin America, an electric cables manufacturer, several hospitals, gold mines, oil companies, cigarette factories, the plot of land containing a pre-Hispanic pyramid in Mexico City, Saks Fifth Avenue stores, bicycle factories, cable TV companies in favelas in Brazil, train lines, construction firms, shares in the New York Times and the largest collection of Auguste Rodin plaster molds in the world.

Weeks after talking to the multimillionaire, the Christmas book man made an appointment with Slim. The tycoon received him in his office in Lomas de Chapultepec, the most traditional of the affluent districts in the Mexican capital. That's the office where Slim has on display a bronze sculpture of Napoleon on his deathbed, a work by the artist Vincenzo Vela, much admired in the late nineteenth century in Paris. According to one of his employees, Slim keeps it there to remind himself that he is a mere mortal.

When the man handed him a copy of the publication, Slim examined it carefully and glowered at the invoice. He said he could not pay that price because he thought it too high. The amateur photographer assured him he would not be making a profit, that his production costs were real. At his desk, where there is no computer or device whatsoever, Slim took a pencil and piece of paper, added and subtracted numbers, and worked out the amount he was willing to pay. The Christmas book man was haggled down to the last cent by the richest Mexican in the world.

During one of our interviews, Slim told me he could not remember the episode narrated by that character, who asked to be kept anonymous out of fear of reprisal. In Mexico, many people know things about Slim, but those willing to speak freely about him do not abound. That's why it's easier to find legends than true stories about this man who studied civil engineering using electronic calculators, an object about which the future millionaire wrote his honors thesis, envisioning a bright future.

The Christmas book story is one of the many which, between truth and fiction, are told time and again at business meetings to remind people of the "Slim style" when negotiating. Another funny anecdote that does the rounds among the same circles is that of the time when Slim haggled for hours with a seller in Venice just to get a discount off some souvenir.

"Yes, the Venice thing did happen, but the prices aren't the point. I went into a shop and got chatting to an old seller, an heir of the Venetian tradition. I believe in having real conversations with real people. First I struck up conversation with the seller's son, and then the man himself appeared. Then the conversation got a bit long," Slim clarifies regarding that haggling episode, witnessed by a group of Mexican intellectuals who were with him. "I'm not a souvenir shop owner. I wasn't in the store buying merchandise to resell it. I'm interested in the costs, the sales schedules, the marketing, the business plan, that kind of thing, but not because I want to buy. When you shop for souvenirs you do so at leisure, but I don't normally go around buying things."

For Slim, what he did with that Venetian seller was not haggling, but "to enter in communication with an entrepreneur, people who do business."

To give a better idea of his negotiation style, Slim himself created a list of guidelines that his employees and some followers I know try to follow to a T. In 2007, when I first requested a formal

4

interview with him, one of his 220,000 staff kindly replied that my request would be considered. Among the documents attached to the message was the one in which the magnate explains the principles of his business conglomerate:

1. Simple structures, organizations with minimum hierarchies, human development and internal training of executive functions. Flexibility and speed in decision-making. Operating with the advantages of a small business, which are what make big businesses great.

2. Maintaining austerity in times of plenty strengthens, capitalizes and accelerates the development of a company; at the same time it avoids bitter, drastic changes during times of crisis.

3. Always active in modernizing, growing, professional development, quality, simplification and tireless improvement of productive processes. Increase productivity, competitiveness, reduce spending and costs, always guided by the highest global standards.

4. The company should never be limited by the status of the owner or the administrator. We should not feel like big fish in little ponds. Minimum investment in non-productive assets.

5. There is no challenge that cannot be overcome when working as a team, with clear objectives and knowledge of the tools available.

6. Any money that goes out of the company evaporates. That's why we reinvest the profits.

7. Business creativity is not only applicable to business, but also to solving many of our countries' problems. Which is what we do through the group's foundations.

8. Firm and patient optimism always bears fruit.

9. Times are always propitious for those who work hard and have the means to do so.

10. Our first premise is and always has been to remain acutely aware that we can take nothing with us when we depart from this world, that we can only do things while we're alive, and that an entrepreneur is a creator of wealth, which he temporarily administrates.

Slim gives this kind of advice in his speeches. It was not difficult for his media advisers to figure out that herein lies his potential for popularity: in encouraging others to dream of becoming millionaires by following his steps. Thus, the mogul delivers formulae, tips and secrets to the business world, where his holding company, Carso, controls firms dealing in food, car parts, merchandise, detergents and cosmetics, machinery and electric and non-electric equipment, non-iron metals, mining, paper and paper products, rubber products, chemistry and communications. These and other business areas make Carso the industrial group with most shares on the Mexican Stock Exchange.

"Historia de Grupo Carso" ("History of Grupo Carso") is the title of a document he wrote to share how his empire evolved. It is dated June 1994, and he gave it to me personally—with some notes he made by hand, in pencil—in spring 2015 to help me understand the way in which his business conglomerate operates. Grupo Carso's business principles include working without any corporate staff (since the company should always be localized at the production plant, operations and sales, and with minimum operational expenditure). It also specifies that investment should always go into the production plant and the administration and distribution teams, never into corporate assets.

Slim explains:

> The aim is to reduce the hierarchy to the minimum, bringing the directors as near as possible to the operations, and having them work for that and not for corporate structures. We try to combine executive activity with the interest of shareholders through a delegate of the president of the committee, who, working in conjunction with the directors, will seek to constantly optimize investments, strategy and expenditure.

Beyond his business profile, Slim also has a political side. Since 2006, that political profile has come under increased scrutiny, although he has never seemed too worried about how drastically he divides opinions, nor does he seem overly concerned with explaining the origin and development of his megafortune directly to the press. However, "How does it feel to be the richest man in the world, in a country where 50 million live in poverty?" is one of the FAQs the businessman answers in a dossier that his PR team gives to journalists when they request an interview. "To me this is not a competition. I don't think in those terms. When I die I'm not taking anything with me. Creating wealth, and ensuring its distribution, is a legacy that will remain," writes Slim. Other FAQs are equally deadpan. "Is it true that Carlos Salinas de Gortari sold you Telmex in return for a favor?"

But most of them are indulgent. The last one is: "Why have you not put yourself forward as a presidential candidate?" Slim could have put there a phrase that I've heard him say during his speeches: "I believe a businessman can do with one dollar what a politician cannot do with two or more."

How did this son of a Lebanese merchant get formally involved in the world of business after studying civil engineering at a state university? In 1965 he bought the bottling plant Jarritos del Sur; he then created a brokerage firm, a construction company, a mining company, a real estate operation and property development company that he called Carso, the name he would later use for his entire empire, fusing the first letters of his and Soumaya's (his late wife's) names. His first strategic purchase was a graphic arts company called Galas de México, of which he bought 60 percent in 1976:

> At the time of purchase, Galas presented very difficult conditions: workers on strike, 1,700 clients and 25 percent of the sales depended on a single one of them, numerous products, obsolete equipment, clients annoyed about the strike, suppliers who would not send goods due to lack of payment, overdue payments to banks and creditors, unpaid tax agreements and social security, in addition to various labor disputes and a lack of industrial experience.

It was with this purchase, and 10 percent of the tobacco factory Cigarrera La Tabacalera Mexicana four years later, that Slim started to garner notoriety in the national business community. Grupo Carso was formally constituted in 1980, and between 1981 and 1984, during a period of financial crisis in Mexico, his consortium made important purchases, a move that Slim defines as the "Mexicanization of companies." The term reflects the nationalism that tends to feature in his language. The tycoon writes:

> During those years, and seeing as many large national and foreign investors did not want to continue their investments, it was viable to acquire a majority in several businesses at prices well below their real value, and even Mexicanize some of them, including Reynolds Aluminio, Sanborns, Nacobre and its subsidiaries. Later we Mexicanized, in terms of equity and operations, Luxus, Euzkadi, General Tire, Aluminio and 30 percent of Condumex. Another way in which we Mexicanized companies was by selling them to other Mexicans, as was the case with Química Perwalt in 1983, and La Moderna in 1985.

The 1980s are considered pivotal in the development of his business conglomerate. Slim enthusiastically tells the story of this growth:

> As we all remember the 1980s was a critical period in our country's history. There was a lack of confidence in Mexico's future. At the time, while others were refusing to invest, we decided to do so. The reason Grupo Carso made this decision was a combination of self-confidence, confidence in the country, and common sense. Any rational and emotional analysis told us that doing anything other than investing in Mexico would be an atrocity. You cannot bring up and educate your teenage children (or of any age) with fear, lack of confidence, and buying dollars.

Slim equates this period of risky buying with a purchase made by his father: "The conditions in those years reminded me of the decision my father made in March 1914, at the height of the Revolution, when he bought 50 percent of the business off his brother, risking his entire capital and future."

In actual fact, the conditions differ greatly between these two scenarios. While Slim's father had lived through the revolutionary chaos, the tycoon made his immense fortune within the framework today's dominant ideology: neoliberalism. It was during the intensive application of neoliberalism in Mexico, through the so-called Washington Consensus, that Slim amassed a significant share of his capital.

What is the Washington Consensus? It's a term colloquially given to the economic model imposed by world powers on developing countries. One of the best definitions provided comes from Indian writer Pankaj Mishra, who describes it as "the dominant ideological orthodoxy before the economic crisis of 2008: that no nation can advance without reining in labor unions, eliminating trade barriers, ending subsidies, and, most importantly, minimizing the role of the government."

More than any other businessman in the region, Slim took advantage of this turning point in history, when economies that until the 1980s had been tightly controlled by political regimes began to open up. He became the most emblematic representative of Latin American capitalism.

2

Forbes

The list of the world's richest people as compiled by *Forbes* magazine states that, in 2014, along with Carlos Slim, the richest Mexicans in the world also included Germán Larrea, with $14.7 billion; Alberto Baillères, with $12.4 billion; Ricardo Salinas Pliego, with $8.3 billion; Eva Gonda de Garza Lagüera, with $6.4 billion; María Aramburuzabala, with $5.2 billion; Antonio del Valle, with $5 billion; the Servitje Montul family, with $4.8 billion; the González Moreno family, with $4.7 billion; and Jerónimo Arango, with $4.2 billion. The combined fortune of these nine Mexican multibillionaires is $65.7 billion, less than the $72 billion that Slim was worth that year. In Mexico, there is no one who comes even close to disputing his leadership in the *Forbes* list.

The novelist Eduardo Antonio Parra once told me that Slim was not the first Mexican to become the richest man in the world—it was Antonio de Obregón y Alcocer, who, in the viceregal Mexico of the sixteenth century, amassed an enormous fortune exploiting the La Valenciana mine in Guanajuato, which at the time was the greatest silver producer on the planet. The systematic exploitation of its miners, who worked in semi-slavery conditions, made Obregón a figure of great renown in the colonial era, so much so that he was named a Count by King Carlos III of Spain. According to Parra, the Count of La Valenciana was so rich that for his daughter's wedding, he ordered the path from his house to the church to be paved with gold.

De Obregón y Alcocer does not appear in an interesting *Forbes* issue where a series of variables are used to calculate who have been the seventy-five richest people in the history of humanity. This list is topped by John D. Rockefeller and includes Tsar Nicholas II of Russia, magnate Andrew Carnegie, automotive financier Henry Ford, pharaoh Amenhotep III of Egypt, oil tycoon Jean Paul Getty, "robber baron" Cornelius Vanderbilt, King William II of England, Empress Cleopatra, Walmart founder Sam Walton, Roman senator Marcus Licinius Craso, and Carlos Slim himself.

Slim is not only an immensely rich man: he is also a strategist, a trait he demonstrated from an early age. His honors thesis for his degree as a civil engineer was titled "Applications of lineal programming to some civil engineering problems." In addition to championing the use of electronic calculators, it provides a detailed analysis of the way in which the bloodiest wars in the twentieth century transpired. Young Slim's thesis begins thus:

> The fundamental intention of this research is to describe some of the techniques developed after the Second World War as well as to briefly describe some of their applications to civil engineering. These techniques[...] constitute extraordinary tools that greatly aide common sense and allow directors in general to make more rational and objective decisions (without ever replacing the human element) while making it possible to play out the potential outcomes. The effectiveness of these tools depends on the precision of the data provided and the choice of technique applied.

After acquiring control of Telmex, formerly owned by the Mexican state, and sole provider of telephony services in the country, one of Slim's tactics was to use the capital generated by the growth of mobile telephony in Mexico, which in two years went from 8.3 million to 96.2 million users, in order to economically strengthen his company, América Móvil, and, with the enormous cash flow he possessed, purchase new telecom companies in Brazil, Argentina, Peru, Chile, Ecuador and Colombia. This way, the captive Mexican consumers were to Slim what the La Valenciana silver mine was to de Obregón y Alcocer in the sixteenth century, and Slim capitalized on this situation to expand his empire beyond Mexico. In 2010, Slim's empire would have 259.3 million customers in eighteen Latin American countries, including Brazil's two main mobile phone and landline companies: Claro and Embratel.

This "silver mine" has allowed Slim to expand his various investments such that he now controls, through his mining company, Frisco, an area of land equivalent to six times the capital city of Mexico.

However, around his seventy-fifth birthday, Slim experienced slight setbacks in his Latin American expansionism. A Panamanian judge had ordered that some of his properties be seized, due to a legal controversy over the concession he received to build a hydroelectric plant during the government of Martín Torrijos. Around the same time, the Uruguayan government revoked the concession of his telecom company Claro, due to matters of legitimacy, according to an official announcement. José Mujica, one of the most celebrated presidents in the world, declared publicly before he left office that he did not wish Slim's company to become the owner of communications in his small South American country.

And in July 2015, the non-governmental organization PODER, which promotes business transparency and has offices in Mexico City and New York, published a damning report signed by Omar Escamilla Haro, which questions the mining rights in the land owned by Slim:

> In Mexico, the law prohibits the existence of "latifundios," defined as land tenure for commercial estates exceeding 150 hectares of irrigated cotton cultivation or 300 hectares of land used to grow banana, coffee, agave, rubber, palm, vine, olive, quinine, vanilla, cacao, nopal or fruit trees. However, the agrarian and mining laws and regulations never establish the amount of land that a company can legally own. This basically eliminates the classification of latifundios for property in the hands of companies. That said, if we use the amount of land in the hands of small proprietors as a parameter of analysis, we can establish that the main shareholders for Minera Frisco, Carlos Slim and his immediate family, own land that can be classified as a latifundio.

However, the question for many Latin American political analysts was not whether Slim would be capable of continuing to accumulate more money in his remaining years of life, but what would become of that stratospheric fortune.

"Antonio de Obregón, Count of La Valenciana, seems to be a forgotten character in Mexico's history... How do you think posterity will treat Slim?" I asked the writer Eduardo Antonio Parra. His reply:

Slim is aware that many in Mexico and Latin America despise him and he wants to do something about it. He may go down in history as a good benefactor, but that depends what he does from now on. What I think stands out about him is how he gets involved in everything, not just the telecom business. I found out that one of his companies is going to expand into the sewage system in Mexico City. That man can make money even out of shit!

3

Success

In today's world, where there are 1.4 billion people living on less than a dollar a day, what kind of success does it mean for just one person like Carlos Slim to accumulate a fortune of around $80 billion? As Albert Camus writes in *The Fall*, success is easy to obtain. The hard part is to deserve it. Slim smiled dispiritedly when he spotted the word "success" in my notes for our interview, and read me part of a letter he wrote in the '90s, addressing young people: "Achieving success in material, business or professional terms: that is not success. Success is balance, harmony, family and friends, which are what matters."

I asked him to talk about success in its most basic definition. "I think happiness is a path," he said. "And along the way we fall, get stuck, encounter severe difficulties, and what we need to do is focus on becoming stronger through these crises so we can keep moving forward." Then, seemingly moved, he described his life philosophy: "The important thing is to love life and everything it has to offer. Not to narrow-mindedly focus on just one project or activity, but rather to love life, to experience and understand life itself, because it's by experiencing and understanding it that you enjoy life more profoundly."

"What would you say to people who view you as an example of success?"

"Look, if success is seen as a way of having a family, an active family that works and has feelings and a sense of responsibility, in which all family members love each other deeply, I believe it's a very good example: having a very functional, close-knit, deeply loved family, with good relationships, and I'm talking about 'family' in the broadest sense, because I believe it's important for all of us to have one, and old friends you can depend on. In that sense, it's good to be able to serve in a way as an example, especially when it comes to a way of life. I think that anyone who enjoys any kind of privilege, whichever it is, has a duty and social responsibility..."

"But I think the admiration some people have towards you is not because of your family, but your huge accumulation of money. To many, that is a symbol of success."

"Maybe, but I don't think money is a symbol of success, because you can have a lot of money, and yet be miserable and alone. Someone said of a person: 'He was so poor, so very poor, that all he had was money.' I think that sums it up very well. Also, we need to make a distinction between money and business. It's one thing to have X million or billion in the bank, or in cash, or in investments, or in whatever you like, and it's another to have a business, where what you have is an important investment for society."

Slim went on, now commenting on the difference he saw between the concepts of income and wealth. He characterized income as the fruit of wealth, while wealth should be managed in such a way that it bears fruit, so that it can be distributed among others. "It's the fruit that should be distributed, not the wealth itself. Does that make sense?"

"I think so."

"If you distribute all the shares of Pemex among Mexicans tomorrow, what would each Mexican do?" Slim's example wasn't accidental. Pemex (Mexican Petroleum) is the previously state-owned company that is currently entering a period of competition, since the government opened up the energy market to private investment. Slim's is one of the companies that will participate.

Slim claims that if Pemex shares were distributed out among all Mexicans, most who received them would sell them immediately: "They'd sell them, because what you want is to have a better life for your family. So the important thing is for Pemex to be a very efficient, prudent company that creates more wealth, and for the fruit of the wealth that is being created to be partly reinvested and partly redistributed. Just as in private companies. When you create wealth, it's about the wealth staying within society."

In Slim's view, the important thing is that wealth "generates employment, generates more wealth, generates services or important assets for society, and when there are shareholders, that they participate in the product and that the taxes remain, and that there is still an independent part of the company—I believe we as businesspeople have that obligation. Even if sometimes the business cooperates in some way to resolve important social projects."

"That sounds interesting: in a time when there's a love for easy money, for consumerism, you, one of the richest men in the world, have this vision, which seems contrary to what you represent to many people."

"What matters is not that people possess wealth, but what they do with it and what kind of wealth it is. If what you have is a lot of money in cash or investments to amuse yourself and hang out, you turn into a kind of social parasite. That's quite different to the situation of a businessman who is working on the development and structure of the company. So, taking Americans as an example, some of them [Warren Buffet and Bill Gates] are going to donate half of their capital. I say: OK, but why half? Why not 70 or 80 percent? It's not so much the percentage that I might object to. My question is: Why don't they give their time? Why not, instead of giving money, give time and commitment, so that together, with the money they have, they might solve some problems? All that money being donated to people is not functional, it doesn't solve anything. Maybe it's just to make themselves feel good or avoid feeling ashamed of having resources, of having wealth."

In the same train of thought, the man who has accumulated a fortune equaling the GDP of several poor countries, concluded by telling me about his view of his own wealth: "I am not ashamed of what I have, although many are critical because they say I'm favored and this and that, but ask me whatever you like about that and I'll answer."

4

Khan

It's understandable that a multimillionaire like Carlos Slim, who is so omnipresent in the life of Mexicans and Latin Americans, should be an object of over-the-top adulation and gratuitous praise. Opinion on him is divided between the indulgence of intellectuals, politicians and artists, who see him as a nationalist benefactor, and fierce attacks from ordinary citizens, who have no other choice than to be his customers because he owns the vast majority of the products and services they consume. Then they let off steam by telling jokes, such as the typical: "Baby, it doesn't pay to argue on the phone for hours on end. Carlos Slim will make a tidy profit, though." The reach of his power extends even to the realm of domestic arguments, and the only thing left to do is laugh.

But in the business world, one of the things that stands out about Slim is his ruthlessness. A very close associate of northern Mexican entrepreneur Lorenzo Zambrano, the late president of Cemex, told me that he and Slim were friends until the cement mogul decided to buy a small percentage of the telephone company Axtel, a Telmex competitor. Not only did this cause their personal relationship to cool, but Slim decided to invest in Cementos Moctezuma to compete against his former friend.

In 2010, on the centenary of the Mexican Revolution for greater social justice spearheaded by Emiliano Zapata and Pancho Villa, Slim celebrated his seventieth birthday accumulating so much money that he was seeing earnings averaging $2 million per hour—a fact that he downplays and explains away as a part of the period we live in:

"Now we are in a new era in which what matters most is combating poverty," he says. "It used to be a moral and ethical problem: now it's a financial problem. The great Chinese progress is bringing 20 or 30 million Chinese people out of poverty and marginalization every year. What China has done is fight poverty through capitalism. Everything is capitalism. People who talk about 'savage capitalism' are on the wrong track. Everything is capitalism. There is state capitalism or private capitalism. Or the capital within pension funds, which in the end is private. Capitalism is fundamental for investments to take place. A friend of mine used to say: 'What is capital? It's what you earn minus what you spend.' That is what ends up forming our capital, and societies need to develop theirs, as China is doing."

Slim is the highest representative of a concept that has not been well-researched but is a distinct reality: Latin American capitalism. It is in this region of the world where Slim has made the vast majority of his investments, although he has participated in other regional markets. In Spain, he has purchased real estate companies such as Realia de Valencia, the Oviedo football club or the Catalan construction company Fomento de Construcciones y Contratas. Austria and the Netherlands are other European countries where Slim has invested in the telecom sector.

But the expansion of Slim's empire has by and large focused on a region of the world where the word "democracy" was first heard in earnest only a couple of decades ago, and where the law of the jungle sometimes prevails above all others.

Perhaps this is why I was not surprised to find out that Slim likes the stories of the Mongol emperor who ruled one of the largest empires in the history of humanity. *Genghis Khan and the Making of the Modern World*, a *New York Times* bestseller written by Jack Weatherford, is one of his favorite books, and he gifted me a copy after the following explanation:

"This book was interesting to me because Genghis Khan didn't change the laws or the religions of the countries he occupied and he allowed free trade. He was savage when it came to conquering, but that was only when there was resistance, and in that he was no different than others."

For a few minutes Slim relates some of the Asian emperor's military strategies. He tells me, for example, how he destroyed a European army that was much more heavily armed than his own. He explains how Genghis Khan sent out some of his cavalry to threaten confrontation. Soon after, the cavalry pretended they were losing and began to retreat, drawing the enemy army forward, so that as their troops followed they started to lose their original formation, their cavalry separated from the infantry until they came to a place where the rest of Genghis Khan's warriors waited in ambush, ready to kill the cavalry first, then the infantry. "Genghis Khan and his men managed to undermine the cohesion of occidental European armies; they knocked the bottom out of them by displacing and undoing their formations, tricking them into thinking they were already victorious, and taking advantage of their slow speed, because they were very heavily armed, very burdened. Genghis Khan was an extraordinary strategist."

"Don't you feel like there's a similarity between you and Genghis Khan? You are the first Latin American businessman to become the world's richest man, a position that had only previously been occupied by men from more developed countries. Do you feel like a modern Genghis Khan of sorts?" I ask.

"No, no. In an agrarian society there were wars, ransacking, conquests, slaves. Those were completely different paradigms, and he was a great conqueror who went far. Which is strange, because his own society was more primitive; that is, he was technologically behind those he conquered because he relied on the speed of the horse and on people's courage, attacking with bow and arrow on horseback, with very astute and sometimes very aggressive battle and conquest strategies, and he sought to conquer also through negotiation. Those were times of war and he fought against armored armies, which he defeated despite them being technologically more advanced. Genghis Khan filled a very important stage in history, and his was the greatest conquest in the world, greater than that of Alexander the Great: Genghis Khan was the man who most transformed the world in the second millennium."

5

Money

Carlos Slim gets up from the table, where we are talking about the various influences he has had in his life, and pads over to the library, which takes up a section of his massive, carpeted office. He points out a few books.

"Look, this one about Baruch is interesting. And this one about Ling, who created a conglomerate and ended up bankrupting it, but it's interesting to see how he did it. This one's about Vesco, who ended up keeping a fund and then ran away to Cuba. It's a great book because it describes the crisis of the '70s. This one's about Ford. Here's the one about Don Pepe Iturriaga that I was telling you about the other day. This is a book about Getty, and this is the other one about Getty that I read when it was featured in *Playboy* magazine."

The Mexican millionaire picks out a dog-eared paperback from the shelf: *Así hice mi fortuna,* by American oil tycoon Jean Paul Getty, first published in English as *My Life and Fortunes* in 1963. As Slim flicks through it, I notice the title of the first chapter: "How I made my first billion dollars," and see that there are sentences and paragraphs underlined in black ink. It's one of the few books in Spanish in this section of the library, where most books are in English, which Slim has been reading and speaking since he was young.

"Was Getty your main role model in the business world?"

"Not at all! Not my main role model. Baruch comes before him. And Rockefeller before Baruch," he replies, and again turns to his books. "Look, this is the book about Rockefeller's grandson, and the one about Chrysler is over there somewhere. You learn from all of them, and as I say, you learn from the good and the bad. In this book, for example, there's a good analysis of Gates when he was starting out. The author gets it spot on. He says: 'This guy's not merely selling, he's developing his business properly.' This one, for example, is *Paper Money*."

Slim reads mostly biographies, books on business, sports and finance statistics, as well as history. The books are tightly packed in a heaving, six-shelf bookcase that takes up the whole of one of the walls of his 900-plus-square-foot office, very near the house in which he's lived for forty years. On display in his office are family photos, classical paintings, and a Spartan desk that Slim hardly ever uses, since he prefers to work at a table strewn with documents and sometimes diabetic chocolate wrappers. Although he is shortsighted in his right eye, he has perfect vision in his left, allowing him to read without glasses at his seventy-five years of age. He often interrupts our interviews to show me some of his books or documents kept in this library. If, as Borges said, we are not what we have written but what we have read, these interruptions from Slim are more revealing than some of the things he says, as they reflect part of the personality of a Mexican whose methods of wealth accumulation are questioned by many, and whose fortune, according to researcher José Merino's calculations, could support the poorest 10 percent of Mexico's households for almost fourteen years.

One of the books he pointed out the first time we met in his office was *Mr. Baruch* by Margaret L. Coit, published in English by Houghton Mifflin in 1957, the year Slim began his civil engineering studies at the UNAM. It's the biography of Bernard Baruch, an American financier who became a millionaire in the early twentieth century by speculating on the sugar market, and who was nicknamed the Lone Wolf of Wall Street because he acted outside the financial institutions of the time. Baruch then unexpectedly left Wall Street for Washington, DC, to work in politics, and he served as a war adviser during the governments of Wilson, Roosevelt and Truman.

Another of the biographies Slim has read is *Ling: The Rise, Fall, and Return of a Texas Titan*, by Stanley H. Brown. Published by Atheneum in 1972, it tells the story of Jim Ling, an electrician from Oklahoma who, with only a high school education, became one of the great corporate speculators and the creator of Ling-Temco-Vought—one of the world's largest conglomerates—until it went bankrupt with the 1970s crisis in the United States. There is also *Vesco*, by Robert A. Hutchison (Praeger, 1974), about Roberto Vesco, a fascinating and contradictory character, son of an Italian father and Yugoslavian mother, born in Detroit, who didn't even finish high school—although at age thirty, thanks to his remarkable salesmanship, he became a millionaire, even if he did then scam a Swiss company for several million dollars and flee to the Caribbean: first to the Bahamas, then to Costa Rica, and eventually to Cuba, where he was warmly received by the revolutionary government until he likewise scammed a nephew of Fidel Castro and landed in a Havana jail.

The Crash of '79, a financial thriller by Paul E. Erdman (Simon & Schuster, 1976), is another of the books that Slim showed off. The blurb on the back cover says: "Erdman knows about the intrigues of international high finance. No one is better placed than him to describe that world. With an expert hand he leads the reader to the power centers of today." And there is *The Fords: An American Epic*, by Peter Collier and David Horowitz (Summit Books, 1987), about three generations of the family who created one of the greatest automobile empires, focusing on intergenerational conflicts.

By businessman Jean Paul Getty, whom Slim has been following since the 1960s, he has two books: the autobiography *A mi manera* (Grijalbo, 1977) and *Así hice mi fortuna* (Sayrols, 1987), whose first chaper is titled "How I made my first billion dollars."

"I see there's also poetry in your library," I say when I notice a book by the popular Mexican poet Jaime Sabines.

"We edited this one. Well, his secretary edited it and we published it. Look, if you want to talk about poetry, this one is interesting," he says, as he shuffles over to the far right of the bookcase, where he picks out a volume by Khalil Gibran.

Slim asks if I want him to read a poem by the Lebanese author on giving, and I say yes, knowing that he did the same in 2007 to *Time* magazine journalist Tim Padgett when asked about his way of doing philanthropy.

And so, standing next to his bookshelves, his blue tie loosened and his sky-blue shirt monogrammed with his initials, one of the richest men in the world starts reading a poem.

All you have shall someday be given;
    Therefore give now, that the season of giving may be yours and not your inheritors'.

You often say, "I would give, but only to the deserving."
    The trees in your orchard say not so, nor the flocks in your pasture.
    They give that they may live, for to withhold is to perish.

Khalil Gibran, known in Mexico as Gibran Khalil Gibran, a Lebanese immigrant in America who wrote in English and published *The Prophet* in 1923, is one of Slim's favorite authors. Others on his list are contemporary Mexicans such as Ángeles Mastretta and Carlos Fuentes, who fictionalized part of his relationship with Slim in *La voluntad y la fortuna* (*Destiny and Desire*), one of his last books. Slim and Fuentes used to meet frequently before the writer died. Slim also befriended the late Colombian Nobel-Prize-winning author Gabriel García Márquez.

Other high-profile acquaintances include American ex-president Bill Clinton, scientist Stephen Hawking, historian Hugh Thomas, futurologist Alvin Toffler, strategist Nicholas Negroponte and the Spanish socialist ex-president Felipe González, who is also his friend. All of them have visited the billionaire's house in Lomas de Chapultepec, some of them on a Sunday or Monday night, which is when Slim's children—Marco Antonio, Patrick, Soumaya, Vanessa and Johanna—meet for dinner and chat about different topics with international personalities of science, literature and politics. Since 2002, Fundación Telmex has organized an international symposium in Mexico City. Slim invites some of the people he knows or admires to deliver a keynote speech that only the young interns and specific staff from his companies have access to. The list of speakers is as long as it is diverse, and reveals the kind of convening power Slim possesses, as well as some of his interests and passions. In 2002, for example, the legendary football star Pelé was a guest, while in 2003 guests included Alvin Toffler, ex-president Bill Clinton and basketball player Earvin "Magic" Johnson. In 2004, guests were Mikhail Gorbachev, the last Soviet president, and from the United States, former secretary of state Madeleine Albright. In 2005, actor Goldie Hawn and Argentinian ex-football player Jorge Valdano were guests, while in 2006, a year of troubled presidential elections in Mexico, the symposium did not take place.

In 2007 the international catwalk of Slim's acquaintances was set in motion once more and guests included singer Gloria Estefan, athlete Carl Lewis, and Carly Fiorina, CEO of Hewlett Packard. In 2008, actor and activist Jane Fonda was invited, and, also from the United States, Colin Powell, former secretary of state. Between 2009 and 2013, the list of guests included former president of Chile Ricardo Lagos, tennis player Anna Kournikova, actor Forest Whitaker, cofounder of Twitter Biz Stone, journalist Larry King, filmmaker James Cameron, former UN secretary-general Kofi Annan, president of the US Federal Reserve Alan Greenspan, former secretary of state Condoleezza Rice, basketball player Shaquille O'Neal, Brazilian former president Luiz Inácio "Lula" da Silva, trainer Joséph Guardiola, former British prime minister Tony Blair, writer Deepak Chopra, swimmer Michael Phelps, cofounder of Wikipedia Jimmy Wales, actor Al Pacino, founder of Facebook Mark Zuckerberg, actor Antonio Banderas, and former secretary of state Hillary Clinton.

This list of characters is as varied and contradictory as the image of Slim tends to be. As a man who says he is politically neither on the left nor the right, it would seem that his political geometry is determined solely by capital.

———

We return to the tour of his library.

"These here are books I've read, lots are about business, but I have many more books at home," Slim clarifies as we walk past one of his bookshelves.

"And what else do you read?"

"Lots of things."

"Do you read economic theory?"

"No, I rarely read theory. I don't like it."

"So you're an omnivore?"

"Look, these here are art books."

The businessman who built one of Mexico's biggest museums, which carries the name of his late wife Soumaya, points at the shelf holding mostly gifted volumes that he has decided to keep in his library, a few of the hundreds that arrive each year and that pile up, along with other kinds of gifts, in a room next door that functions as a customs office or sorting heap.

We continue walking and Slim remembers something. From between the book *Historia de la deuda exterior de México* (*History of Mexico's Foreign Debt*), written by Jan Bazant and published by El Colegio de México in 1968, and the biography *Hammer*, by Armand Hammer and Neil Lyndon, he picks out an old volume entitled *Geometría analítica y cálculo infinitesimal* (*Analytic Geometry and Calculus*), by F. Woods and F. H. Bailey (UTEHA, 1979).

"This is my book from second year in college," he says, proudly.

Then appears *La Reina del Sur* (*The Queen of the South*), a novel by Arturo Pérez Reverte about a woman from Sinaloa involved in international drug trafficking. Slim explains:

"This is out of place. There are others here I haven't read, either... Look, this one's very good. Look at what a lovely title it has." I read on the cover *Reinas, mujeres y diosas. Mágicos destinos* (*Queens, Women and Goddesses: Magical Destinies*), while Slim rips off the plastic wrapping that still covers it.

"We published it at Sanborns and the cover is a painting from the museum," he says, and continues searching. "*The Peter Principle*, this is a great one." He shows me the book, whose author is famous in the business world because of his adage: "In a hierarchy, every employee tends to rise to the level of their incompetence. The cream rises till it sours."

In this same section there is a beautifully illustrated book about modern warfare, which Slim says he just read and that I should also read to my son. There is a biography of the Kennedys and the book

25

Outliers, by Malcolm Gladwell. He asks me if I have read it. When I say I haven't, he says I should and gives it to me. I take it and eye the subtitle on the cover, not wondering whether it might be a hint: "Why some people succeed and others don't."

Slim is not only a voracious reader, but also one of the biggest booksellers in Mexico. Sanborns, his chain of about 200 restaurants and department stores, includes the country's biggest network of bookshops, which implies that for authors and publishing houses it is vital to establish a commercial relationship with the company, currently headed up by Patrick, the youngest of his sons.

"If your book is not in Sanborns, it does not exist. It's that simple," said an experienced publisher I have worked with a number of times. For years there have been rumors that books are censored if Slim or his inner circle find them uncomfortable. But Slim says this is untrue and cites an example: Daron Acemoglu and James Robinson, MIT and Harvard professors respectively, wrote *Why Nations Fail*, in which they include a small section about the owner of Telmex. "Slim has made his millions in the Mexican economy in large part thanks to his political connections. When he has ventured into the United States, he has not been successful." This section made Slim consider the possibility of undertaking legal proceedings to force a public retraction from these professors, who come from two of the most prestigious universities in the world and whose book has been praised by several Nobel Prize winners in economics.

A man who did take legal action against the publishing house was Jacques Rogozinski, who led the privatizations as head of the Office for Divestiture of Public Enterprises during the government of Salinas de Gortari, the period during which Slim bought Telmex. Rogozinski objected to the phrase that said, "Even though Slim did not put in the highest bid, a consortium led by his Grupo Carso won the auction," and managed to get the publishing house to remove it from the following edition.

"Despite everything, we're selling that book at Sanborns. It sold 700 copies at 349 pesos," said Slim.

"You've never blocked a book?"

"Well, yes, there was just one time when we didn't sell one."

"Which one?"

"I can't remember his name, but the author told us that if we didn't do this or that, he was going to stand outside Sanborns to sell it himself, just to attract publicity. So we sold it for a while, just to get him off our back."

"Do you mean the journalist Rafael Loret de Mola?"

"How do you know?"

"Well, because he publicly denounced it in the 1990s."

"Yes, it was a sort of pressure we weren't keen on, but he's a good guy; he's a bit weird and all, but a good guy."

In addition to being a reader, seller and even occasional publisher of books, Slim might soon become the author of his own biography. The first time I interviewed him, one of the things he clarified was that he was writing a book about his life and family too, and that in that task he was being helped by his nephew Roberto Slim Seade, "a kind of personal secretary," son of his late brother, Julián, and formal manager of the family's hotel companies.

"I'm writing the only authorized biography that will exist, just that right now I have other work to do," he cautioned at the time. "I will answer any questions you have, but regarding your book all I ask is that you don't put in too many lies."

———

Vicente Fox was the PAN (National Action Party) politician who in 2000 ended the seventy-two years of uninterrupted government by the PRI (Institutional Revolutionary Party). Slim, who says he voted for the PRI in those historic presidential elections, financially supported Fox's campaign. After winning the elections, Fox governed Mexico between 2000 and 2006, maintaining a close relationship with Slim, which was evident not only in the lack of regulation of Slim's telecom monopoly, but also in the appointment of former Grupo Carso employees to key government departments. One such person was Pedro Cerisola, a former Telmex executive who became minister of communications and transport.

During those years, Slim was regularly invited to meetings at the official presidential residence and office of Los Pinos. On one of those occasions, after a lunch meeting, Slim visited the library and for some reason, one of the leather-bound books caught his eye. The title on the spine was "Leonardo," and he went to have a closer look. He picked it out of the shelf, opened it, and found a handwritten note on the first page: "This book was donated by Linda H. de Slim." It was a biography of the famous Italian inventor and artist, and donated by Slim's mother, Linda, to the presidential library in the '70s. Slim showed me a facsimile of that biography of da Vinci that he had made. As well as showing Slim's special connection with books, this episode is also revealing of the Slim family's long-standing close ties to the presidency at Los Pinos.

"So, is this the library where you keep your most prized volumes?" I ask.

"Look, I don't have a uniform mentality. I am very plural."

"But this is a special library, and it's interesting to see it, because, as they say, 'By your books you will know thyself.'"

"No, you won't get to know me, because these are also books here about all the stupid things you can think of," he scoffs, and then resumes the tour of the library. "Look, here is the annual report from the Banco de México 1994. Why '94? Because here is the history of the devaluation," he shows me a series of economic indicators in tiny print and points out the date: March 21. "Here is Colosio, here the reserves, and how far they are taken. Here is the 'December error,'" he says, alluding to the mishandling of the sudden devaluation of the Mexican peso that took place that month. This was a factor that, along with the political instability following the assassination of PRI presidential candidate Luis Donaldo Colosio and the Zapatista uprising, led to a severe financial collapse of major international consequences, known as the "Mexican peso crisis." The IMF managing director called it "the first major crisis of the twenty-first century," and it has been argued by some that one of the underlying causes was the too-rapid process of banking liberalization in the country.

Then he pulls out a hardcover book. It's the memoirs of George Bush Sr. On the first pages there is a dedication, but all I manage to read is: "Family and friends," and a date, May 2006.

"This book by Bush is out of this world. Did you know that he and Gorbachov made a deal?"

"To end the Cold War?"

"No, no, not just that. They also agreed to bring democracy

and freedom to the whole world. What happened in Chile—Pinochet's resignation—was their doing. So was Panama—the fall of Noriega—and everything that happened throughout Eastern Europe—the Prague Spring. A fascinating read."

Another of the signed copies that Slim shows me is *Leadership*, by Rudolph Giuliani, former mayor of New York, famous for implementing repressive policies. I barely manage to read the final words in Spanish: "With admiration and friendship," and then the signature of the author, who is now a security consultant. Near Giuliani's book is *El desacuerdo nacional* (*The National Disagreement*), by Manuel Camacho Solís, the Mexican politician who in 1994 acted as an intermediary between the government and the Zapatista Army of National Liberation (EZLN). Slim reads the dedication to me: "To Carlos Slim, who can see the forest for the trees and turn what he imagines into reality, with my friendship and determined conviction of reaching an agreement to grow with justice."

We carry on along the bookshelves and he takes out a bound manuscript whose cover says, "*Revolutionary Wealth*, Alvin Toeffler."

"Alvin Toeffler asked me to take a look at this before it was published."

He flicks through the volume, where I notice some handwritten notes in the margins of the greatest contemporary futurologist, who is a friend of Slim's.

"And did you make any corrections?"

"It has some numbers errors."

"And did Toffler make the changes?"

"No, because in the end I didn't get them to him in time."

Unlike the book *Why Nations Fail*, of which Sanborns bought the small amount of 700 copies, the Spanish print run of *Revolutionary Wealth* was bought almost in its entirety by Slim's chain.

The tour of his library continues, and at some point we are right in front of the book *Los retos que enfrentamos* (*The Challenges We Face*), published in 2014 by former president Felipe Calderón, but Slim ignores it. Meanwhile, he picks out with enthusiasm an old volume entitled *Desarrollo estabilizador* (*Stabilizing Development*), by Antonio Ortiz Mena, and exclaims:

"This is excellent!"

I

"What will you do with these books?"

"Do you mean what will my children do with them when I die?"

"Well, you could also do something before then."

"Do you mean am I going to donate my collection? Nope."

"Why not give it to the reading library at UNAM?"

"No, we have studies centers."

"Or the University of Austin. For example, the politician Bill Richardson just donated his library to them."

"But in the United States, they buy them."

"True, Gabriel García Márquez's library was bought there for $2 million."

"Twelve million?"

"No, $2 million."

"No, that's too cheap."

"And Bill's?"

"I think he donated it."

For a brief moment Slim remains silent, as if thinking about what will happen to his books in the future.

But he doesn't speak further on it.

———

"I've never worn glasses. I've been reading with my left eye since I was young."

"And why did you never get a laser operation?"

"In those days there were no operations."

"And now?"

"Why would I get operated if I read fine with my left eye?"

"I got the operation a year ago and it changed my life."

"Sure, but in ten years you'll be back to where you were."

"But I will have had ten years of not wearing glasses."

"Yes, but you're going to live fifty more. You'll have a tough time, kid, believe me… No, my eyesight is fine, I can read fine. Let's see, look, get me something in fine print."

Holding up some financial documents in fine print, the magnate starts reading out loud to perfection.

———

I asked two successful businessmen in their thirties, separately, whether they thought it was interesting to know what books Slim has in his library. Despite the generational gap and the fact that they are critical of the billionaire's dominant role in the business world, both said yes. After I'd mentioned some of the titles, one of them told me he'd started to look for them to read them soon, while the other one was amazed because he didn't know most of them, despite being an avid reader of books about finance and business strategies. The titles I found in Slim's library, where the most repeated word was "money," included *Money: Whence it Came, Where it Went*, by John Kenneth Galbraith (Houghton Mifflin, 1975); *The Money Machine: How KKR Manufactured Power and Profits*, by Sarah Barlett (Warner Books, 1991); *Paper Money*, by Adam Smith (Dell, 1982), *Super-Money*, by Adam Smith (Random House, 1972), *Common Wealth: Economics for a Crowded Planet*, by Jeffrey D. Sachs (Penguin, 2009), *The Warren Buffett Way: Investment Strategies of the World's Greatest Investor*, by Robert G. Hagstrom (Wiley, 1997), a Spanish edition of *The Peter Prescription: How to Make Things Go Right,* by Laurence J. Peter (Plaza & Janés, 1991), a Spanish edition of *Up the Organization: How to Stop the Corporation From Stifling People and Strangling Profits*, by Robert Townsend (Grijalbo, 1970), and *The Money Lords: The Great Finance Capitalists, 1925–1950*, by Mathew Joséphson (Weybright and Talley, 1972).

Of all the titles in this section, the one that intrigued me most was a Spanish edition of *Winning Through Intimidation*, by Robert J. Ringer (V Siglos, 1974), first published in English in 1973. My book dealer told me it would be difficult to find, but he would help me find it for a thousand pesos. I asked the same bookseller how much he thought he could get for a 1960s edition of a book by Getty underlined by Slim; he replied that it would be worth between 50,000 and 100,000 pesos.

I also talked about the list of over 100 books that I identified in the library with Daniel Gershenson, a prominent independent activist and critic of Slim's monopolistic practices. Gershenson, who lived a large part of his life in New York, was of the opinion that "his selection of titles is quite conventional; indistinguishable from that of any rich dude from Wall Street (a 'master of the universe,' as Tom Wolfe would call him), who might also be a baseball or basketball fan."

Of the dozens of sports books that are also in Slim's library, Gershenson pointed out that the billionaire had a biography of Ty Cobb, the Detroit Tigers' player who was nicknamed the Peach of Georgia and considered by experts to be the best baseball player in history, even above the famous Babe Ruth: "Cobb was a cantankerous, confrontationally racist, and belligerent player in Major League Baseball, which was segregated until 1947, when Jackie Robinson—the first black player—was hired by the Brooklyn Dodgers." Known for his violent tendencies and his spikes-up displays of cruelty in an era when those "character traits" were highly valued, Cobb was a man who, according to North American folklore, twisted the rules and grabbed undue advantages for the sake of achieving his goal: to win at all costs.

A "dirty" baseball player, but a winner. The ultimate accolade within gringo pragmatism.

II

6

Telmex

Anyone can become a millionaire overnight out of sheer luck. But to reach the top of the list of the world's billionaires takes half a lifetime of effort and, according to modern Western mythology, requires the profile of a generous, creative and audacious man. Bill Gates is seen as an IT genius, Warren Buffett as an infallible investor, George Soros as a rebellious and chic millionaire. Carlos Slim is known for being one of the richest men in the world in a country with 50 million poor. Perhaps this is why, rather than believing in the value of his work, his critics compare him to the Russian oligarchs, who multiply their fortunes through corruption and receive business advantages under the shadow of power. The *Wall Street Journal* attributes Slim's fortune to his monopolistic practices. The magnate has denied this time and again, although in Mexico there is a very popular notion that without the help he received from the government he would never have reached the heights of the world's richest.

During the May 1 Workers' Day Parade, 1989—when the PRI regime still went to great lengths to create the display of thousands of workers parading down cities' main streets—then-president Carlos Salinas de Gortari, watching the event from the Palacio Nacional balcony, asked the director of the state-owned company Teléfonos de México (Telmex) to stop marching and come up to the balcony to watch the workers' contingents together. A simple gesture like this, for the PRI, held the key to the future: the government was preparing to privatize the company. A year and a half later, on December 11, 1990, Slim was presented as the winner.

If social media such as Twitter and Facebook had existed back then, *Carlos and Charlie's* would have become a trending topic—the popular joke alluded to the never-proven fact that Carlos Slim was in reality a front man for Carlos Salinas de Gortari in the purchase of the national telephone company. The first exhaustive journalistic criticism of the irregularities was *Operación Telmex* (*Operation Telmex*), by Rafael Rodríguez Castañeda, current director of *Proceso,* a weekly political analysis magazine. In his book, the journalist predicts the creation of a telephone monopoly with limitless gains. He also quotes a *Business Week* article, published in July 1991, that states:

> rumors and allegations of nepotism surround the entire privatization process. In response, the government did the impossible to create an image of impartiality. For example, in the cabinet meeting that would decide the new owners of Telmex, the three bidders were named A, B, and C. But everyone knew who was who. "We're not selling oranges here," said a secretary of state.

According to this theory, there were political motivations behind the conditions for advantageous monopoly: the government needed to demonstrate that selling state-owned companies was profitable, and sought to consolidate and maximize Telmex in order to show it off as a success story, instead of creating free-market competition. According to this theory, Slim's success as a businessman was supposed to signify the success of the PRI regime's privatization policy.

A 1990 document entitled "Regulatory aspects of the privatization of Telmex" outlines the evolution of the regulations around the sector throughout the twentieth century in Mexico:

1938 General Communication Law
• Telephony franchisees were foreign
• Existence of two telephone companies, two public networks

1948–68 Stability and development
• Telmex is created by merging the two existing companies
• Annual growth rates of 10 to 14 percent

1968–81 Political crisis—Major intervention from the State
• Establishment of a new franchise (1976)
• Nationalization of telecommunications (establishment of the regulator-operator duality)
• Deterioration of tariffs, political and labor relations
• Growing tax burden

1982 Start of restructuring of the economy
• Start of process of change to establish a modern regime
• Correction of public finances
• Opening of the economy
• Democratic reform

1988 Change and opening
• Breaking of the duality regulator–operator
• Deregulation
• Privatization processes

Independent specialists in telecommunications say that a significant amount of the privatizations that took place during the 1990s in Latin American and in the former Soviet republics occurred in a very similar fashion. When companies ceased to be a state monopoly, two or at most three new major shareholders would enter, fusing an experienced operator with a huge financial backer in order to administer the existing telephone networks, because creating new infrastructure was not economically viable. An even more radical, often cited theory regarding monopolies in telecommunications is that they were "natural" because of the large-scale investment required in order to maintain a certain efficiency. However, it's worth noting that with the networks already in place, as is the case now, it is possible to maintain efficiency and generate greater competition.

During Salinas de Gortari's term of office, nearly 1,000 public companies were privatized—Telmex, the only telephone company in the market, was the most profitable, and the most controversial. Until then, Slim was known only as another businessman supporting Salinas de Gortari from the start of his election campaign. He was under fifty years old and the only thing widely known of his biography was that he had started out working as broker in the stock exchange and had made his fortune by buying companies in crisis and turning them around almost miraculously, inspired by the so-called Modigliani-Miller theorem, which encourages buying and operating companies even if they are financed by the sale of debt.

The purchase of Telmex included favorable clauses that gave the businessman control over the company, and the monopoly of its service, during the period that saw the greatest number of new landline purchases in the country. Buying Telmex in 1991 cata-pulted Slim as a public figure in Mexico, and perhaps contributed towards the normalization of evil that Nobel Prize-winning author Octavio Paz attributes to the PRI in his essay *El ogro filantrópico* (*The Philanthropic Ogre*).

The transition from a nationalistic to a free-market economy in Mexico can be compared to what Russia experienced during Perestroika. In the midst of these changes, both countries saw for the first time the emergence of multimillionaires who took center stage in the political and social life of the nation. Many of these wealthy men protagonized a type of capitalism where influence peddling occupied the void left behind by a lack of strong laws and government. For this reason, when under international scru-tiny, the Mexican multimillionaires of the twenty-first century are seen as more akin to the Russian oligarchs than to Buffet, Soros or Gates, even though the conduct of the latter three has also been questioned, like when Soros launched a speculative attack against the pound sterling in 1992, known as Black Wednesday, causing severe damage to the British government. It is no secret that Gates has also consolidated a monopoly with Microsoft: nine out of ten computers in the world are manufactured by his company. The dif-ference is, he went on trial in the United States for his monopolistic practices and, over time, became the greatest philanthropist that has ever existed, giving away more money annually than the entire budget of, for example, the World Health Organization.

Analyst Gerardo Esquivel created a report for Oxfam and the organization Iguales, entitled *Desigualdad extrema en México: concentración del poder económico y político* (*Extreme inequality in Mexico: concentration of economic and political power*), which was published in 2015. In it, he cites an Organisation for Economic Co-operation and Development (OECD) study, which concludes that between 2005 and 2009, thanks to Slim's telecom monopoly, Mexicans were $129 billion worse off (an amount equivalent to 1.8 percent of the country's yearly GDP), a fact attributable to the lack of competition and high concentration of the market within an openly dysfunctional legal system. "Evidently, the weakness of Mexican institutions," writes Esquivel, "has contributed to the sharp increase in the country's widespread inequality. The entire Mexican population paid extortionate telephone rates due to the monopolistic power of Mr. Slim's companies."

When Slim submitted his tender for Telmex, he didn't even make the *Forbes* list he now tops. The story is often told by his admirers that when he received the state-owned company he was a well-established businessman who possessed an admirable down-to-earth quality in his style of working with people. His defenders also recognize that Slim had a close relationship with Salinas de Gortari since his times as secretary of programming and budget, and the tycoon has never tried to hide the fact that he is a PRI sympathizer.

My interviewees often described Slim as a businessman who was sharp, nationalist, austere and a loyal PRI supporter who, a year after purchasing Telmex, achieved a net worth of over $1 billion, with which he entered, for the first time, into the exclusive club of those on the *Forbes* list.

Since he appeared on the global scene, one of his main critics has been the *Wall Street Journal*, though they have their own agenda in their editorial questions, according to some specialized journalists, such as Diego Fonseca: "*WSJ* tends to speak for Corporate America, which has been wanting to get its hands on Telmex for a while." The author of *Joséph Stiglitz detiene el tiempo* (*Joséph Stiglitz stops time*), a narrative profile of the economist, explains that now the bulk of the value of Slim's telecommunications businesses is increasingly international, particularly when it comes to mobile telephony, Internet and data, with a more promising future than fixed landlines, and that telecom monopolies are almost "naturally occurring" in deregulated economies due to the scale of business (the high cost of investing in landlines in the past and, more recently, the arrival of mobile telephony).

Fonseca explains:

> At least in the twenty greatest world markets there is one "incumbent" (a company with vast shares as compared to the rest, as it was the buyer of a privatized asset) during the opening. These incumbents have handled at least 60 percent of each market. Many of them are private and many others are partly state-owned. (An example: Telefónica, which has thrown bombs at Slim for his "monopoly," has historically been dominant in Spain, and is a company of mixed public-private capital.) As the infrastructure becomes optimal and the markets increase their client numbers, the weight of the incumbents is reduced. That makes the Mexican phenomenon more complicated, because after almost twenty-five years, recently with the start of 2014, Slim would reduce his enormous share from 70 percent to 49 percent, a share which is nearer to what telephone companies possess in the main European markets, for example.

Since Slim reached the top of the ultrarich, he insists, when speaking at conferences in the United States, that he does not run a telecom monopoly because in Latin America, for example, he is competing against Telefónica de España, and has competed at different times against Vodafone, Verizon, AT&T and MCI World Com. In fact, he often goes even further to suggest that there are no monopolies anywhere in the world: "It's just that there are some companies that are bigger than others," he says.

Telmex represented "very difficult professional and financial challenges," Slim explains in his document "History of Grupo Carso." At the time of purchase, the telephone company was operating "with huge deficiencies in service, obsolete equipment, a deteriorated exterior plant, a huge demand that was not being met, and combined subsidies of painful adjustment. All this was having huge consequences on the social and economic life of the country." Then he revealed that his investment was financed through unsecured debt for $500 billion: "The first public private offer for $307 billion, an increase in capital of $500 billion, and another public international offer for $1.094 trillion in January 1993."

The businessman says that consolidating the Mexican controlling company "was a difficult task due to the investment amounts and terms (five to ten years), and negotiations with our technological partners. Southwestern Bell and France Telecom were particularly complex, although we have not had any problems since the agreements were finalized. No doubt, the more you discuss and define the conditions of a partnership, the less problems you encounter further down the line."

For Jacques Rogozinski, who led the privatizations during the government of Salinas de Gortari, what happened with Telmex and other state-owned companies was a normal process considering the context:

In Mexico, the potential buyers who had access to the kind of resources required to purchase and operate Telmex and other state-owned companies and banks constituted a very small group of businessmen: the income distribution, the lack of savings, and the absence of loans for local businesspeople by the national and international banks, among other factors, did not allow (and still do not allow) for the development of a broader network of large businesses. On the other hand, whether there is a greater or smaller number of stakeholders does not depend on Mexico: all over the world, purchasing large companies is something that can only be done by a handful of large-scale corporate groups with extensive knowledge of the sector and a group of financial partners with sufficient capability to provide the capital in the long term. In Mexico, that market is still very small.

If anyone wanted to participate in the processes of purchase and sales of state-owned companies, they had to have a huge financial backing and belong to the country's corporate elite. Therefore, they also needed to have political connections with those in power, including at the presidential level. This happens in all countries. It would be absurd that if Bill Gates or Mark Zuckerberg call the president of the United States, he refused to take their call. And it is equally naïve to suppose that, in private conversation, the president of a nation would not pay attention to the needs of the most important businessmen in his or her country.

7

Privatization

The term "technocrat" was coined by H. G. Wells in one of his science fiction novels published in the early twentieth century. Now it could be defined as a science or technology expert with a great deal of power or influence over the government, regardless of political or ideological convictions. The term has been applied at various decisive moments in Mexico's political life to Jacques Rogozinski, who completed his PhD in economics at the University of Colorado.

Rogozinski was working for the Mexican National Lottery in the 1980s when he received the invitation to become part of the central sector of the federal government of Mexico from Pedro Aspe, an MIT economist and one of the main members of Carlos Salinas de Gortari's team. As president of the PRI party, between 1988 and 1994 Salinas de Gortari sold most of Mexico's state-owned companies, including Telmex.

"Hey, why don't you come and work with me? Cut the umbilical chord already," said Aspe, who was then secretary of programming and budget in the cabinet of Miguel de la Madrid, the president in power prior to Salinas de Gortari. That is how Rogozinski and Aspe were tasked, in early 1988, with the mission of studying privatization around the world. Rogozinski recalls Aspe's request: "All I want you to do is travel and research what different countries are doing with privatizations in general, and some in particular, such as telecommunications."

During Salinas de Gortari's presidential campaign, Rogozinski visited countries like Italy, Germany and Chile, although he focused mainly on the privatizing processes taking place in France and England. "As you know, Mrs. Thatcher was the figurehead of privatization and she was the one who got furthest with it," says Rogozinski. "I also had the opportunity to visit France and see how they had done it, although they had not exactly privatized the company, instead they had modernized the entire telephony department of France Telecom."

After his travels, Rogozinski reached the conclusion that Mexico had no other choice than to privatize the majority of its state-run companies. In his diagnostic report, he considered that during the government of Luis Echeverría (1970–76) the state-owned sector had grown excessively. The government was operating 1,100 companies, which included everything from a milk factory to a bicycle factory to steelworks such as Altos Hornos de México.

"Why the heck should the government be running, for example, a factory producing piña colada mix?" asks Rogozinski. "And then you had the problem of the steelworks, except those produced practically nothing and it was the most outrageous waste of money. For example, in Sicartsa, a steel plant in Michoacán, you produced 100 million tons of steel and lost $100 million producing it. Obviously it makes more sense to shut it down."

It's important to remember that even before doing his research, Rogozinski was already in favor of privatization. "But not evangelically," he clarifies. "It's not that the government couldn't have any public companies. With the Second World War, when there was no more steel left in the world, and when in Mexico there was not enough technology, or enough people with that financial capacity, a decision was made for the government to create steelworks. I think that was brilliant, because the United States was consuming all the steel. What is not clear is why we should applaud that fifty years later—you still have that company under the control of the State, when you already have steel coming out of your ears."

After his exploration of the neoliberal universe, Rogozinski concluded that it was best to start the privatization process with the smallest companies. "That way, if you stick your foot in it, there's no catastrophic consequences," he explains.

With that idea in mind, one of the first privatizations he oversaw was El Mirador de Acapulco, a hotel owned by the Mexican government and located beside the iconic cliff of La Quebrada, popular with daring local divers. But Salinas de Gortari had his eye on the telecom sector especially.

During the interview Rogozinski offered me in his office at Nacional Financiera, the government body he leads for Enrique Peña Nieto's government, he showed me a document in English entitled "Policy Options for Restructure in Telecommunications Industry Structure and Regulation in Mexico."

"What's the date on it?" I asked when he showed it to me.

"December 10, 1988."

That was just months after the contested general elections, in which widespread allegations of electoral fraud led to massive protests. Already, with Salinas de Gortari as president, Rogozinski had a diagnostic report under his arm and plenty of resources to help the new administration begin the bidding process. Telmex was one of the main targets.

"Why the heck would you not want to privatize a company where practically all local calls were free and long distance financed everything else? What's more, the way the company was organized for long distance calls was a disaster: if you wanted to make a call from Monterrey to Nuevo Laredo, because of the way Telmex was structured, the call had to go from Monterrey to Mexico City and from Mexico City to Nuevo Laredo!"

Speaking of the north of Mexico, the industrial conglomerate Grupo Alfa, the most important consortium in the country at that time, had conducted its own research on the national telecommunications sector, aiming to take over Telmex. Rogozinski recalls meeting with the businessmen in Monterrey and realizing that at the time the consortium had two very strong internal groups: one formed by young people and another, more traditional one. A member of the latter was Bernardo Garza Sada, then president of Grupo Alfa. The businessmen were considering submitting a bid for Telmex and invited Rogozinski to travel to Monterrey to talk about that possibility.

Rogozinski went there, and while they were eating sushi, Bernardo Garza Sada received a card from his assistant. The businessman excused himself, saying that the minister of finance, Pedro Aspe, was on the phone.

When he returned, Rogozinski said jokingly:

"Don't tell me the minister of finance called you to say you're in hot water over your taxes?"

"No, it's worse than that," the president of Alfa replied seriously.

"What do you mean, worse?"

"He just informed me that Mr. President, Carlos Salinas, has just decided that the steel industry will be privatized, and now bidding for Telmex is definitely out of the question. We are going to focus on the industry we know about."

In the end, Alfa did not take part in the bid for Telmex. The other two consortiums that participated along with Grupo Carso were Grupo Gentor, led by another Monterrey businessman, Javier Garza Sepúlveda (a childhood friend of Salinas de Gortari), as well as Accival Casa de Bolsa, owned by banker Roberto Hernández, in partnership with Telefónica de España and the company GTE.

The political columns of certain Mexican newspapers used to be the platform through which the PRI regime would communicate the decisions made by the president or government officials regarding sensitive issues. Telmex was one of them, and reading the columns from those years, you get the impression that the favorite candidate and likely winner in the bid was not Slim but Roberto Hernández, who already possessed a significant amount of shares and was on the company's board of directors. Hernández's defeat caused the relationship with Slim to cool, although the banker adhered to social convention and in the end published a newspaper spread that conceded the process.

"Numbers are numbers in this bid! There's no two ways about it," says Rogozinski when explaining that Slim won because he submitted the best bid and not because he received any presidential help.

"So, to what do you attribute the widespread perception that the bid was rigged?"

"I'll explain why that perception was created. I recommend you read my book *Mitos y mentadas de la economía mexicana* (*Myths and Mockery in the Mexican Economy*). Selling ideas using the media has become an efficient mechanism for developed nations, dominant businesses, important politicians and many others to kick away the ladder for others. In the public discourse of government functionaries, businesspeople and intellectuals kindly offer needy nations access to the ladder, but only in private do they kick it away. And here I give several examples. None of this is new: in the 1990s, global multilateral organizations such as the IMF [International Monetary Fund] and the World Bank, mainly financed and controlled by developing countries, defended the thesis that it was desirable to privatize national businesses. The spokespersons of the Washington Consensus claimed that countries need not worry about the need of new owners: all the global companies were presented as prophets of progress, as voluntary militants in favor of developing countries. If you got distracted, you might start believing that the world was full of good Samaritans. And the media were one of the most useful tools to spread these ideas, but time has demonstrated the fallacy."

Before the Telmex bid, according to Rogozinski, Slim was very reluctant to participate. President Salinas de Gortari himself and minister of finance Pedro Aspe invited him to accompany them on a tour in Japan and they discussed the subject during the long-haul flight.

"When Salinas, Aspe and Slim returned from the trip to Japan, the secretary said to me: 'I think we've managed to persuade Slim, but he still hasn't fully made a decision; can you go and convince him.'" A few days later, Rogozinski went to see Slim in his home. "I was with Slim in his home, which by the way had a pool that never had water in it, and he says, 'If I enter and win, it will change my life and I don't know if that's what I want. The whole family gets together every Sunday at home. I'll talk to them this Sunday, and on Monday I'll let you know what I've decided.'"

Rogozinski returned on Monday and Slim said he would submit a bid. So, on November 15, 1990, he presented his proposal to purchase Telmex. He did it through Grupo Carso, S.A. de C.V., according to the original documentation consulted. Grupo Carso's proposal included Seguros de México, S.A. de C.V. (Segumex), France Cables et Radio, S.A. ("France Cables") and Southwestern Bell International Holdings (SBIH) Corporation. The offer was to buy Telmex Series AA shares at $0.80165 per share, for a total of 2,163,040,972 AA shares, together with a stock option for Telmex Series L shares. Grupo Carso and Segumex participated with the majority of the Mexican group package, while France Cables and SBIH underwrote in equal parts the total of the foreign group. The purchase of all the shares and the stock option was carried out through a special trust fund.

The formal proposal with which Slim won Telmex states that the group of investors "wishes to support the development and spread of knowledge in the field of telecommunications in Mexico, for which purpose it proposes to establish, carry out and finance education programs and training in said field, acting through the appropriate Mexican institutions." It also clarifies that the offer was under the condition that, by December 7, 1990, the company SBIH would waive certain restrictions imposed by the courts of the United States of America, referred to as "Modification of Final Judgment-MFJ."

Slim and his partners attached to the proposal a "modernization plan" and a "joint-venture association contract," which specified the equity participation of each one of the members of the consortium. "In its totality," says the text by Slim and his partners, "they comprise a powerful and singular combination that meets all the necessary attributes to make Telmex one of the top telecommunications companies in the world." It goes on to provide a profile for each of the shareholders:

> Grupo Carso is one of the most important industrial conglomerates in Mexico, with a successful track record in the management and modernization of complex businesses. France Cables, wholly owned by France Telecom, which in turn depends on the French government and is considered among the main international telecommunications companies, has widely demonstrated its ability to rapidly and effectively modernize large-scale telecommunications systems. SBIH is a wholly owned subsidiary of Southwestern Bell Corporation, a publicly listed stock corporation recognized in the industry as a leader in network operations management and development of mobile communications and telephone directories.

Other documents that formed the offer include a series of receipts for the deposits left as security for $50 million, copies of authorizations and powers of the members of the consortium, and the sales contract of the members of the consortium in case the government accepted the offer and the trust agreement of Grupo Carso, France Telecom and Southwestern Bell. Slim and his partners also clarified that, should they win the bid, they would need to discuss with the government aspects of the concession titles of Telmex and the business service, as well as technical assistance contracts.

Jaime Chico Prado, who at the time was one of Slim's associates, signed the formal proposal and provided as his address 1020 Sierra Vertiente, in Lomas de Chapultepec in Mexico City. The message ends with a succinct list of motives: "We have a great deal of interest in the challenges and opportunities that the privatization of Telmex represents, and we would like to underline our absolute dedication to the task of collaborating with Telmex and the government to develop a world-class telecommunications system."

One little-known aspect of Slim's formal proposal to purchase Telmex is the special participation of a group of Mexican entrepreneurs. The document states that other shareholders—through Grupo Carso, on behalf of third parties—were businessmen Agustín Franco (and family), Miguel Alemán, Rómulo O'Farril, Bernardo Quintana, Antonio y Moisés Cosío, Ángel Lozada Moreno, Manuel Espinosa Yglesisas, Antonio del Valle, the Mary Street Jenkins Foundation, José Miguel Nader, Claudio X. González, Antonio Chedraui, Ángel Demerutis Elizarraraz, investors from Sinaloa, such as Ignacio Cobo, and investors from Tabasco.

Rogozinski claims it is wrong to state that Slim purchased Telmex in 1990: "Salinas de Gortari's friend was not the owner of Telmex. If Southwestern Bell had not decided to contribute $72 million more to the group's offer, the owner would have been Roberto Hernández. In other words, the privatization did not favor any friend of the president, but was won by an American businessman! Ed Whitacre III offered more money than the rest. The silence around this is deafening. And if you don't believe me, you have one advantage: Mr. Whitacre is alive. He has invited many people to go and interview him, but no one has wanted to do so. Why? Because then their false tale about the government handing Telmex to Slim will fall to pieces."

The day after my interview with Rogozinski, I requested an interview with Whitacre III. At the date of publishing this book, no response had arrived. And reading Rogozinski's book, I found a table preceded by the following text:

The press never mentioned that American shareholders earned two dollars for each one that Slim received, nor did it pay too much attention to the composition of the share capital of Telmex by the end of the privatization process:

- 10%: Southwestern Bell
- 5.23%: 32 Mexican investors
- 5.17%: Carlos Slim
- 5%: France Telecom
- 4% reserved for the workers (50,000 people)
- 70.6% was in the New York and Mexico stock exchanges

Truth be told: Salinas's "friend" was not the owner of Telmex.

8

Monopoly

On December 11, 2014, exactly twenty-five years after Carlos Slim purchased Telmex, former president Carlos Salinas de Gortari, upon request from the newspaper *El Financiero*, responded to some often-asked questions about this sale with an article published in two parts under the title "Telmex, a successful privatization that was later questioned." The reason the still-powerful ex-president decided to delve further into this point, as he writes in his introduction, is that it coincided with "the fresh perspective of the great telecommunications reform in 2014."

In the article, Salinas defends the privatization conducted by his government and cites favorable opinions from the World Bank. The interesting part is that he goes on to question the lack of regulation of Telmex by the governments that followed his term of office (Ernesto Zedillo, Vicente Fox and Felipe Calderón) and quotes recent surveys (which he does not identify) in which "most users complained despairingly about cut-off calls, undue charges, not enough coverage, lack of connectivity and disconnection of the service for no reason." The politician, who a wide sector of the population in Mexico at some point believed was the person behind Slim, concludes his text saying that, "to many, Telmex has become the 'black beast' of Mexican private companies."

Throughout the article, the ex-president rules out that the privatization of Telmex was done for ideological reasons or that it produced a greater concentration of wealth in Mexico. He also contends that the process was not rushed, nor that it sought to benefit hidden partners. Likewise, he argued that the funds obtained never disappeared from the treasury. This is the position that Salinas has defended in other texts and public speeches. However, Salinas's last three arguments are direct accusations against Slim, as he claims that Telmex in fact is now a private monopoly, citing a study by the OECD: "Telmex controls 80 percent of the market in landlines and 70 percent of mobile telephony. It is a company with dominant power throughout all sectors of the market (landline, mobile and broadband networks) and across all the regions of the country." The OECD concludes that Telmex, the dominant operator, "enjoys lasting power over the market that the competition is not denting and which is equally not limited by regulation in any efficient way."

The ex-president also states that Telmex "is now an inefficient and abusive company" and he again quotes the OECD document:

> Its prices are too high: Mexican users pay more than most member countries of the OECD. The case of broadband, the most important one technologically, is the worst: the prices are among the highest and the rate of coverage is lower with very slow speeds. Telmex has profit margins double those of the OECD, and in exchange it occupies the last place in coverage and the last in investment per capita. High costs, high prices, bad quality, and few options have a negative impact on the welfare of all Mexicans.

Finally, Salinas claims it was not the privatization of Telmex— made during his government—that catapulted Slim to his position as richest man in the world:

> Slim did not inherit his fortune from Telmex. He took advantage of neoliberal deregulation to consolidate his business in the emergence of a new sector, mobile telephony, and entered as a dominant player in that sector across Latin America (Argentina, Colombia, Ecuador, Guatemala, among others.) The fortune is in América Móvil, which was never a public company. In 2012, that company was worth over $100 million. Telmex, on the other hand, fifteen years after it was sold, had the same value in real terms, when taking into account the size of the investment made during its expansion.

During one of my interviews with Slim, I ask him about this. The tycoon tells me he knows of the article but has not read it, so in order to have his opinion I read him some extracts. As I do so, he interrupts:

"It's a lie. He's just covering his own back and everyone else did it all wrong. He says Telmex is inefficient. What does being inefficient mean if competitors have come in, such as Telefónica, AT&T, Verizon, Vodafone? Do you think it's very inefficient if none of those companies have been successful?" Then he takes a document from the table. It's an OECD report. He flicks through it until he finds a graph: "This is the income per minute per country. Mexico sells at two cents and only these countries sell at one: Telefónica sells at nine cents in Spain. Are we being abusive by selling at two cents?"

"Salinas also quotes OECD documents to question Telmex…"

"Well, José Ángel Gurría—former secretary of the OECD—was paid 90,000 euros to do a study in which he cut América Móvil to bits and said we were the worst and whatever else, but they're correcting it now."

"So, what was Salinas's motivation to write this article?"

"He wants to prove that he's brilliant and beyond reproach, that he did everything by the book and everyone else is shady and moronic, and that Telmex is a piece of shit."

"Does that mean there is no longer a relationship between you and Salinas?"

"No, I do see him… I saw him the other day and told him he was telling a whole lot of lies."

"And what did he say to that?"

Slim makes a flustered reply and then asks me not to publish what he just said.

Then he completes his answer.

"Maybe I'll read the whole thing he wrote and point out the lies to him one by one. He wrote for *El Financiero* to get on the right side of Televisa and the television networks. He was a puppet again. Anyway, if I start arguing, considering the state of the country, I'd only be adding more tension to the current situation."

"Beyond what Salinas says, there is the widespread perception that the government handed you a monopoly…"

"That's the lie that gets repeated over and over. Look, in this case my competitor was the beneficiary. In the terms of the call for tenders, he was benefiting, because it said you could give shares as payment or as a guarantee, and we had nothing and he had 10.6 percent of the company... There was a brokerage house that owned 10.6 percent before, because the point was that the amount we offered for the company was far above what it was worth a year prior. You have seen that, right? How much it was worth?"

Slim's main competitor for the purchase of Telmex was Hernández, who at the time owned Banamex. Before the privatization of the state-owned company, the brokerage house Accival, of which Hernández is a partner, bought Telmex shares until it obtained 10 percent.

In those years, Hernández was the favorite candidate to win the bid for the Mexican telephone company. However, he did not lose out entirely: in December 1984, Telmex had a market value of $316.8 million. Hernández and the other Accival partners, whose names are not all known to us, having accumulated a good amount of Telmex shares prior to the privatization, saw how the value of their investment was going through the roof.

"When Telmex was privatized, 20.4 percent was sold to private investors," Slim says, as he does some calculations on a piece of paper. "Of which 10.2 percent was to foreign investors, and of the rest we had about 5.2 percent in Carso and Inbursa, of which I owned about 60 percent. So in reality I had about 3.7 percent. They said it was mine, but I only had 3.7 or 3.8 percent of Telmex."

I also asked Rogozinski about the article penned by the ex-president whose government he had worked for:

"Well, and what do you want me to say?"

"Your opinion on the article."

"Regardless of what it says there, I want to say that Telmex was a successful privatization. Look, you may criticize all you want, but what you cannot criticize is that today, if you need a phone, you get it installed within days, if not hours."

"The ex-president recognizes that aspect of the privatization process, but says that afterwards Telmex became inefficient, monopolistic and so on, because there was no regulation."

"Look, my point of view on that subject is this: is there a regulation problem? Yes, but not because there was none, but because it was not enforced. There's a difference, even though the end result is the same. The average citizen doesn't care. I can accept that some of the aspects criticized about Telmex that are due to the lack of regulation enforcement. What I do not accept is that Slim does not invest."

...

"Explain to me why you want Slim to invest more. If he invests more, his service will improve, and if his service improves, more people will move to Telcel, and if more people move to Telcel, he will make more profit, which is not bad, but aren't you complaining that Slim is a monopolist, that Slim is dominating? If he does what you say, will he become more or less dominant?"

...

"But, is it a monopoly or not, as the ex-president Salinas claims?"

"That's another of the old wives' tales. Let's see, does Telmex provide 100 percent of users in Mexico City? No. Is it 80 percent? No. Maybe 60 percent. Let's say it has 60 percent. From 60 percent to 100 percent, there is a huge jump. Now, in the tiny, remote village of Quinchunchu, Telmex has 100 percent. Sure, maybe in that place. Why? Because nobody else is investing there! Telmex may be dominant in some places and in others it may be monopolistic, but that's not because it wants to be, it's because Telmex is obliged to go there. Nobody else wants to go there and nobody will. So the question becomes about how to pull that village out of a monopoly if no other service providers want to go there because it's not profitable. The problem is 100 percent political."

9

PRI

On Sunday, July 2, 2000, a former Coca-Cola CEO, Vicente Fox, won the presidential elections in Mexico as candidate for the right-wing PAN. For the first time in over seventy years, the PRI had lost the country's most important elections. That day, Carlos Slim went to the national headquarters of the party that had fallen out of favor, and was photographed with PRI leaders such as Enrique Jackson and Jesús Murillo Karam, before saluting the defeated presidential candidate, Francisco Labastida Ochoa. The upset expression on the tycoon's face coincides with the story that some current PRI leaders have told regarding his disappointment on the night when the international community was commenting on Mexico's transition to democracy.

Octavio Paz said that the state created by the PRI was a faceless and soulless master who did not subjugate the people like a demon, but like a machine, and that as the evil grew, the evildoers stopped being exceptional and became smaller. We Mexicans summarized that period by saying: "The PRI used to steal, but at least they allowed others to steal too." The central power in Mexico, Paz explains, did not reside in private capitalism, in trade unions or political parties, but in the state. The poet called it the "secular Trinity": the state was the capital, the labor and the party, with the state belonging to an administrative technocracy and a political caste being led every six years by a different all-powerful president.

However, with Salinas de Gortari as president, the PRI again experienced a drastic change in its relationship to capital, and it publicly acknowledged, without any nationalist complexes, its closeness to the business community. That administration created a government department whose name was still reminiscent of Soviet bureaucracy: the Commission for Financing and Equity Consolidation. The aim of the commission would be to fundraise for the PRI among businessmen. Slim appears as one of the board members on a 1988 party document. Around the same time, the public charity Gilberto was being registered, headed up by first lady Cecilia Occelli de Salinas, with the purpose of helping the thousands of people affected by hurricane Gilberto, which devastated entire cities and villages. Soumaya Domit, Slim's wife, also sat on the board of directors.

During the years in which Slim opened his wallet for the PRI, he rose to the *Forbes* club as if by private elevator. Before Salinas de Gortari's term of office ended, according to the newspaper records of the time, Slim donated at least $25 million to the official party for Ernesto Zedillo's electoral campaign, who would go on to become the next president of Mexico. In February 1993, Salinas de Gortari hosted a dinner party at which he asked Slim and other multimillionaires for that sum to ensure the triumph of the PRI in the following elections, and to allow it to retain tight control over the country the way the party had done ever since its creation in 1929—with each incumbent president naming his successor. After the Mexican Revolution overthrew Porfirio Díaz's thirty-year dictatorship, the Institutional Revolutionary Party had in effect established its own dictatorship, despite running formal elections each year.

The newspaper *El Economista* was tipped off about the meeting, and published the news under the headline: "PRI sets quotas for big businessmen." Days later, the former president of the Inter-American Development Bank (IADB), Antonio Ortiz Mena—in whose mansion Salinas de Gortari's meeting with the multimillionaires was hosted—offered a press conference in which he explained that the PRI had been linked to government since its inception, but that now that circumstance was coming to an end, which was why the political institution needed an independent economic life.

It was no coincidence that such an important event was hosted at the home of Ortiz Mena, who had been the regime's minister of finance for twelve consecutive years. He represented the PRI's old administrative technocracy, which was breathing its last. Other multimillionaires present at the meeting were Carlos Hank Rhon, Claudio X. González, Emilio Azcárraga, Alberto Bailléres, Roberto Hernández, Adrián Sada and Lorenzo Zambrano. Slim was the only one of them who had long been a part of the PRI's Commission for Financing and Equity Consolidation.

A year after that dinner party, with the elections underway, Slim was approached by a small group of reporters in the Constellations room of Hotel Nikko, during an event in support of Luis Donaldo Colosio's recently launched campaign for the presidency of the republic. With the shadow of Telmex's sale still lingering, the subjects of the financing of the PRI and the Zapatista uprising were the main points on the national agenda.

"How much will you donate to the PRI?" one of the journalists asked Slim.

"It's not interview time."

"Later, if you prefer."

"No, I'd rather send you a document where I summarize my position regarding the country."

"Tell me about Telmex. Cuauhtémoc Cárdenas says that if you win the elections, the company will again be put to public tender."

"But I only own 2 percent of the shares of the company: 75 percent of the shares belong to small owners. I can prove it."

"Cuauhtémoc Cárdenas says the tender was conducted incorrectly. What's your opinion?"

"That that's a whole load of hogwash, along with all the other nonsense that man spouts. He's being ignorant, quite frankly, and what's more, not admitting it. I can send you documents for everything."

"Sir, instead, please tell me about it."

"No, no. Interviews don't allow people to work in peace."

"What's your opinion about the conflict in Chiapas?"

"I'll send you my document in due course."

Over twenty years after that tumultuous 1994, I asked Slim if in 2015 he still considered himself a PRI supporter.

"No, I was never a member of any party," he replied.

"But you were: you appear formally as a member of the PRI's Commission for Financing and Equity Consolidation."

"Yes, I was invited. It was a way in which... Look, there were two things: they wanted to separate, because the Ministry of Finance provided the funds for all the parties, all of them, except the PAN, which was using different model. So I imagine it was an attempt to do things differently."

"Were you a member of the PRI's Commission for Financing?"

"Yes, but we never held a meeting, to my knowledge."

"Have you never considered yourself a PRI supporter?"

"Not me. I voted for the PRI for president and PAN for members of congress and senators. Always. From when I was twenty-one. That's the way I've voted."

"Is the PRI of today the same as it used to be?"

"We'd need to speak in more detail about that, but the PRI changed every six years. That's like asking: is the current prime minister of China the same as the former prime minister. What China is doing now is the way the PRI used to do things."

10

Heart

Ten years before becoming the wealthiest man on earth, Carlos Slim was at death's door with a heart condition. In the fall of 1997, the tycoon looked so thin and weak that his close friends worried they might never see him again in his office doing calculations on three calculators at a time. And those close to him couldn't get used to the idea of not seeing him review financial reports from all over the world with the impassive gaze of a shark hunting its prey. He traveled in secret to Houston, Texas, accompanied by his wife, to have one of the valves in his heart replaced. It was considered a low-risk operation.

He went to the Texas Heart Institute, an Adventist medical center directed by Denton Cooley, who was famous for having carried out the first artificial heart transplant. The surgical team leader was Michael Duncan, and the doctor in charge of operating, Paolo Angelini, was an Italian cardiologist who had studied in Mexico, spoke passable Spanish and to whom Slim took a liking. When they were finishing the open-heart surgery, the seam on the new valve broke. Slim suffered a hemorrhage that the specialists battled to stop, transfusing thirty-one bags of blood. During the twenty-four hours that followed, Slim breathed with the help of a ventilator. His immune system was vulnerable and he caught pneumonia. Within a couple of weeks, the businessman lost over forty pounds.

It was almost November 2, and as is traditional in Mexico for the Day of the Dead, all the newspapers published humorous obituaries in rhyming verse—known as *calaveras*—for well-known living figures. This is the *calavera* that *Reforma* published for Carlos Slim:

Death in the end will always win
even if you mess with its affairs.
That's the story of how our Slim
left the Forbes' list of billionaires.

The dead are looking all encumbered
all because of Carlos' numbers:
since he went and bought the graveyard
the price rise caught them off their guard!

By all appearances it seemed that, regardless of the *calavera*, the main headlines that fall would announce the death of the then-richest man in Latin America, who, at age fifty-seven possessed a fortune of $6.5 billion. Some of his associates believed that he had in fact died, and spread that rumor. Others thought that Slim's rivals, such as the banker Roberto Hernández, divulged the news to destabilize his shares in the stock exchange. Slim's PR team had to issue a press release to clarify that the owner of Telmex was still alive and all was business as usual throughout his empire:

Mr. Slim Helú underwent a scheduled cardiovascular procedure in October. During the recovery process he contracted pneumonia, which he is recovering well from. The businesses and institutions in which Mr. Slim is a shareholder continue to operate unchanged, with the same administrative structures.

Doctor Héctor Castañón, head of intensive care at Hospital Siglo XXI, traveled to Houston to support his recovery. Slim stayed several weeks more in the United States before returning to Mexico to continue his rehabilitation at his home in Acapulco, where he celebrated his fifty-eighth birthday with a small party on January 28. From there he would leave for Cuernavaca and finally return to Mexico City.

Meanwhile, the daily battles around his growing empire

continued. On his birthday, a grassroots organization in Mexico City, the Asociación para la Defensa de Tlalpan (Association for the Defense of Tlalpan), through actress Jesusa Rodríguez and former congressman Marco Rascón, lodged a criminal claim against Slim at the PGR for the building works that were being carried out at the archaeological site of Cuicuilco, in the capital of Mexico. The unhappy neighbors were demanding a ten-year jail term for the president of Grupo Carso for the damages that his business was causing to the most ancient pre-Hispanic city in the Valley of Mexico. Around the same time, Telmex was facing a string of public legal disputes with the companies AT&T and MCI, which had started competing in the Mexican long-distance calling market.

However, Slim's main worry at that time was whether he would be fit enough to continue directing his businesses. At some point, he even told some of his associates that he was considering retiring from his financial operations altogether. What he did instead was to accelerate the transmission of responsibilities to his three sons, who took on the most senior roles within Grupo Carso. Carlos was thirty-one years old, Marco Antonio was thirty, and Patrick was twenty-nine when they were named presidents of strategic areas of their father's empire. Other members of Slim's family were also placed in key areas of the group, such as the directorship of Telmex for Héctor Slim Seade, son of Julián, Slim's elder brother. The four young men had studied at Universidad Anáhuac, educational bastion of the Legion of Christ.

Fructuoso Pérez, a friend of Slim's since their college years, found out about the supposed death of the millionaire in a newspaper. He soon confirmed the news as fake and afterwards, he got all the details about what had happened, from Slim himself. He says that the tycoon gets in a bad mood when he remembers that period: he used to get impatient with the hospital and the ineptitude of nurses and doctors. Still, "for him it was a new lease of life. It made him think about making changes."

Slim almost never talks about what happened during those days. Not even with his closest friends, although he sometimes mentions a Cuban doctor.

"Was it a Cuban doctor who saved your life in 1997?" I ask Slim in an interview.

"That doctor appeared after they said I'd gone belly up. The same day a resident doctor, quite young, of Argentinian origin, was the one who came to the rescue even as the others were gathering the family to tell them I'd snuffed it."

"Why did they say that to your family?"

"I wasn't... I was in a very bad way. They probably left me in the room thinking I was not going to get better and then it was an Argentinian who helped me. Then there were several crises because they gave me a glass of orange juice and I got pulmonary aspiration. And afterwards I was treated by a Cuban doctor—Dr. Guillermo Gutiérrez—but at another hospital, at the University of Texas. I stayed there for three months. Then I wanted to get back to Mexico as soon as possible. They told me to ease back into things, so I went to Acapulco first and then Cuernavaca. Then Mexico City. These are painful experiences, but you survive thanks to your love of life and the support of your family. My wife was very intelligent, as are my children."

In October 1992, five years before the problems with his heart valve, Slim had already undergone an initial cardiovascular surgery, supervised by Dr. Teodoro Césarman, the renowned cardiologist of former president Luis Echeverría and the Mexican comedian Cantinflas. After that operation, Slim decided to spend his recovery at his mansion in Acapulco. The press knew even less about that operation, having only recently become interested in the millionaire because he had won the Telmex tender. A few days after being discharged, he was admitted again. The surgeon, Michael Duncan, a member of Cooley's team, saved him on that occasion—the second time he found himself at death's door, in 1997.

Slim's health was not yet a matter of speculation in the stock exchange. When admitted for surgery, his wife Soumaya playfully checked him in under the false name Carlos Delgado (the Spanish word for "slim"), to prevent him from being recognized. The only people who knew about the surgery were Soumaya, their children, and their friends Ignacio Cobo and Juan Antonio Pérez Simón. Months earlier, the latter had also undergone surgery and recommended Slim put himself in the hands of Césarman's team.

During his initial recovery period, Slim had several relapses. He became depressed. He grew a beard and dressed scruffily. In those days, when he was just thirty-third on the *Forbes* list, he told his friends he felt like giving up business. He even told Pérez Simón that he no longer cared about anything. In January 1993, Cobo and Pérez Simón rented a plane and took their partner and friend to the Texas Heart Institute.

After Slim had his heart "tied up," he continued business with renewed energy. That hospital now receives regular donations from him, perhaps an emotional exception to his pragmatic philosophy regarding generosity.

In 1997, after his operation and near-death experience, it appeared as if he might retire from business altogether. A decade later, however, he had become the richest man on earth.

11

Soumaya

Just two years after escaping death, Carlos Slim would go through another tough test. His wife, Soumaya Domit Gemayel, fell ill as a result of a congenital kidney disease, passing away on March 7, 1999, at the age of fifty.

Soumaya's funeral was officiated by Bishop Onésimo Cepeda, who, before taking up vows, used to be a banker and Slim's partner at Inbursa; by Jesuit priest Sergio Cobo, brother of his friend Ignacio Cobo; and by Legion of Christ founder Marcial Maciel. The wake at the family home in Las Lomas was attended by then-president Ernesto Zedillo and the majority of the Mexican political elite. A glaring absence was that of former president Salinas de Gortari.

While Slim researched different places around the world for remedies and treatments for chronic renal failure, his wife faced the disease with a strength admired by those around her. During the last months of her life, Dr. Francisco Ruiz Maza, head of the Hospital Español Nephrology Service, helped Soumaya write a manual for other patients like her. The book, titled *La verdadera alegría es la tristeza superada (True Happiness is Sadness Overcome)*, has a restricted distribution to certain hospitals and foundations, where doctors offer it to patients diagnosed with the same illness from which Slim's wife died.

The fifty-four-page, no-frills chapbook, which includes illustrations of Mexico's beloved comic actor Cantinflas, begins with Soumaya requesting those diagnosed with chronic kidney failure to stay calm, saying that a positive attitude will minimize uncertainty.

In addition to the message in the introduction, the publication explains how the kidneys work, the kinds of treatments available and the medications used. The last chapter is a reflection entitled "To my family," in which Soumaya suggests the ideal kind of relationship between the patient and their loved ones:

TO MY FAMILY:
I would like to ask a few things of you:
1. Love: to feel loved is more important to me now than ever.
2. Understanding toward my spells of bad temper, my limitations, my need to rest.
3. Practical help to me keep going.
4. Joy: to enjoy life even more than before. To combat the atmosphere of pessimism and sadness that emerges when one finds out about these things; through music, entertainment, a sense of humor, etc.
5. Trust in the fact that I can improve and become better day by day, despite having this problem.
6. Challenges so that I don't feel useless, so that I don't remain in an environment of overprotection, which only leads me to have a passive and self-destructive attitude. Please, do not ask me all the time how I feel and let me do the things I can and should do. Don't help me when it's not essential; instead, ask me to do all the things I am capable of, even if they take me some effort.

Thank you very much for helping me, this way, to become a better person each day.

Slim and Soumaya were married on April 28, 1966, at the church of San Agustín, in the Polanco district of Mexico City, where they both lived before they met. He was twenty-five years old and she, seventeen. There was no party, just a religious ceremony, because one month prior to the wedding Soumaya's father, Antonio Domit, had passed away. The vows before the civil judge were given in private, but all the bride and groom's relatives and friends were invited to the church ceremony. The event was covered by *Emir*, the magazine of the Lebanese émigré community in Mexico in those years.

The title of the article is "Domit-Slim wedding was a huge event," and throughout the text it is evident that, because of their respective family origins, the person of interest is Soumaya and not Carlos.

Soumaya is described thus: "The beautiful bride is the daughter of Don Antonio Domit, the late Lebanese industrialist, and the distinguished Doña Lily Gemayel, widow of Domit, widely known and highly esteemed in our social circles," while Slim is described thus:

> The groom is, on his part, a magnificent young man who honors the Lebanese colony. Responding to the intellectual prestige of his forefathers, on the side of his mother, among whom there are many brilliant jurisconsults and people of letters who have brought light to our beloved motherland, Carlos Slim, an engineer, is also a brilliant lecturer at UNAM. His reputation as a talented mathematician is on the rise.

Soumaya was accompanied to the altar by her brother Pedro and her grandmother Emile Gemayel, who had traveled from Lebanon. Slim was given away by his mother, Linda Helú, and his older brother, Julián, representing his late father.

The priest, Marcial Maciel, was at the time the young, up-and-coming founder of the Legion of Christ, an institution of the Catholic Church that reached a very powerful position within the Mexican elite. Soumaya would maintain a close relationship with the Legion of Christ and Maciel till her last day; she didn't live to hear of the scandals of corruption and pedophilia committed by Maciel, for which the congregation fell into disrepute in the early 2000s, and which eventually prompted the Vatican to take action.

Soumaya Domit and Carlos Slim had six children: three boys—Carlos, Marco Antonio and Patrick—and three girls—Johanna, Vanessa and Soumaya. The "seventh child" was Grupo Carso.

It has been twenty years since Slim became a widower, and although the press has been curious about whether he might remarry, and there has been some speculation about possible candidates, from Mexican actresses to members of Arab royal families to divas of world cinema, Slim continues to affirm his enduring love for his late wife.

12

Gemayel

Carlos Slim's late wife came from one of the most powerful families in Mexico's Lebanese community. Soumaya and her brothers Lilo, Pedro, Antonio and Muchel were children of businessman Antonio Domit and Lily Gemayel. Antonio Domit, like hundreds of Lebanese people, left his country at the start of the twentieth century fleeing war and a lack of business opportunities. After making his fortune in Mexico through manufacturing and sales of footwear, he returned to Lebanon in 1946 for a spell to explore the possibility of doing business there. During the journey he met Lily Gemayel, daughter of a sheikh and niece of Pierre Gemayel—founder of Al Kataeb, a nationalist movement and political party that took inspiration in the Spanish phalange and Italian fascism. Pierre Gemayel was also the political leader of a powerful Maronite community, the Maronites being the largest Christian denomination in Lebanon.

Antonio Domit and Lily Gemayel were married in Beirut, Lebanon, on Thursday, February 6, 1947, at the Saint George Cathedral. The magazine *Emir* described the event thus: "The union of the beautiful Lebanese lady and the great Mexican industrialist constituted a social event without precedent."

Unlike the discreet wedding between Carlos Slim and Soumaya Domit, the matrimonial union of Antonio Domit and Lily Gemayel was quite the event. Antonio Domit arrived by car to the Gemayel family residence, followed by friends and journalists who formed an impressive caravan of vehicles for the time. Lily came out wearing a white dress adorned with orange blossoms and walked to the car, where she sat next to her father Michel, who held her arm during the journey. Meanwhile, Antonio traveled with Pierre Gemayel, the Phalangist leader, who was best man at the wedding. They all advanced to the cathedral in Beirut, escorted as well by the local police. The cathedral had been decorated with hundreds of flowers, rugs and tapestries. Lily walked to the altar accompanied by her godmother, Samia Aboussouan, daughter of the former president of the Court of Cassation, while Antonio walked down the aisle beside his best man, Pierre Gemayel. Among the guests were former presidents, ministers of the Lebanese government, generals and members of parliament. The vicar of the Maronite Church in Lebanon, Abdala Khouri, was in charge of blessing the union. Then a secretary read the special message sent by the Maronite Patriarch, reflecting on the Lebanese emigration to America:

We are proud of the example that you have set, loyal son of the Lebanese man who abandons his motherland pushed by the love of work and progress, but who always carries in his heart his love and loyalty toward Lebanon. The children of Lebanon carry abroad their talent, energy and honor, and live among people whose language and customs they do not know; but they do not take long to learn the language and take the best of their customs, in the end occupying high ranks and important positions. They keep their link with the motherland, follow its situation closely and offer their help to see it become prosperous and glorious. There are times, such as this case, when they return to their country to choose their life partner, a young lady from the noble Lebanese families.

We congratulate you, and ask God to make your marriage joyous and give you many children so you may educate them in the love of God and Lebanon, and increase their joy in the union with their life partner.

In witness whereof, we repeat our congratulations to you and your relatives, and wholeheartedly give you our apostolic blessing.

Bkerque, February 6, 1947
Antoun Pedro Arida
Patriarch of Antioch and all the Orient

At the end of the religious ceremony, the wedding party was held at the Sisters of Besançon School, where Lily had completed her studies. They spent their wedding night in the village of Chtaura and then traveled to Egypt by plane for their honeymoon. A month later, they embarked on their journey to Mexico, stopping in Paris along the way and then in New York, where they met with the city's Lebanese community, headed by Salloum Mozarkel, director of an Arab-language newspaper called *Al Hoda*. Finally, on May 4, their plane touched down in Mexico City, where they were welcomed by a mariachi band, a group of workers from the footwear factory, and a number of relatives led by Pedro Domit, Antonio's brother.

A few days after the wedding they gave an interview in their home for the magazine *Emir*. Lily Gemayel gave it in French: a "beautiful, exquisite, almost polychromatic French, which denotes the presence of a select, cultivated spirit, and a clear and well-organized mind." The conversation began with the question about the genteel nature of the Lebanese colony in Mexico and praise for them from Lily, who then spoke about her nostalgia for Lebanon:

The past few days, walking around the capital, standing before panoramas of incomparable beauty, there were moments when I felt I was in Lebanon itself. What I love most are the flowers, the trees, the blue sky. Blue is my favorite color, and when I landed in Mexico, the first impression that my spirit perceived was that: lots of flowers, lots of trees, a blue sky of breathtaking depths, that reminds me of the sky of the Mediterranean. Flowers, trees, blue sky... If I had nothing more, that would already be enough for me to love Mexico.

During the same interview, Antonio Domit spoke of his journey and reencounter with Lebanon, celebrating the independence achieved by his country, and then lamenting the unfavorable economic situation, derived from a cycle of depression and postwar uncertainty. When the *Emir* journalist asked him whether there was any organization that unified Lebanon's political aspirations, Domit responded:

> Yes, there is. In Lebanon's national panorama, there is one organization that stands out vigorously—a movement that brings together at its core several tens of thousands of members, in which Lebanon can perhaps find its firmest hopes. It is not, in itself, a political organization. It is a movement of national forward momentum and projection, whose members sacrifice themselves for their ideals and make contributions from their own funds, and entirely give up on personal profit and advantages, and if we are to speak of politics, in the end, it should have no other meaning than that which serves to tackle the vital problems on whose solution the present and the future of Lebanon depend. That movement contains the most expansive and wholesome part of the Lebanese youth, the new ideas, the new style. That movement is called Al Kataeb.

Al Kataeb was founded in 1936—the year when legendary black athlete Jesse Owens won four gold metals and broke two world records at the Olympics in Berlin, to Hitler's dismay. The right-wing, anticolonial movement's motto kept with the times: "God, fatherland, family." Pierre Gemayel, Antonio Domit's best man and uncle of Soumaya, fervently claimed the Phoenicians as ancestors of the Lebanese. As years went by, the movement turned into a political party and, in the 1970s, Bashir Gemayel, cousin of Soumaya and son of Pierre, created a paramilitary wing called the Lebanese Forces, a counterpart of today's Muslim Hezbollah guerrillas.

Bashir became president of Lebanon in 1982 with the backing of Israel and the rejection of thousands of Palestinian refugees from the war in their homeland, living in temporary camps in Lebanon. A few weeks after taking office, Bashir was murdered. His brother Amin replaced him and, in retaliation, the Phalange followers of the Gemayel family attacked the refugee camps of Sabra and Shatila, killing, according to the Red Cross, 2,400 Palestinians in front of the occupying Israeli troops.

But Antonio Domit didn't live to see this; he died of a heart attack in 1966—and a month after his death, his widow, Lily Gemayel, went dressed in black to the wedding of her daughter Soumaya and Carlos Slim, an engineer whose only claim to fame was his talent in mathematics, and who married into the most aristocratic family of the Lebanese right wing.

13

Exodus

In Mexico, Carlos Slim's style is often explained with some hackneyed phrase revolving around the stereotype of the stingy Arab. When I traveled to Lebanon in 2008, a professor told me the story of an American who arrives at a lamp shop and sees one he likes. He asks the price and the sales person answers, smiling, that it's $50, an extortionate price for that kind of lamp, but the client nonetheless accepts, saying he'll take three. The sales person is deeply offended, admonishes the customer for not haggling for a better price, and refuses to sell him a single one. In the commercial culture of the Middle East, haggling is so essential it's impolite not to do it. However, in Mexico and almost everywhere else in the world, if a multimillionaire haggles as a general rule, he is bound to build a reputation as a miser.

All jokes aside, Slim may not be solely a product of Lebanese culture, but he is greatly admired in a community that prides itself for having a nose for business and a knack for entrepreneurship. He'd scarcely be recognized on the streets of Beirut, even though he has key personal links with the recent political history of the country: his cousins-in-law Bashir and Amin Gemayel are two of the most controversial Lebanese presidents of recent times. Unlike his wife's surname, Slim (or Salim in Arabic) has no lineage whatsoever... though of course things have changed.

One man in Lebanon who does know Slim's story is Issa Goraieb, editor-in-chief of *Le Journal*. A Lebanese man with a generous gaze, he was born in Mexico in the mid-twentieth century, in the town of Matías Romero, Oaxaca. Goraieb believes that the major famine experienced in Lebanon between 1910 and 1915, caused by the Turkish invasion, marked the following generations, especially those who emigrated to the American continent fleeing hardship, and who built their own support networks, as did Slim's father.

If Arab cultures have a reputation as hard bargainers, the Lebanese who migrated in the early twentieth century continued to hold those shortages in their memory and were even more cautious. Lebanon was part of the Ottoman empire between 1516 and 1920, comprised of what is present-day Syria, Israel, Jordan, Palestine and Turkey. In 1864, Lebanon achieved autonomy, to become a silk provider for France, but lived through civil wars between Maronite Christians—followers of the hermit Saint Maroun—and the Druze, an Islamic religious group.

Slim's father, from a family of peasant silk producers, was born in the village of Jezzine; after emigrating to Mexico, following his older brothers José, Elías, Carlos and Pedro, he became a prosperous fabric merchant. He then participated in the foundation and senior management of the Lebanese Chamber of Commerce, where the favorite buzzword in business management was "austerity."

The Lebanese diaspora in Mexico generally established itself in street peddling of costume jewelry and textiles, in particular lingerie. The installment-payment system known as "abono" became their trademark. Door-to-door sales and flexible payment plans allowed them to earn up to triple the cost of the products, eventually allowing them to formally establish wholesale businesses. During Mexico's recurrent economic crises, thanks to the liquidity of their operations, the Lebanese were able to accumulate valuable assets.

Their exodus to Mexico began in the early twentieth century, at the height of the dictatorship of Porfirio Díaz, who argued that the country needed more and "better quality" laborers and encouraged many foreign communities to settle. Some nationalist sectors were opposed to the idea. *Progreso Latino*, a 1905 magazine cited in a study by researcher Angelina Alonso, demanded that 3,000 people be stopped from disembarking from the Middle East because they brought "no more industry than their arms, nor greater aspirations than theft and begging."

III

Years later, many Lebanese merchants took advantage of the Mexican revolutionary period to consolidate their businesses. Because they were not obliged to take sides, they became providers for both the army and the rebel factions, mainly of uniforms and clothes. However, xenophobia was also increasing and in the 1920s, during Mexico's first oil boom, politicians and working-class leaders began lobbying to stop the arrival of more foreigners. In 1924, president Plutarco Elías Calles forbade the arrival of Chinese and Japanese people, while on July 7, 1927, the Interior Ministry extended the prohibition to the immigration of workers of "Syrian, Lebanese, Armenian, Palestinian, Arab and Turkish origin." A few years later, this suspension was canceled, but Lebanese immigrants were pressured to work in farming rather than commerce. By that time, Lebanon had gained independence from Turkey, although it remained under the French mandate until the end of the Second World War.

A strongly patriarchal system is one of the predominant features of the Lebanese diaspora's business dealings in Mexico. The father or elder brother controls the family and the businesses, while the women are consigned to sales activities, and marriage helps establish bonds of alliance with other families.

This style of organization, which is evident in Slim's family and reflected in those of other businessmen of Lebanese descent, has more to do with their survival as a foreign community than as a strategy for the accumulation of wealth, according to Luis Alfonso Ramírez, whose book *Secretos de familia* (*Family Secrets*) explains that the function of Lebanese women, in their role as housewives, is to protect, acquire and reproduce the family status:

> They are in charge of gaining access in social circles to "the people of noble birth" or otherwise create other equally prestigious circles. They devote themselves to building an image of their husband and children through their participation in charity foundations, service clubs and religious associations. Through their wives, the men invite the archbishop or other businessmen to dinner.

Some Lebanese people who came to Mexico at the same time as Slim's father were not initially aware that the American continent was composed of different countries. Many of them actually wished to migrate to the United States, not Mexico, explains the researcher Angelina Alonso in *Las aventuras del paisano Yusef* (*The Adventures of Fellow Countryman Yusef*), a classic book on Lebanese immigration in Latin America. They traveled to the port of Beirut with kefir, chickpeas and jars of pickles to sustain themselves during the long journey. After passing the Suez Canal, the ships went to Italy through the Strait of Sicily, eventually reaching the port of Marseille in France and then departing toward America. Some of them disembarked in New York and others in Veracruz, the most important port in the Gulf of Mexico, where all they needed to enter the continent was their passport.

Not all the migrants were fleeing poverty. "There are families like that of Slim, Gemayel or Domit who were wealthy but left due to political differences or simply because they liked the idea of emigrating from Lebanon to explore new places; but their motivation was not the search for a better quality of life because they already had that," says María Elena Buendía in her research on Lebanese migrants in Mexico.

Slim's father, Julián Slim Haddad, disembarked in Mexico at Veracruz, as he himself declared a few years later at the registration of foreigners with the Migration Service. His real name was Khalil, but he changed it to assimilate better in his new environment. Among migrants seeking a certain phonetic equivalence for better assimilation, the name Boutros became Pedro, Mayrem became María, and Youssef became José. Other Lebanese communities radically altered their identity. In confidential documents from the civil intelligence agency in Mexico, there are records of a Lebanese man called Mahamud Hamis Bacharroch, who took the name Hilario Quintero to do shady deals in Zacatecas, while in Tamaulipas, the most infamous loan shark went by the name Alejandro González to facilitate business, even though his real name was Oly Corand Assad.

Carlos Slim Haddad, the uncle and namesake of the richest Mexican in the world, did not have children and applied for naturalization on April 15, 1924. He stated he was of legal age and married, and gave his address in the Roma district in Mexico City. Six years earlier he had applied to the public works department for a permit to build a new bedroom in addition to a room for his chauffeur. The name he used was Carlos Beshara Slim, with the following explanation:

> Because I was born on the day of St. Charles Borromeo, on November 4, and because the language of my name is not easy to pronounce, especially for people who are accustomed to speaking in Spanish, finding myself in this republic, I have used in addition to my mentioned name (Beshara) the name Carlos and since my arrival, and with the purpose of facilitating being called by a name that is of easier pronunciation and in addition because I truly already go by the name Carlos, I wish to be known by my full name: Carlos Beshara Slim.

One of the witnesses named on his Mexican citizenship application was Antonio Letayf, a reference which would have guaranteed immediate approval, because he was the first Lebanese migrant to become a Mexican citizen in 1899, via a letter signed by Porfirio Díaz. Letayf's name became the best recommendation that a newly arrived Lebanese immigrant could hope for.

The dictator Porfirio Diaz's sympathy for the Lebanese people did not prevent many of the immigrants from participating in the Revolution that overthrew him. With Pancho Villa, a Lebanese man named Rechid Kuayes climbed to the rank of colonel and died in combat. Other Lebanese people to join the Zapatista revolutionary ranks included Miguel Kuri, member of staff of the general Emiliano Zapata, as well as Colonels Félix Fayad and Tufic Daher, Majors Jorge Atala and Antonio Karamel, and Lieutenant Elías Mena.

In Mexico, Lebanese migrants demonstrated their ability to adapt to the political environment. That has not changed.

IV

14

Don Julián

When Julián Slim Haddad arrived in Mexico in 1902, he was four-teen years old and his brothers lived in Tampico. The first member of the Slim family to arrive to the country was José, Julián's eldest brother, who arrived in 1893 at the age of seventeen, according to the statement he gave at the official migration register. Five years later, José opened a store at the port, where he received his other brothers before Julián: first Pedro, and then Elías and Carlos. After a series of disagreements, especially with Pedro, José left Tampico for Mexico City in 1904, in search of new business. The newly arrived Julián went with him. Not long afterward, Pedro, Carlos and Elías joined them in the capital and again worked in partner-ship to open a haberdashery and silk store, although they also began to seek and buy properties for sale and resale, which yielded high profit margins. They also ran into conflict: in January 1909, their company, Slim Hermanos, was sued by the company Giórguli and Duadietel, of Venice, Italy, for not paying for a huge amount of stock they had purchased.

In the capital city, the Slim brothers took advantage of their con-tacts within the government of Porfirio Díaz, to the point where they were nearly in charge of collecting tax from the city's street vendors. The proposal document, signed by Elías Slim Haddad, owner of the La Cruz haberdashery, reads:

> Should the tax authority believe this pertinent, our request is
> simply that we be habilitated to collect all tax from street vendors

in Mexico City and other towns of the Federal District; that we be vested with the legal faculties to do so and for this purpose be obliged to pay a fixed amount, delivered monthly and to be set by the government, taking into account the current amount collected. Knowing, as the authority knows, the vast number of street vendors who engage in tax evasion, whether because they are not known to the inspectors, or because of the various schemes they may make use of, our proposal should be perfectly convenient.

In view of the favorable business prospects opening up to him and his brothers, on April 7, 1908, José Slim applied for Mexican citizenship. He was thirty-three years old and then single, so the following year he decided to travel to Lebanon to find a wife and bring her to Mexico. He found her. Her name: Zaquie Karam.

Upon his return on March 10, 1911, José granted Pedro full control of his business, La Mariposa de Oriente, the largest haberdashery in the capital. "Thousands of street peddlers and retailers bought at La Mariposa," says an article in *Emir*, "located on the intersection of Corregidora and Academia streets, and Slim's merchandize was sold all over the Republic."

While José was in charge of planning new businesses and taking fierce legal action against their debtors, Pedro managed the daily affairs of the haberdashery: "Mr. Pedro Slim, in addition to his extraordinary memory prowess, had an admirable understanding of people's psychology, and was renown for his personal knowledge of his clientele. He used to give each one of his numerous clients the credit he judged to be the most appropriate. His calculations were almost never mistaken."

In a document written by Slim himself, which he gave to me during an interview, he says that that same year, 1911, his father Julián Slim Haddad started a business with his brother José, who was thirteen years his senior. The name of the company was the aforementioned La Mariposa de Oriente. In the beginning they each owned half of the shares, but in May 1914, Julián Slim bought the other half off his brother José. According to the magnate's text, by January 21, 1912, just ten years after being founded, this business had merchandise valued at over $100,000 and had purchased almost ten properties in the historic center of Mexico City, opposite the Palacio Nacional. Slim calculates that the current value of the shop would be over $5 million, and the properties worth around $20 million.

To Slim, his father "was ahead of the business philosophy of his time, because he possessed a profound knowledge of the sector. Already in the '20s, he was talking about efficient commerce, defined as selling large volumes with tight profit margins and providing payment facilities, which is a factor that's still not being incorporated by large discount stores."

In February 1920, at the young age of thirty-three, Pedro Slim died of Spanish influenza. His widow, María Amar—who died a few days later—inherited, together with their children Pedro, Munir, Isabel, Victoria and Carmen, the most important haberdashery of Mexico City, in addition to property and cash funds. Immediately after Pedro and María's deaths, José Slim was granted power of attorney over his brother's estate, took over the management of La Mariposa de Oriente, and legally adopted the children. He then issued a series of debt collection lawsuits against his brother's defaulters and tenants.

By then, José Slim was one of the most prosperous members of the Lebanese community in Mexico. In 1923, he founded the first Lebanese chamber of commerce, although those close to Carlos Slim claim it was his father, Julián, who did so. What we do know is that José Slim traveled to Paris on two occasions as a representative of this chamber to advocate for the independence of Lebanon.

In the mid-1930s, José fell ill from diabetes and decided to return to Lebanon with his wife, Zaquie, in 1939. His nephew Pedro was with him through his recovery period. Convalescing and far away, the eldest of the Slim brothers became benefactor to a number of Lebanese families who had recently arrived in the country:

The distinguished businessman Don José Slim, who has been in Lebanon for two years, left instructions to his legal representative in this capital, Mr. José Meouchi, to distribute the sum of 600 pesos monthly to families in need. Mr. Meouchi has carried out the order and will continue to do so. Every month, in a closed envelope, he makes the delivery to the people specified. This is true philanthropy, because Mr. Slim does it in secret and it has only been made known to the public by the beneficiaries themselves.

When he died, part of his fortune was being used to build a Mexican house in Lebanon. During the government of Lázaro Cárdenas, José Slim was designated a Mexican consul in Lebanon, but he never took up the position due to his illness, of which he would later die. The obituary dedicated to him in *Emir* reads:

Serene and a master of self-restraint, he never said a word about the large amounts of money with which he helped a large number of families in need each month, spreading wealth generously; very few knew of the amounts and the benefits that were distributed by Don José. And by his orders, these donations are to continue for an undefined amount of time.

Thirteen days after José Slim's passing, a mass was held at Balvanera cathedral, officiated by the archbishop of Mexico, Luis María Martínez.

The cathedral was decorated with a high-end but austere funerary arrangement. Curtains were draped from the main domes, forming four sections; and the columns of the main altar, the frontispiece, the communion rail and pulpit were draped also in black, while at the foot of the altar a great catafalque was raised with a coffin of walnut wood, on which the chevalier medallion of the Légion D'Honneur was affixed in the center.

Their heir was his nephew Alberto, who José Slim had legally adopted as a son.

By the 1940s, the youngest of the Slim Haddad brothers had garnered prestige as a businessman in his own right, and like the rest of his brothers, had accumulated a significant amount of capital. What set him apart from his siblings is that Julián married the daughter of one of the most prestigious Lebanese men of the time. Linda's father was José Helú, director of the most influential newspaper in the community and president of the exclusive social club Círculo Libanés in Mexico.

Julián Slim's father-in-law arrived in Mexico at the beginning of the century with his wife Wadha Atta, with whom he traveled to Parral, Chihuahua, where Linda Helú was born. The revolutionary spirit was picking up around those years and their business was destroyed by arson, leading the family to flee the north of the country. Before they settled in Mexico City, José Helú remained for a season in León. Once in the Mexican capital, he connected with businessmen who were close to Porfirio Díaz and started to prepare the newspaper *Al Jawater* (*The Ideas*), whose first issue, printed on a Sudal Mexik machine, came out on July 24, 1909.

Al Jawater was published on Wednesdays and Saturdays, although in September 1910, because of the centenary of Mexican Independence festivities, as decreed by Díaz's government, it was printed every day. Finally, a couple of years later, in the heat of the Revolution, *Al Jawater* stopped circulating.

José Helú's next venture was to found the Círculo Libanés social club. In a licensing application submitted on October 16, 1913, the intellectual applied for a license for the venue located at Avenida 16 de Septiembre, for a bar, restaurant and gambling, as well as pool, bowling, chess, dominoes and backgammon.

José Helú and Wadha Atta had four children: Ángela, Carlos, Linda and Antonio. Ángela and Carlos died at young ages, while Linda married Julián Slim and Antonio became a very successful crime writer and rose to fame when he began working in the world of film.

Due to the experiences he'd had, the maternal grandfather of the richest Mexican in the world became one of the best-informed men of the country during those turbulent years. He published essays from time to time, focusing mainly on Middle East issues—particularly against the annexation of Lebanon, which had long been on Syria's agenda.

It appears that the Syrians understood that their activities in favor of the annexation of Lebanon were useless and detrimental to their interests, because they abandoned the idea and set to work resolving their internal problems with the mandate. With this policy they earned the sympathy of all Lebanese people, who will add their efforts to that of their neighbors and their brothers of tongue, and work together united for the progress and happiness of their two nations when the time is right for a political union, which may perhaps take place with the good-neighbor method, with conviction and equality of rights and obligations.

Ten years after his death, *Emir* published an article in his memory, saying: "Without demeriting anyone, but with an opinion full of integrity, we can currently say, in the Arab journalism of Latin America, there is no other writer with the strength and character of Don José Helú. No one has been able to fill the vacuum he left behind."

José Helú was also a poet. This is one of the last poems he wrote:

> In my lifetime, I never found myself bereft
> of friends who showed me loyalty and grace
> now I've crossed the threshold gate
> of Mystery—*how many will be left?*

Linda Helú married Julián Slim in August 1926. Their first daughter was Nour, born in 1930. Afterward came Alma, Julián, José, Linda and Carlos, who was born on January 28, 1940. Julián Slim Haddad, influenced by his father-in-law, José Helú, became very involved in politics, in particular advocating for Lebanese immigration in Mexico. In the archives of the department of migration we can see that a large percentage of the Lebanese people arriving to the country named Julián Slim as a reference. Some of those who did so between 1930 and 1932 were Ana Amar Haddad, Porfiria Meneses, Dolores Mansur, María Guaida, Zakieh Asmar, Loreto Kuri, Miguel Atta, Isabel Assaz, David Chartani, José Abud, Eva de Barquet, Gurban Assuad, Miguel Naged, Teófilo Zhil and Sakis Tannous. In that same decade, Julián was one of the key organizers of an event celebrating the work of Andrés Landa y Piña, head of the migration department, for being a "true friend of the Lebanese people."

Along with his work as an activist, Julián was a frequent visitor to the courtrooms, in which he sued businessman Manuel Echavarría before the Fifth Court because he did not want to give up his shop, located at 2 Tacuba Street, where Echavarría had set up the bar Salón Correo. More lawsuits from Julián Slim can be found against Carmen Hernández for not paying rent, or against Takumi Namba for wood that was not delivered for some bookshelves; the list of lawsuits lodged in the official archives goes on and on. His wife, Linda Helú, also appears there—like when she sued the Compañía Industrial Manufacturera because it refused to vacate the family property at 155 Ámsterdam Street, on the corner with Ozuluama, in the Condesa district. This company was represented by Prudencio Guízar Valencia, brother of Bishop Rafael Guízar Valencia, who initiated Marcial Maciel into religion.

Aside from his work as a businessman, Carlos Slim's father led an existence that was widely covered in the media, particularly among the Lebanese socialites settled in Mexico City. On February 12, 1943, his cousin Alfredo Harp and Suhad Helú were married at the residence of Tufic Sawyeg, "a well-known industrialist and brother-in-law of the bride, as he is married to Mary Helú de Sayeg." The witnesses of the union on groom's side were Miguel Abed, José Meouchi and Miguel Atta, while for the bride it was Tufic Sayeg, Carlos Slim Haddad—uncle of magnate Carlos Slim—and Assad Bujali.

After the legal ceremony, the religious ceremony was held at the church of La Coronación, opposite Parque España in Condesa.

Suhad Helú arrived at the church on the arm of Julián Slim Haddad. The bride was wearing "an elegant dress of white taffeta, dotted with pearls and embroidered with silver threads, complemented with a classic headdress and a delicate veil that highlighted the bride's refinement." Suhad was followed by the maids of honor, Therese Harp, Nour Slim, Mimi Helú and Almita Slim, "Therese in a dress of pale pink tule; Nour in pale blue; Mimí, in tan; and Almita, in salmon. All in the same style of mohair with silver embroidery."

The residence of Tufic Sayeg was also the location for announcing the engagement of Nour Slim, the eldest daughter of Julián Slim

Haddad and older sister of Carlos Slim. In its classic pompous style, *Emir* published the following note:

Nour is the daughter of Julián Slim and Mrs. Linda Helú de Slim. Is it necessary to add anything else apart from simply mentioning those names? If anyone stands out for his dynamism, hard work, endless capability for work, for his entrepreneurial spirit, his affiliation to what is represented by the prestige and honor of the colony, that man is Julián Slim, who has performed certain roles of responsibility to perfection. Nour Slim, who has featured in our pages more than once, has endeavored with her generous youth to work toward noble and plausible causes; and that is why there is nothing but appreciation and sincere friendship toward for her for her merits, and appreciation for her virtues.

Commentary on the event has the exaggerated tone that the community's publications maintain to this day, and in which the Slim family is continually present:

The bacelorette party reception that the friendly couple offered for Nour is now catalogued as one of the most brilliant, jubilant and lovely in the social annals of the colony. Of Mrs. Maruca and her organization skills, all that can be said is that she was fantastic. The magnificent residence of Mr. Tufic Sayeg and his wife was very well attended by the most distinguished people. Notable figures in the cinematographic world of Mexico (the Grovas, the Bustillos Oro, Antonio Helú, etc.) highlighted with their presence the brilliance of the party.

All of Carlos Slim's sisters were regular faces in the Lebanese socialite magazines. An article entitled "The young ladies of the Slim residence" says:

Around us still lingers the brilliance of the singular success of the Lebanese young ladies with their party at El Patio, an enterprise that had required organization skills and had demanded they employ a great deal of time in the preparations, when the Club Femenino Libanés, indefatigable in its charity work, prepared the event at the residence of don Julián Slim. The invitation to this regular soirée came from the distinguished young ladies Nour and Alma Slim, enthusiastic members of the club who participate actively in its work. The vast hall of the Slim residence offered a magnificent setting for the gathering of the Lebanese ladies. But the entire expanse of the stage was necessary to shelter the very large group of delightful young ladies who gathered there to continue to contribute their grains of sand in assisting the disadvantaged. The Slim residence is as much a home to the colony as is memorable the head of the household, Don Julián Slim. All of Nour and Alma's guests felt at home there, and the entire evening was lively, with everyone chatting in groups.

Another wedding in the Lebanese community that captivated the community's imagination in the 1950s was that of Antonieta Daw and "Miguelito" Nazar; they would become one of the greatest symbols of police repression in Mexico during the 1970s, a time known as the "dirty war," in which Julián, Carlos Slim's older brother, also participated. Daw and Nazar were married at the church of Santa Teresita del Niño Jesús, accompanied by their parents, José Daw and Adela Gastín de Daw, as well as Pedro Nazar and Hacibe Hajj de Nazar. The families of both were originally from a Lebanese village called Kaitouly.

At the agreed time, Antonieta descended from the nuptial carriage, radiantly happy, on the arm of her father. She wore a red dress in the style of Louis XIV, á la Madame de Sevigné; the bodice was tailored with a brocade and silver with pearl borders; the skirt, crepe of ivory colored gauze; the headdress, pearly with an exquisite illusion veil, designed and created by Henry de Chatillón; the bouquet of white orchids with tuberoses. On her neck she wore two exquisite strings of pearls, and her headdress was completed with a pair of diamond earrings. The wedding dress was designed and created by Mrs. Nagibe, widow of Mitry.

Among the guests was José Nazar, uncle of the groom and based in the border town of Reynosa, Tamaulipas, accompanied by his wife, Caffa M. de Nazar. José Nazar would be a key figure in the groom's future, who, thanks to Nazar's help, would eventually have a long career in the Mexican intelligence service and spend the last days of his life judged as a killer of members of the government's opposition.

However, on their wedding day, which was attended by 250 people during a reunion celebrated at a restaurant, Nazar was radiant and youthful: "The party lasted the whole night and the bride and groom retired in English style to head to Acapulco, where they spent their honeymoon." Among the guests were the families of Slim and Domit. Antonio Domit gifted the newlyweds a standing lamp, and Elías Slim, a mirror and jewelry box.

Another of the great weddings of the period was that of Adela Seade and Jorge Sayeg, whose witnesses were President Adolfo López Mateos and Julián Slim—the magnate's older brother—who had started to work for the secret police. At the time, Fernando Gutiérrez Barros was beginning his career as subdirector of the Federal Security Directorate. He rose through the ranks for arresting and then liberating Fidel Castro and Ernesto "Che" Guevara during their time in Mexico, before they conducted their revolutionary expedition to Cuba on board the Granma.

The social life magazines of the period also published tragic news, such as the deaths of Slim family members, most of them due to heart conditions. Emily Meouchi, wife of Elías Slim Haddad, died at the age of sixty-two of a heart attack and was buried at the French Cemetery of San Joaquín, in the crypt of Julián Slim's family. Her obituary reads: "How aristocratic she was! Of congenital, delicate and clean aristocracy, which emanates from beautiful souls refined by the flames of love. And how generous Doña Emily was in that divine gift of maternal love!" Alberto Slim, who inherited the fortune of Pedro and José Slim Haddad, died of a heart attack during a dinner at the Mónicas restaurant. He was fifty-six years old and a consummate socialite. A few years before his death, Alberto Slim was in New York with his cousin Carlos, who would spend a season there during his gap year, after completing his degree in civil engineering at the UNAM.

———

In June 1953, Julián Slim Haddad died of a heart attack. His funeral ceremony took place in the Palacio de Bellas Artes. The event was officiated by Joséph Naffah, in representation of the minister Khalil Takiedine, and Juan Aun, director of the newspaper *Al Kustas*. Los Madrigalistas, an orchestra of twenty musicians directed by Luis Sandi, played "Halleluja," "Velada trágica," "Tan dulce ha sido" and "Gloria," among many other songs. His obituary in *Gemas de Líbano* magazine describes the businessman thus:

> Don Julián Slim was the living example of the immigrant who was in so much need of this America of ours; he loved both Lebanon and the land where he spent most of his life, a country so dear to him that he asked for the warm refuge of the Valley of Mexico to be the final resting place for his bones. And it is here, in this land of ours which became his own by dint of love, that he will rest forever; but also in our hearts will his memory live forever more, because his memory will be with us as we walk along this path, aiding us when we falter, encouraging us through our frailty, revitalizing us in our hour of need, and always being an example.

Sheik Nacif Fadl spoke in Arabic about Julián Slim. So did Roberto Cossío, who in the name of "the Mexican people" said:

> I'm not here to offer my condolences to the widow, Mrs. Linda Helú, nor to her children and other relatives; nor to give my condolences to the Lebanese community as I feel I myself am a part of it, and I am also in need of receiving those condolences for this irreparable loss which fills us all with pain; I come, therefore, with my homage of tears, to offer due tribute to the father, the friend, the fellow Lebanese man who has just departed toward the shores of eternity.

15

Al Kataeb

The father of the world's richest Mexican, Julián Slim Haddad, was not only a prosperous businessman who was well connected to the government of his time, he was also a follower of Al Kataeb, a Lebanese organization that, in those days, received covert financial support from an Israeli government that was keen to gain political power over Lebanon. The Israelis, who had initiated hostilities against the Palestinians, were supporters of Pierre Gemayel, Slim's uncle-in-law, as an ally in Lebanon. According to declassified documents that journalist Berry Morris made public in *The Jerusalem Post* in the early 1980s, the intermediary between the Gemayel family and the Israeli government was Elías Rababi. It was under the auspices of this alliance, years later, that the Sabra and Shatila massacre would take place on September 14, 1982.

The English journalist Robert Fisk, who covered the killings for *The Independent*, has written at length about these events, declared by the UN General Assembly an act of genocide:

> I recall the old man in pyjamas lying on his back on the main street with his innocent walking stick beside him, the two women and a baby shot next to a dead horse, the private house in which I sheltered from the killers with my colleague Loren Jenkins of the *Washington Post*—only to find a dead young woman lying in the courtyard beside us. Some of the women had been raped before their killing. The armies of flies, the smell of decomposition. These things one remembers.

The pact between Israel and the Lebanese Phalange movement had been in place since 1948, according to documentation revealed first by the *Jerusalem Post* and later by the *New York Times*. The man who oversaw the agreement, Rababi, was in Mexico that same year, after his meetings in New York. In Mexico City, Rababi's delegation was received by the father of Carlos Slim, who was photographed with them in his living room. "Magnificent and warm reception of the Kataebists at the Slim residence" is the title of the *Emir* article about the social event.

> Don Julián Slim—so highly esteemed in the colony for his patriotic fervor, his entrepreneurial spirit, his cordiality, and the enthusiasm with which at all times he makes himself available and provides his invaluable support and collaboration when it comes to the pursuit of noble causes—did not want it to be merely a private social occasion... An event that departed from official protocols and allowed the delegation of Al Kataeb to perceive first-hand the closeness, sympathy and love with which the colony spontaneously gathered round to freely express its faith in the destinies of Lebanon and the patriotic crusade undertaken by the youth legions of Al Kataeb.

The article also states that Slim's mother, Linda, and his sisters Nour and Alma, "educated in the choicest social disciplines," were in charge of looking after the guests, offering "the finest wines and liquors, and delicious platters artfully arranged and presented in the style of Oriental, French and Mexican cuisines." Slim's father dedicated the toast to the "illustrious" delegation of Al Kataeb (whose members included Jean Kaf, Abdo Saab and Alfredo Yazbek) and encouraged the Lebanese youth based in Mexico to fulfill the destiny that had been set into motion by the older generations:

> They should be aware that Al Kataeb works with civic pride to maintain the glories and independence of the homeland of our elders. The youth born in Mexico must and should preserve, along with love for the land where they were born, their devotion and fervor for the land of their forefathers, from which they have inherited a spirit and virtues that gave days of light to civilization.

Elías Rababi was the last of the delegation to speak. He started by addressing Julián Slim, thanking him for his words, as it was evident that they were spoken from the heart:

> He compiled glossaries for topics explored by the great orators and poets of the past, both in Spanish and in Arabic, and found in his expressiveness and in his eloquent command of the language an accurate phrase, a fair comment, a proper consequence and deduction for all subjects, revealing himself once more as the most brilliant improviser in the Arabic language we have heard in recent times.

After that night, the Phalangist delegation returned to Lebanon. "What is Al Kataeb?" asks a propaganda leaflet published after their visit to the Slim family residence:

> It is not just one more of the many associations that exist, and much less is it a political party. It constitutes, quite simply, a national organization that groups together the cream of the crop from the country's youth, in terms of both their physical and their spiritual aptitudes, and represents a movement of such impetus, vigor and projection, that new legions continuously join the organization to strengthen its ranks. Al Kataeb currently has more than 60,000 members. Its motto, "God, Fatherland, Family," summarizes its principles and objectives. God, who is faith and awareness of our destiny; Fatherland, which is commitment in struggle and sacrifice; Family, which is love and loyalty.

Al Kataeb has been erased by the magnate from his official narrative. I ask him about it and he gives me this definition of the Phalangist organization: "Al Kataeb was very important in the independence of Lebanon and what I have seen in documents is that there is a great link between France and Lebanon, which continues to this day."

"But there are allegations and documents published by the *Jerusalem Post* establishing that Al Kataeb was financed by Israel to secure control over the area."

"I don't know. I have doubts and it may be that they gave them weapons, but I think they also had their own financing, which I believe came from Arab countries. Arab countries were very... Lebanon used to be what Dubai is now."

"Your uncles-in-law Bachir and Amin Gemayel were accused of being responsible for the massacre of Sabra and Shatila."

"They were my mother-in-law's cousins. Look, I think it was a full-blown war and there were killings all over the place and even... in Lebanon there was a terrible civil war. There were lots of deaths on all sides. What surprises me is that it ended. I think that was in '82 is when a bomb was placed in the building where Bachir lived and everyone died. It was a very violent war, there were lots of deaths, and I don't know if there were deaths and massacres on one side and the other. We are talking about full-blown wars here."

"Do you follow politics in Lebanon now?"

"Not in detail. I pay attention to the underlying issues, and we have a few initiatives there. We have a foundation that works in social and educational activities. We don't make any distinctions between the different groups that exist. We carry out activities at various locations, we don't look at whether they are Catholics or Muslims."

"Your father and some other members of your family were followers of Al Kataeb."

"My father wasn't a huge follower, I don't think so."

"I have a photo of a welcome reception he offered them."

"What we've seen (and we have hundreds of letters and papers and documents) is that my dad was not a radical, not at all. There are many countries that separated the church from the state, some in the eighteenth century, and others in the nineteenth, such as Mexico, and that was a huge achievement. Now we are seeing the religious problems of the Middle East. In Iran, since the Shah left, we are seeing a lot of religious fanaticism. I think in Lebanon there are Catholic and non-Catholic parties, and Muslim parties, but in the end there have always been people living there who were Catholic, Muslim, Jewish, Shi'ite and Sunni and Druze."

"From the documents consulted it can be understood that your father was an activist."

"I think my dad was not an activist, not even close. Maybe some Maronite organization visited and he offered them a reception, because, that's the thing, my dad was a fervent Maronite. He didn't go to church every day, though. He did enjoy going now and then, but to small churches and that was it."

16

Racism

"What do you get if you multiply a Lebanese man by a cat?" was a scornful popular joke in the Mexico of the first half of the twentieth century, when Carlos Slim was born. The answer: "Seven mink coats." But other, more overt forms of racism were also present. José Vasconcelos, the greatest man of letters of the time—minister of education and rector of the Universidad Nacional—published the 1937 essay "What is communism?" in which he condemned the mix of Mexican and Lebanese races:

> Saying a single word against the *gachupines*—Spanish settlers in America—at the time in which Don Ramón settled here, was ungentlemanly and disloyal, because precisely in those days there was brutal persecution taking place in our cities and villages; our own *gachupines* were being increasingly replaced by communist Jews, who now operate in small-scale industries and a large sector of commerce, but speak English; and by the Syrian-Lebanese, who do not improve our race, but rather worsen it.

His criticism, which reflected the country's increasing xenophobia toward the "Arabs," provoked a heightened reaction from the Lebanese community, as well as interesting self-reflection. In *Emir*, Leonardo Kaim listed thus the qualities of the Lebanese people:

> *Physical qualities.* The Lebanese man, in general, is perfectly endowed; he is strong, beautiful, white of race, manly, resistant and blessed with longevity.

Moral qualities. His religion is Catholic. He is of good customs (and when he does not already follow them, he is wonderful at assimilating the good customs of his host country). He possesses an innate kindness. His good sense, his desire to always be frank and sincere, his endeavor to make the best choices, his wish to be useful and make himself likeable make him a considerably valuable man.

Spiritual qualities. He possesses a very rich cultural tradition. The magnificent Arab literature is his daily bread.

Others responded to Vasconcelos, pointing out that, if he looked at how the Lebanese in Mexico managed their wealth, he would see they differed greatly from other foreigners because they liked to spend their money in Mexico, rather than accumulate it to spend in their country of origin. They also pointed out that the Lebanese people were not displacing Mexican workers, because instead of taking up jobs, the Lebanese started businesses and hired Mexicans: "You will have seen that there is no industry, trade or profession in which there is no one born in Lebanon or of Lebanese descent. They work in all the sectors of the country's economy. In all of them except for bars, *pulquerías*, cabarets."

Emir defended the honor of its community and, over several magazine issues, reported some of the things that Mexican presidents have said about the Lebanese people:

> Our ports will always be open to welcome them, because they come
> to our country without the backing of battleships and cannons.
> Porfirio Díaz

> I have always considered that the Lebanese colony is the one that
> tends to best assimilate with the Mexican people.
> Venustiano Carranza

> Not only do we keep our ports and borders open to you, but also
> our hearts; please be assured that you will be provided with all
> kinds of guarantees.
> Álvaro Obregón

We should sell cheap like the Lebanese do and we will surely not
lose. Our people require cheap merchandise to be able to dress as
is due.
Pascual Ortiz Rubio

It was not until May 19, 1943, when Vasconcelos, also author of
La raza cósmica (*The Cosmic Race*), responded to the criticisms via
a letter sent to the Lebanese community:

I cannot and should not take back my statement about the Spanish
being, as an emigrant, the superior and most desirable race. That
does not mean we cannot love people or migrants of other races
and hold them in great esteem. I have Syrian-Lebanese friends, but
up until now the Syrian-Lebanese race has not been able to demonstrate a kind of cultural prowess and spiritual development that is
comparable to the Spanish.

Years later, President Adolfo López Mateos would coin the
most well-known phrase on the topic: "Whoever doesn't have
a Lebanese friend or relative should go and find one." By 2000,
there were half a million Mexicans of Lebanese descent—some
of them well-known artists such as Salma Hayek, Astrid Hadad,
José María Yazpik and Demián Bichir, or businesspeople across
a wide range of sectors such as Carlos Slim, Antonio Chedraui,
Alfredo Harp Helú, Kamel Nacif, José Sulaimán and Jean Succar
Kuri. President Vicente Fox upheld the tradition of vindicating the
Mexican-Lebanese people by saying: "The Lebanese community is
more Mexican than molé."
Slim does not remember being the target of any kind of racism
due to the origin of his parents: "Not in high school and university.
Maybe in primary and secondary school they would say something
to you. Sometimes they called us 'Turks.'"
After telling him about Vasconcelos's opinions of the Lebanese
people, Slim says he remembers seeing it in the homes of his relatives: "I met Vasconcelos in person, but I never chatted with him,"
then his secretary brings him some copies of a speech typewritten
by his father. "This," Slim points out, "is a defense of the Lebanese

community that my father made during the government of Ruiz Cortines, when there was an intent to pass a decree against the Lebanese."

I leaf through the speech, which is about eight pages long, and I ask him for a copy, but Slim says he will only give me one page, because he would rather keep the rest for the autobiography he is writing.

In his speech, Julián Slim Haddad expounds on the entrepreneurial philosophy of the Lebanese of the time, arguing that their system, which relied on selling at high volumes with razor-thin profit margins, establishing direct relationships with the customers, and purveying reasonably priced, unadulterated products, while providing credit and payment facilities, was precisely the reason the Lebanese communities, "thanks to their love of work, their industriousness and their experience," had become so prosperous and successful. He also argued that the fact that Lebanese merchants always act with absolute integrity and "adjust their actions according to the strictest rules of morality and honesty," constituted, with their business philosophy, an infallible protection against the kind of "selfish capital that exploits the people." He goes on to argue that it is only thanks to Lebanese capital that a long list of economically depressed, "unwholesome" or remote, sparsely populated areas had seen any kind of resurgence. After building his argument, he explains that other traders were creating a hostile environment for their own gain:

> We understand that our business may not be viewed in friendly terms by other large-scale traders similar to our own, and that is so because, from the moment we hold as an invariable rule to sell cheap and with tight margins, providing payment facilities and acting with absolute integrity, it is not possible for another business intending to extract handsome profits to accept a competitor that forces it to reduce its huge margins and exaggerated earnings. For this reason, Mr. Minister, may we put forward for your consideration the vested interests of those traders who, incapable of accepting modest profits, create around us an environment that is detrimental to our interests, which will necessarily exert an

unfavorable influence on us. Fortunately, this is easy to combat by means of the evidence we will supply in abundance for your fair consideration, in order to modify what refers to us in the ministerial agreement at hand.

V

17

Childhood

Carlos Slim tells me that he only felt discriminated against for being Lebanese during a brief period in his childhood, which transpired at 51 Cerrada México, in the neighborhood of Condesa. He attended nursery school and part of primary at the G. B. de Annes School for boys and girls, just two blocks from his house. When he was seven years old, his family moved to the neighborhood of Polanco, on Calderón de la Barca street, coincidentally also at number 51. Then he went to a boys-only school directed by Augustinian priests; there, he attended from the fifth grade of primary to the third grade of secondary. From age ten, in addition to studying, Slim used to accompany his father Julián to the historical center to help him with work and learn the ropes. It was during that time that his father used to send him around to other stores in the area to keep tabs on the prices of his competitors, "and I felt like a spy because that was after the Second World War. So I looked at the prices of our competitors and then returned to my father's store and made a record of the prices," he says during an interview with Larry King.

When Carlos was just thirteen years old, his father died of a heart condition. But before he passed away, Julián Slim Haddad had provided the young Carlos with a basic financial education, as he says in his official biography:

> In late 1952, and with the objective of administrating our income and expenditure, my dad assigned us the task of administrating a savings book that he reviewed with us every week. Following this

rule, I administrated my personal accounts for many years. Thus, in January 1955 my estate was worth $5,523.32 and by August 1957 it had increased to $31,969.26, and it continued to grow as I invested mainly in shares of the National Bank of Mexico, on occasion using credit, in such a way that by early 1996 my personal capital was more than $5 million, not including the family estate.

While Slim was buying stock in the National Bank of Mexico from age twelve, his childhood was not without troubles. He recalls that in primary and secondary school, some of his peers tried to bully him, and in that context he got into his first fistfight.

"I was quiet, but not a pushover. In sixth grade of primary school, the class bully was pestering us (the bastard was actually about two or three years older than us; he was such a pain in the neck). So I stood up and gave him a thwack, and his father, who was the prefect (it was an Augustinian school), did the most intelligent thing that could have been done: during playtime he had us all wear boxing gloves and got us to fight for the entire break."

The magnate was eleven years old at the time and the Augustinian school where he was studying was Instituto Alonso de la Vera Cruz. The second time he got into a fistfight was in secondary school. He says he can't even remember the reason for the fight: all he can remember is that his rival was "a very aggressive kid." He can't remember whether he won or lost, either.

"Look, in those days it wasn't about winning or losing. There were no rules for knocking out or anything. The point was to resist. Afterward, you didn't know if you hit the guy more or if he hit you more, but the point was to hold out. So you didn't know if you won or lost."

I asked him if during his college years he had fought again, as a former colleague of his told me that Slim got into a fistfight with another college student in the bathrooms of the Palacio de Minería during an annual ball.

"No, I wouldn't have got into a fight. I was a lecturer at the college! How was I going to start fighting? Let alone in a bathroom. You go in there to do other business, not to fight," he laughs. "At college there were almost never any fights. Well, not in my college, anyway. Maybe from time to time you'd see a gang at parties and so on, but at the college itself I don't remember ever seeing a fight. You see, the wonderful thing about university as opposed to high school is the atmosphere of camaraderie between the most diverse social classes. Maybe you had a car and the other one didn't have a penny, but there was friendship."

The magnate says that his parents always prioritized his education and that one good decision they made was to enroll him in small schools, where there were five children per class and not more than forty in the whole school.

"Before fourth year of primary, me and my brothers were put in a very famous school that was near the Sheraton. It's called Escuela Inglesa para Varones (English School for Boys). I couldn't bear it and didn't last ten days there. My parents were intelligent enough to respect that, because I needed more freedom. I've always needed more freedom."

Slim says he had a good relationship with his older brothers, Julián and José ("Pepe"), but he liked to be alone at school and in the parks: "I was never in the same school as Julián. He was a few years older. With Pepe, he went to the English school, and then returned to this one—Vera Cruz—and then, when we moved houses, I kept going to Vera Cruz and Pepe returned to English School. And Julián, I don't know when he was transferred from the English school to Cristóbal Colón. I don't know when Julián studied there. Pepe and I started in Alonso de la Vera Cruz. I started in fifth grade, and he, in first of primary. It was here in Palmas, where San José de la Montaña was."

When José and Julián completed their secondary school studies, their father took them to Monterrey to study at the newly created Instituto Tecnológico y de Estudios Superiores de Monterrey; however, one month after installing them in the northern Mexican city, Julián Slim Haddad passed away and Slim's brothers returned to the capital.

"If you look at yourself as a child, how would you define yourself?"

"Well, I was very free. I never felt repressed."

"What kinds of things did you dream of? What did you like doing? How did you dress?"

"Normally. Like any other child. Jeans weren't in fashion the way they are now. We wore them instead when my dad took us to his work."

"What did you wear at college?"

"Trousers, a shirt and sometimes a jacket."

"Did you have a favorite pair of shoes?"

"No."

"Were you not very fussy in that sense?"

"Nobody was. What we wore was a bit more informal. Some guys did wear a leather jacket."

"What were your hobbies?"

"American football. I was very good at running the ball, but I was always put as tackle. So I never played. Just as a tackle sometimes. We played *tochito* (touch football) and I liked running the ball, I was good at it."

What Slim most likes to say in public about his childhood is that he opened his first checking account when he was twelve years old—the same age he started buying shares in the National Bank. When he starts telling me that story, he pulls out an old notebook, in which there are faded inked notes, and goes into a kind of trance:

"Look, when I was sixteen years old, my mum gave me $50. So I invested that. This used to be my wage: 200 pesos... When my father passed away, the one who took over managing the family's finances was my sister, who was very diligent. My sister studied very hard at school. My other sister, Alma, left school and started working with my dad at age eighteen. She was very young. Look how ugly my handwriting was. Here my Dad told me off for crossing out so many things. Here he told me off, too. Here, when my father passed away, I made a list of the shares that the family owns. My dad had 1 percent of the National Bank, which was $16,667. This is from when I was thirteen years old."

"And what was your dad like? What's the sweetest memory you have of him?" I say, trying to steer the conversation toward his father's human side.

"For example, this is my first balance sheet," the magnate goes on, getting more and more excited. "Dad used to give us five pesos as pocket money and a little black book that I can't find, dear me. It's like this, little and black. I think I took it home."

He turns to his nephew, Roberto Slim, who is present at the interview. "Look for it at home, in the little office at the front, where the dinette is." Then he continues: "Here I made my first balance; when I had forty shares of Banamex, I had 6,600 pesos. That was my capital. I was fifteen years old: 6,600 pesos, minus 1,000 that I owed my mom. This is the balance of January, of March. This is from 1995. And here I wrote: cash balance: 600 [pesos]; late payment, gift, salary... I also had a little sweets shop and these are my sales. These are my daily expenses. Watch glass replacement, shoe polish, bus fare; phone call, twenty cents (see how expensive that was!); sandwich, sixty-five; taco, lime; bus, twenty-five. Two marbles for Chinese checkers, 3.50 [pesos]. These are my first balance sheets. I did all this in memory of my dad, I think, because he used to make us fill out these notebooks."

"So it makes sense that you were so interested in the electronic calculator at the time, as it allowed you to process all those numbers every day."

"What we used was the slide rule... Look, by May I had duplicated my capital. Here I had 22,000 pesos. The truth is I've never needed any money in my life. For purchasing the shares, my mom lent me 1,000 pesos; 31,000 pesos. These were shares in the National Bank. Here I already had 300 instead of forty. These were my stamps. Oh, this is when they asked me to administer family matters. How long do you think I administered them?"

"You still do, I guess."

"Of course not: sixty days!"

"Why?"

"Because they were too demanding."

Slim shows me a document written by his brothers where they reminisce on the time when Slim stopped administering family matters: "Thanking him for wasting his time for our benefit. Two months into his mission, during which he did not charge any fees." Then he says, "See, I didn't even want my brother as a business partner, much less would I have strangers as partners now. Around that time my mom gave me a loan to buy shares. I think it was a loan for 500,000 pesos. I said to her: 'Instead of keeping it in the bank, give it to me, I'll give you 10 percent.'"

"And what was your mom like?"

"My mom was very courteous, very kind, very sociable, very dutiful, very conscientious, very attentive, because my dad said to her before he died: 'Don't get into business and don't give any loans or guarantees.' And my mom was religious about that. She left us lots of properties and shares."

"What do you feel you learned from her? What character traits did you inherit from her?"

"Her sense of family justice. She never gifted me anything if she didn't give the same thing to my other siblings. Or when I got married, when I bought my wife a big ring, ooft, she got so angry!"

"Was she jealous?"

"No, not at all. She was worried my brother's wife might be upset because the ring my brother bought was smaller, because there was a difference in the rings. She was fair. We had a beautiful plot of land of 21,000 square feet. So when I was about to get married, I had a construction company. I asked her to loan me the land so I could build a house there, and I would move out once it got sold. She asked why she should give me a loan and not my brothers. She had an incredible sense of justice and equality. She was also very sociable and everyone loved her, but the rules were the rules."

18

Youth

Carlos Slim's business influences also come from places less distant than Lebanon. After completing his civil engineering studies at the UNAM, he found inspiration in the pages of a *Playboy* magazine. One day, among photographs of seminude girls, he read an article by Jean Paul Getty, the first man to accumulate a fortune of over $1 billion. Getty's philosophy around the need to have a "millionaire mentality" to succeed made an impression on the young student. In the mid-1960s, the oil magnate wrote for that magazine about business strategies; the publication encouraged its readers to become consumers and promoted a carefree and hedonistic lifestyle.

Slim's student years at the UNAM in the late '50s and early '60s were a preamble to the student uprising that took place in 1968, with demonstrations and protests culminating in brutal repression where hundreds of students were killed by the army in Plaza de Tlatelolco. Despite various attempts made after the political altercation, those responsible for the massacre have never been brought to justice.

The Faculty of Civil Engineering had a more conservative reputation, though, and remained on the sidelines of the political discontent that galvanized other sections of the university. Around the same time, Getty was advising young people to avoid radicalism at all costs. According to him, that was a game that would almost always be lost.

Slim decided to study civil engineering because at the time the degrees in economics were still focusing purely on rhetoric instead of looking at numbers.

"So what could I study instead? Accounting?" he says, grimacing in response to his own question. "Why did I study engineering? Because I like numbers. That's what I'm good at, the way other people are good at words. Ever since primary school I liked numbers, and in engineering at the time there were no alternative degrees. Maybe given the choice I would have studied engineering administration or industrial engineering."

He also took some courses at the mathematics school in the Faculty of Sciences, but he thought the degree focused too heavily on pure mathematics and he did not complete those studies.

Slim enrolled in the Faculty of Civil Engineering in 1957 after concluding his studies at Preparatoria numero 1 of San Ildefonso, where some teachers made a profound impression on him, such Mr. Mosqueira, who taught physics and cosmography, and Mr. Cordero Amador, nicknamed "el Sonrisal" (the Big Smile), who taught world history.

In 1954, the UNAM's imposing university campus—Ciudad Universitaria—had just been inaugurated, so his generation saw the launch of what is now one of the most important public universities in Latin America. Around 1,350 students enrolled along with Slim in his first year in the Faculty of Civil Engineering, the vast majority of whom were male, but the cohort dwindled year by year, and only around 300 students completed the degree in 1961. Their lecturers included some of the most prominent practicing engineers of the time, such as Enrique Rivero Borrel, Javier Barros Sierra, Carlos Izunza, Rodrigo Castelazo, Rodolfo Félix Valdéz, Daniel Ruiz and a trio of brothers—Marco Aurelio, Francisco and Jaime Torres Herrera. Other lecturers were Antonio Dovalí, who later became director of PEMEX, the national Mexican oil company, and Mariano Hernández, who received the National Engineering Award.

The political unrest in Mexico City was building, and two of its epicenters were the UNAM's Faculty of Philosophy and Faculty of Law, where latent references to the recently victorious Cuban Revolution abounded.

Slim's longtime friend, Fructuoso Pérez García, remembers those days at the Faculty of Civil Engineering well. I met this amiable engineer through Francesc Relea, former correspondent for *El País* in Mexico. After several requests, Fructuoso agreed to talk on the record, during a long interview at his offices in San Miguel Chapultepec, in Mexico City.

Fructuoso does not remember any major political upheaval in their faculty.

"There were some students who were far left, and they made some waves, but the most they did was to commandeer city buses or try to organize strikes in the other faculties, but it was nothing like what we saw years later, in '68. The Faculty of Engineering was very apolitical. People would show up and try and persuade us but they weren't successful," says Fructuoso, pointing out that most of them belonged to "anti-US organizations." However, the faculty was represented by a left-wing student called Amado Armejo in the UNAM Federation of Students.

Fructuoso's memories of those years border on the idyllic: "We all got along really well with the other schools. For example, next to us was the Faculty of Architecture, on one side, and on the other the Faculty of Chemistry. There were never problems of any kind. The most that could happen was on the day of San Juan, when we had water fight games, and of course, the internal American football competitions, with the Faculty of Engineering against Architecture, or Law, or Chemistry. So there was obviously competitiveness in that sense, but there were no great rivalries. We all commuted together on the city bus, with great familiarity, including Carlos, who was a normal kid."

Slim also remembers it that way. In an extravagant event held in May 2013 at the Palacio de Minería, to celebrate the fifty-fourth anniversary of his graduation as an engineer, the multimillionaire spoke about his college years in front of hundreds of guests—which included the most diverse figures, from the president of the Supreme Court of Justice to the journalist and politician Carlos Payán, and José Narro, rector of the UNAM. In his speech, Slim said:

> Us students came from the most diverse places, all over the country, from the most diverse social and economic classes, from the most

diverse ways of thinking; it was, in short, a mosaic of Mexico as a whole, which also included many classmates from Central America and beyond. Those were the years in which were able to appreciate the importance of public education, which constitutes the best resource that a country can offer its population to improve and make level the opportunities to everyone through quality public education. Thanks to the plurality and diversity of our classmates, and our teachers, we got to know our country better. We interacted in harmony, we developed friendships. And in many cases that friendship, such as the one of our class of '57, after so many years, is still ongoing thanks to our president, Fructuoso Pérez, who I thank for his hard work and boisterous leadership over all these years.

The Faculty of Engineering was also known for holding two very important balls: the spring ball and the graduates ball. A talented student orchestra provided the entertainment at the parties, usually held at Palacio de Minería, located on Tacuba Street in the historical center of Mexico City. In addition to the student orchestra, musicians such as Juan García Esquivel, Juan García Medet or the soloists of Agustín Lara often performed. Two orchestras played in the main patio, and the other two in Tacuba Hall, which Slim and his friends used to call "the maternity ward," because that's where the second-chance exams and proficiency certificate exams were held. Fructuoso remembers that all the guys wore tuxedos and the girls ballroom gowns, for a party that usually went until three or four in the morning.

Slim didn't wear formal clothes all the time, of course. He also liked sportswear, especially baseball, which he played for the faculty team. Fructuoso was shortstop and Slim usually picked the position of catcher during matches against other faculties at the UNAM. There was a good skill level on the team, especially thanks to students from Chihuahua, Guanajuato and Veracruz. Baseball was the favorite sport at the college, although at the end of his studies, some students of that generation dedicated themselves to the world of professional football: Víctor Mahbub was president of the UNAM's Pumas team, and Gustavo Hernández played for the

Diablos Rojos of Toluca, Federico Schroeder for the Atlante and Pascual Ortiz Rubio for the América.

"I'm intrigued by the fact that you played as catcher. I often think it's the most boring position in baseball," I say to Slim in an interview.

"No, it's more boring to be a fielder. The ball never arrives," he laughs. "There's nothing boring about being a catcher. The catcher is the one who guides the pitcher. The combination pitcher-catcher is the most important in baseball. Just imagine: the catcher has to communicate with the pitcher. He has to tell him what each batter is like, where to aim, where to put the ball. That's why sometimes they get their wires crossed and it fails."

"So were you a good catcher?"

"Well, I just dabbled."

"And did you bat well?"

"I was very good at batting and then suddenly, I went into a slump and started to bat poorly. I don't know why if I am short-sighted in this eye," he says, pointing at his right eye.

Slim also practiced athletics during those years. He especially enjoyed track and field, shot put, and javelin and discus throw.

"I love athletics, too. More than baseball, in fact."

"So you watch the Olympics more than the World Series of the Major League?"

"Yes."

"That's revealing. I hadn't heard that. And is shot putting what you like the most of athletics?"

"No, I like the races. For example, you know how fast humans can run, right?"

"No."

"It's about forty kilometers per hour. That's the fastest. Maybe a bit faster in sprints, but in medium runs, of 100 to 200 meters, humans have never reached forty kilometers. Only in relay races: in relays they go over forty kilometers. You're going at forty kilometers, then it decreases at 200 meters, almost the same; at 400 it's still fast, but after 1,500 meters the speed difference between 1,500 and forty kilometers is not much. Whether running 1,500 meters or one mile, the speed does not go down much. Have you seen people run 10,000 meters? They get into a fantastic pace. It's all numbers, you see."

"But tell me something: what do you enjoy more, the action or the numbers?"

"I like watching the athletes, but also the statistics. That's what I said to you at the beginning. The more you know about something, the more you enjoy it. The more you know about music, the more you enjoy it, or if you know about theater, or art, or architecture. So, the more you know about sports, and you know what happened and how they did it, you get to enjoy it more. That's why Jesse Owens... Do you know who Jesse Owens is? The 'black legend.' He ran in the Berlin Olympics and Hitler was furious because he won at everything: he won 100 meters, 200, long jump, but in 100 meters he did 10.3 seconds. Now they do 9.58."

"And all these statistics, do you keep them in files or in your head?"

"I have them all here," he points at his head. "Well, I do have a little graph about the speeds in a notebook."

"But a good part of it is in your head, isn't it?"

"And if it stays there, fine. If it doesn't, I don't mind."

Beyond his sports interests, Slim's academic routine during his early college years was to go to class between 7 and 11 a.m., take a long break, and return at 4 p.m., finishing by 10. Generally, during the midday break he played sports, studied and ate lunch with his friends. Some of his closest friends at the time were Luis Ramos Liñán, José Campa and Sergio Covarrubias, with whom he studied at the Preparatoria n. 1.

According to Fructuoso Pérez, Slim was not at all dull: "He liked parties and he liked girls and everything. He was a regular student, I mean, he was a good student but without being a nerd. He had a gift for mathematics, to the point where he started teaching that subject at college when he was in fourth year."

One of the anecdotes Fructuoso remembers most vividly about Slim took place during a forty-five-day field trip to the United States on board a Mercedes Benz bus. As in any adventure of this kind at that age, practical jokes were the order of the day.

"Every time we talk about this, Carlos ends up in stitches. We were at a hotel in Houston, which was called Shamrock Hilton. We all used to go into each other's rooms and one day Carlos went into mine when I was buck naked. Someone knocked at the door and Carlos said: 'Go on, open, someone's knocking.' So I opened the door. They'd already planned it: Carlos pushed me out to the hallway. The others would open doors and say 'Here, quick!' and I'd run that way and they'd close the door. Then some gringos were coming and I was totally naked. With that prank of his, ooft, they all laughed their heads off."

The purpose of the trip was not tourism, but to visit works of civil engineering as part of the young students' training. The trip's organizer was one of their lecturers, Carlos Insunza, who later became a close friend of Slim's. In the United States they visited hydroelectric plants and road bridges, while in Mexico they went to all the latest, cutting-edge works, such as the Coatzacoalcos bridge in Veracruz, or the La Amistad dam on the border between Mexico and the United States.

"It meant we bonded a lot because we were together all day, we had breakfast, lunch and dinner together, and we had a riot. So we always got into all sorts of antics. We always remember those journeys very fondly."

"What other anecdotes do you remember from those trips?" I ask Fructuoso.

"On a field trip... If this gets published he won't be very happy, but let me see... On a field trip, I can't remember the place, I think it was near Guanajuato, he was driving a car, an old car. Well, not too old, a Ford. They separated from the group because the rest of us were on the bus. And these bastards brought some girls with them."

"From Guanajuato?"

"Yes, some hookers. They brought them in the car all the way to Mexico City. It was a hoot... Anyway, so many anecdotes. He loved it. He was very playful. He liked everything, like a normal person."

In 2007, on the fiftieth anniversary of the year that marked his generation at the Faculty of Civil Engineering, Slim financed a series of celebrations and activities that went on for several days and included everything from a rock-and-roll blowout—where the magnate and his former classmates went dressed in jeans and leather jackets—to spa visits on the outskirts of Mexico City. There was also a lunch party at the UNAM Botanical Gardens, several breakfasts, several balls—some of them with entertainers like Angélica María and Enrique Guzmán—as well as a special concert by the Orquesta de Minería in the Nezahualcóyotl Hall. Slim and his former classmates' activities did not end there. In August 2007, Slim arranged for the remains of the godfather of his generation, Bernardo Quintana Arrioja, president of the Civil Engineers' Association (ICA), to be transferred to the Rotunda of Illustrious People in Mexico City. After the ceremony, the former students held various celebrations at hotels, museums and nightclubs. Slim attended all of the events and tried to appear as an alumnus like any other.

On the occasion of those celebrations, a special edition of *Orbe* —the student magazine of those years at the Faculty of Civil Engineering—was published, with a youthful and defiant Slim on the front cover doing the Tancredo, a bullring act consisting of sitting in a chair in front of a bull, without moving. This happened at the ranch of El Charro on the August 8, 1959.

"Carlos did it to perfection. It's not easy because the bull is charging at you. You shouldn't move because he follows the movement. The thing is to have the balls not to move. And this bastard did it. I've heard him say: 'It was one of the most exciting moments I've experienced in my life.'"

Slim confirmed to me afterwards that doing the Tancredo was "the most spontaneous, strongest emotion I have ever felt." I show him my copy of the 1959 issue and he tells me that he did another Tancredo the following year: "That time the bull charged at me three times and did not touch me. As soon as it arrived to where I was, it would turn around. People thought I'd gone into shock and God knows how many things they made up about me, but I remember the whole crowd went off their nut. That was also at the El Charro ranch, there in the National Army."

Everyone paid into the fiftieth anniversary celebrations, but Slim dispensed the largest amount, as he decided that if anyone could not afford it, he would cover their bill. Fructuoso explains Slim's request:

"I don't want anyone of our generation to not come to the events. I'll pay their share without you telling them. Just tell them they don't need to pay, that there's a fund and that's it, but I don't want you to tell them that I paid."

"That's the kind of guy he is. It's not the amount of money, which to him may be a lot or little or nothing: it's the gesture. He's very generous."

"What are Mr. Slim's birthday parties like?" I ask him.

"They are organized by his children and I've been lucky enough to be invited."

"But are they quiet or more formal, or is there also lots of dancing?"

"No, no, no: just forty or fifty people, friends and family only."

"When he's out and about, it looks like he doesn't have much security."

"He has lots of security, but it looks like he doesn't. He drives his own car, he doesn't go around with a driver. Obviously his bodyguards have to look after him, that's normal. One day he said to me: 'Let's go.' We were going to Toluca Airport. 'You drive,' he says. So I was driving along, and he kept saying 'You're a shocking driver.' I said to him: 'But this piece of shit is so heavy, it's like driving a tank.' Because they are bulletproof, and you're not used to it. You do this and the car—"

"And what kind of car was it? A Mercedes?"

"Yes, a Mercedes, or SUVs, he doesn't give a damn."

"Did he have a car when he was at college?"

"Yes, but a modest one. Some of us were lucky enough to drive a car, not many of us. But did Carlos have a chauffer or anything like that? No, not at all."

"Did you ever imagine at the time how things would turn out for him?"

"How far he would go? To being the richest man in the world? No, we never dreamed of it."

————

Carlos Slim's college peers didn't see him becoming a businessman when they were studying at the UNAM. Some were surprised that in

December 1967, six years after graduating, he invited them to form an investment club. It was unusual, because most of the recent engineering graduates opted to work in construction, the most obvious career path for a civil engineer. It was around that time when Slim, already married to Soumaya, founded Carso and started to work as a stock broker. Some of his friends seem to remember that he told them he had acquired a masters' degree in investment in the United States, although this information is omitted from his official autobiography.

At the time when Che Guevara was inspiring hundreds of Latin American students, Slim's heroes were the likes of Jean Paul Getty, who, in addition to being a millionaire, garnered fame as a motivational writer. In his book *How to Be Rich,* he describes four types of people:

1. Individuals who work best for themselves, rather than for a company.
2. Individuals who strive to become the most powerful within a company.
3. Individuals who aspire only to receive a good salary.
4. Individuals who do not have any need or desire to prosper, and are satisfied with what they've got.

Those who are in the first two categories, Getty explains, will become wealthy because—abracadabra—they have the "millionaire mentality." The American tycoon used to say that the secret to building his fortune was to get up early, work until late, and find oil. The main source of his fortune was Getty Inc., an energy empire which disappeared when it was bought by Texaco, years after his death. Getty also had a reputation for not spending money. In the magnate literature, aside from being recognized as the first-ever billionaire, he is often called "the world's stingiest man."

"I did read Getty in Playboy. It's not that I was looking at the pictures of girls... Well, I looked at them too, but I didn't buy the magazine. They had it in the barber shops," Slim tells me in an interview. "But the businessman I most admire is my dad. When you look at prominent businessmen you might see they have many good things that you can learn a lot from, but when you look at their personal life, they're not that convincing. I think you can learn a lot from everyone by looking at what they do well, but also at what they do wrong. Of the twentieth century, I would say that the best businessman, in my opinion, is Edison. He was a great inventor, he developed the inventions, was a great scientist, and he was probably Mexican, or at least Latino because he was called Thomas *Alva* Edison. And you may criticize him all you like, but he invented everything. Look him up online one day and see how many patents he has."

The same year in which AT&T sent the first experimental telecommunications satellite into space and the Beatles launched their first single, Slim graduated as a civil engineer from the UNAM. His honors thesis, "Applications of linear programming to some problems of civil engineering," is dedicated to the memory of his father. The young Slim opens the last chapter of his work with a sentence that now sounds like an outmoded publicity slogan: "With electronic calculators it is possible to add, subtract, multiply and divide with astounding speed."

His teachers celebrated that project, even though the twenty-two-year-old Slim also attempted to refute Einstein's theories. In the early 1960s, lineal programming was an innovative mathematical model for resolving problems, which is why it seemed like a very advanced subject for an undergraduate, and Slim's research question seemed audacious. The model had been applied in secret by the US Army during the Second World War in order to better organize its military offenses, with an algorithm that allowed a choice among the necessary activities to achieve a goal among all existing alternatives. In his thesis, Slim predicted that electronic calculators would revolutionize the way of doing business in the world. Half a century later, calculators, museum artifacts by now, are still his main tool of choice when closely monitoring his businesses.

The member of a Peruvian committee with which Slim visited Machu Pichu says that after arriving to the sacred city of the Incas, the magnate stood apart from the group for a moment to do some calculations. According to their testimony, after half an hour he rejoined the group and said that he had come up with a new model to implement a system of mobile telephony in South America. Also in Peru, but in Lima, an executive told me another story about Slim, described not as a man who doesn't like losing, but as a man who always wants to win. They were in Lima visiting a museum and Slim asked the executive how many artifacts he thought were on display in the exhibition. The executive said that he had no idea. Slim asked again.

"Thirty thousand," said the man, knowing of Slim's reputation for accurate calculations.

"No," replied Slim. "There are more than 45,000."

Then one of the guides appeared and Slim asked him to tell him the magic number, trusting he would win.

"Thirty three thousand," responded the guide.

Slim glanced at his colleague with exasperation and promised he'd win next time.

During an interview, Larry King joked about whether Slim could read a balance sheet:

"Oh actually, I think I didn't learn that until I was in my twenties. I couldn't understand why what there was on one side was the same as what there was on the other."

"Yeah, why did it have to match?" laughed King.

"Yes. Until I learned that one part is what you have, the other is what your debts are, and the difference is what is yours. It's just arithmetic."

"Simple?"

"Very simple. Anyone could do this."

The conversation ends with King's mischievous smile.

After graduating, Slim spotted a newspaper advert for a course on "economic development and project evaluation" offered in conjunction with the UN, the ECLAC (the UN's Economic Commission for Latin America and the Caribbean), the UNAM and the government of Mexico. In 1962 he began that four-month course, which he completed with a grade of 9.8/10, which surprised his teachers, since the economists studying with him rarely ever received a grade above 8. Because of that grade, he was invited to Chile to take an eight-month course organized by the ECLAC. Slim only attended part of the course, opting instead to skip the introduction and focus on his industrial programming classes.

According to Slim, he really enjoyed his months in Santiago but avoided participating in the theory discussions there: "The ECLAC school was divided; the structuralists against the monetarists, or something like that, which I didn't really understand. To sum it up, some were on the left, others on the right, and both met in the center and coincided. What interested me much more [was] lineal programming because it's about optimizing things: simplifying, synthesizing, and understanding things and making them more efficient."

During his stay in Santiago he took the opportunity to travel around South America and visit Buenos Aires, Argentina, and São Paulo, Brazil, whose urban infrastructure he found impressive. When he returned from South America he focused on completing his thesis and formally graduated as an engineer. He taught at the Universidad Iberoamericana and on the "Fourth course on project evaluation and economic development" of the ECLAC.

The future magnate was then about twenty-three years old. One year later, in 1964, he decided to take a gap year and traveled first to New York, then to Europe and finally to Jezzine, the Lebanese village where his father was born. He stayed in Manhattan hotels and took full advantage of the New York World Fair that was being celebrated that year. He also remembers visiting the New York Stock Exchange and spending time alone in the library reading books about analysis and material in reference to an investment plan called the Monthly Investment Program (MIP). Afterward he traveled to Europe and visited Amsterdam, Paris, Madrid and Rome, until he reached Lebanon, the land of his ancestors.

A few months later, Slim would be ready to return to Mexico and begin his formal career as a businessman, in 1965.

VI

19

Julián

Carlos Slim's older brother Julián was born in 1938 in Mexico City. Of all the other siblings—José, Alma and Nour—it was with Alma that the richest Mexican in the world had the closest relationship, probably because she married a bit later and took care of several family affairs after the death of their father.

Slim says that as a child he did not have as close a relationship with Julián as he did with José, the eldest, nicknamed Pepe.

"Julián," says Slim, "was older and had his own gang. Pepe and I had another group of friends in the park. We played football and baseball, while Julián was more interested in girls. In those days people used to go to Chapultepec to do the rounds in the park and to court their sweethearts. Julián really loved going there."

When I asked Slim about his brother Julián, his son Roberto Slim Seade was present, who, in addition to holding a management position at Grupo Carso's hotel company, worked on special projects as the magnate's personal secretary. A recent project was to organize the eightieth birthday of legendary Hollywood star Sophia Loren, who celebrated the occasion in Mexico City upon an invitation from her friend Slim.

"It was with Alma that I got on best out of all my siblings. Then when I was a bit older I got on better with my friends from high school and college, even more than with my cousins and other relatives," says Slim, who tells me that Julián began a career in the police force working at a now-defunct preventive corporation, which in those years was called Policía Vial. Julián used to patrol the nocturnal streets of Mexico City, such as the Zona Rosa. "One day I bumped into him as a police officer of the Vial in the Zona Rosa. I'd said: 'Look, let's go and ask that policeman where the place is.' I was out to dinner with Antonio del Valle and Soumaya. We went up to the policeman to ask him and it was Julián," he reminisces.

Julián studied law at the UNAM. Soon after graduating he got a position as a police agent for the Public Ministry of the Attorney General's Office of Mexico City (PGJDF). His closest friend since college was Mario Moya Palencia, who reached the position of home secretary and might have been nominated as presidential candidate of the PRI for the 1976 elections, had he not been accused as the politician responsible for the massacre of student protestors opposing the regime during the Corpus Christi celebrations in 1971.

Julián Slim married Magdalena Seade—whose father, Carlos Seade, was one of the first Lebanese migrants to graduate as a doctor in Mexico, along with Lewis Ferreira, from Guadalajara. A now-defunct Lebanese community magazine had published an article on the wedding between Julián and Magdalena, with a photograph of Julián dressed in a suit, with a slight smile on his face, his left hand resting on his chest, and his right arm wrapped around his wife Magdalena, who is wearing a white dress.

Having recently graduated from law school, in 1960 Julián became secretary of the International Lebanese Association, a project launched by his uncle, footwear entrepreneur Antonio Domit, whose "high goal," according to a manifesto disseminated in Lebanese publications was "to achieve the unification and organization of all Lebanese residents in each country, fostering comradeship and sincere and uninterested friendship, between them and between all the Lebanese communities throughout the world." The document was accompanied by a photograph of the eight "prominent men of moral and material solvency" that made up the board of directors. In the center, we see Julián dressed in a dark suit next to Domit, president of the nascent organization.

Julián and Carlos became closer after the death of their father. In 1966, it was Julián who accompanied his brother Carlos to the altar when he married Soumaya. At the time, Julián was already working for the PRI regime's national security agencies. The Attorney General's Office has a file on him, which I obtained after several years of litigation. Julián was a member of the UNAM Law School's class of '57. His name does not appear in the reports of the National Human Rights Commission (CNDH) nor in those of the department specialized in researching political and social crimes of the past. At law school, his honors thesis, "Effects of good and bad faith in Mexican civil law," is not easy to locate, either. It's much easier to get hold of that of his brother Carlos, which begins with the dedication "To my brothers."

Following clues in the documents consulted about the police career of the magnate's brother, it appears that Julián's career was on the rise, but precisely when Carlos started to become known in the business world, Julián disappeared from the public arena. In 1991, when Carlos won the bid for Telmex, (the company of greatest strategic importance in national security, out of all the companies that were privatized during Salinas de Gortari's government), commanding officer Julián Slim Helú practically abandoned his career as a public servant and became a distant memory of whom very little is said.

When I tell the conflict management specialist Fernando Montiel the story of Julián Slim, he says it reminded him in a way of the myth of the brothers Romulus and Remus under which Rome was built: one of the brothers, Remus, is sacrificed so that the other, Romulus, may be crowned king, allowing one of the greatest empires in history to flourish. Julián died on the afternoon of Thursday, February 17, 2011, at the age of 74. The wake was held at his home, located on Sierra Leona street in Lomas de Chapultepec, Mexico City. The news of his death received very little coverage in national newspapers, which were primarily focused on the daily troubles elicited by the so-called War on Drugs, which can be traced back in more than one sense to the "Dirty War" that Mexico had experienced during the 1970s. The day following Julián's death, the front covers of *Milenio*, *El Universal*, *Reforma* and *La Jornada* had photographs of the 30,000 candles lit on the UNAM's main square, during the first protest to take place in Mexico City against

131

the War on Drugs, for the 30,000 violent deaths since December 1, 2006, when Felipe Calderón rose to power. Nor did any of the political commentators mention Julián's death. On the other hand, some pointed out the promise of then-secretary of federal public security, Genaro García Luna, to "clean" the corrupt police forces of the country. García Luna was considered a kind of security tsar in Mexico during Calderón's so-called War on Drugs.

The newspaper that dedicated the most amount of space to the former commanding officer's death, as well as to the funerary acts that followed, was *Excélsior*. According to the article signed by the editors, present at Julián's wake were former home secretary Manuel Bartlett; Banamex president Alfredo Harp Helú; UNAM rector José Narro; Kimberly-Clark president Claudio X. González; chief of the Mexico City police, Manuel Mondragón; and singer Chamín Correa.

Héctor Slim Seade, Julián's fourth son, is the current general director of Telmex. He and his uncle Carlos Slim were the relatives who received the most sympathies after Julián's passing. On Saturday, February 19, they both entered the Panteón Francés cemetery together, where a hearse transported, at 4 p.m., Julián Slim Helú's body in a mahogany coffin. After a brief ceremony officiated for a small group of people, the commanding officer's body was placed in a mausoleum.

Located at the entrance of the cemetery, the monument stands out for its sculpted busts of Julián Slim Sr., the patriarch of the Slim family, and Julián Slim Jr., the police officer of the "Dirty War" who nobody remembers.

———

On January 22, 1975, the young mathematics professor Manuel López Mateos stepped into the Attorney General's Office of Mexico City. He was there to file a criminal complaint against Miguel Nazar Haro and Julián Slim for kidnapping and injuries. They were agents of the police force with the most politically infamous reputation in the history of Mexico: the DFS. The following is an extract of the report written by Captain Luis de la Barreda to protect his agents Miguel Nazar Haro and Julián Slim:

Manuel López Mateos was detained at 10:00 hours on November 29, 1974, by agents of said directorate, and driven to DFS premises to investigate his relationship with a subversive and terrorist organization called Unión del Pueblo, with a significantly large amount of documentation and propaganda pertaining to various subversive organizations having been found in his home.

While being interrogated he stated [redacted section], originally from Veracruz, professor of mathematics at the Faculty of Science at UNAM, where he has always been notorious as a revolutionary element, who has participated since his student years in a variety of movements funded by the Comité de Lucha of the Faculty of Science.

Likewise, he confessed to having served in multiple organizations as an intermediary in the dissemination of propaganda and subversive literature among the studentship, exploiting for such purpose the ascendency afforded by his position as a university lecturer.

During the Cold War, under whose black-and-white logic all dissidents were "Communists," criminal complaints filed at the Interior Ministry were extremely rare: as a first line of defense against enemies of the state, the DFS was untouchable. "To guarantee governance," anything was considered lawful.

The criminal complaint filed by Manuel López Mateos was never investigated.

Thirty years later, in the year 2000, the PRI lost the presidency of the republic to the PAN. The government turnover brought to an end seven decades of party monopoly and marked the start of the current era, regarded as a period of political transition. To investigate the killings, forced disappearances and other crimes committed during the conflict, which is euphemistically called the "Dirty War" (is there such a thing as a "clean war"?) the new government of Vicente Fox created a specialist prosecutor's office. In parallel, a large section of the files of the former DFS were opened; based on these, vast amounts of special reports by the human rights commission were produced, as well as journalistic articles, academic texts and non-fiction books, reflecting on those traumatic years. But few of these efforts translated into real justice. Impunity continues to prevail, now dispersed among the "democratic" chaos.

One of the declassified files kept in the National General Archive—which is housed in the former Lecumberri prison, or "the Black Palace," as it was called back then—contains the internal report on López Mateos's complaint, registered under a preliminary investigation of ephemeral duration: file 8430/SC/74.

The internal DFS report states:

> On January 22, 1975, Manuel López Mateos (nephew of the ex-president) filed a criminal complaint at the Attorney General's Office of Mexico City, against Miguel Nazar Haro and Julián Slim Helú, for the crimes of illegal deprivation of freedom and resulting crimes, for which reason the above Office summons both Nazar and Slim to appear at Desk 15 in order to file their declaration regarding the facts referred to in the complaint.

The bureaucratic tone of the article received an immediate and emphatic response. In the same official document, marked under code 21-500-75, a handwritten note instructed Nazar Haro and Slim Helú on what to do regarding the subpoena from the judicial power, thereby reestablishing order and clarifying the state's priorities: "Do not present yourselves under any circumstances, on orders from above."

And that is what happened.

I shook the hand of Manuel López Mateos in mid-2009 at the lobby of a luxury hospital in Mexico City. He was in the town for a heart examination. The young man who—perhaps emboldened by the fact that he was the nephew of ex-president Adolfo López Mateos—had dared to file a criminal complaint against the untouchable commanding officers of the DFS was now a balding, bespectacled man, and the director of the newly founded Faculty of Sciences of the Universidad Autónoma Benito Juárez de Oaxaca (UABJO). Behind his glasses, his gaze belied the tragic episodes he experienced decades earlier, about which I wanted to interview him.

López Mateos leaned on the arm of his wife, who accompanied him as we entered the hospital cafeteria. After chatting about his birthplace, Veracruz, about our friends in common, and the uprising in Oaxaca in 2006, I asked him about the complaint he filed against Nazar Haro and Slim Helú, who, according to declassified files, arrested him under the suspicion that he belonged to the group Unión del Pueblo, an armed organization whose founders, the brothers Cruz Sánchez, are working clandestinely under the Popular Revolutionary Army (EPR), one of the guerrilla groups still operating in twenty-first century Mexico, along with the EZLN.

López Mateos seemed to lose his concentration. He turned to look at his wife and caressed her face. Afterwards he shared with me a summary of those years: after the student massacres perpetrated by the PRI regime in 1968 and 1971, there was an increase in the number of young people who decided to confront government repression with armed groups inspired by Castro and "Che" Guevara, he said, although the government of Cuba, in those years, had a better relationship with the iconic political police officer of the time, Fernando Gutiérrez Barrios, than with any Mexican guerrilla leader. Then he spoke to me about the revolutionary dream, the liberation of Mexico, and about the authoritarian features of the PRI regime, whose schizophrenic nature—revolutionary but institutional—led Mario Vargas Llosa to call it "the perfect dictatorship."

In 1974, one of those guerrilla groups put a bomb in the Faculty of Sciences at the UNAM, where López Mateos had studied and had just started to teach mathematics. The act lead to several college students being arrested and taken to the DFS premises, suspected of being responsible for the attack. One of them was the former president's nephew.

López Mateos was beaten and imprisoned for twenty-four hours at the DFS headquarters, located next to the monument to the Mexican Revolution. In front of the national mausoleum holding the remains of Pancho Villa and other national heroes, agent Miguel Nazar Haro tortured the "suspect" who is classified in the files as a "revolutionary element," although while he was being beaten he was called a "goddam agitator."

Two months later, López Mateos decided to report the agents who arrested and beat him.

"Did Julián Slim Helú also torture you?" I asked.

"Carlos Slim's brother? No, he didn't beat me."

"In the complaint you filed, you included his name," I said, as I handed him the document.

"He was there too, but he didn't beat me. It was just Nazar Haro."

After hearing his story, it was hard not to think of the title—referenced in Quevedo's verse—of a novel by Argentinian ex-guerrilla fighter and writer Miguel Bonasso: *La memoria en donde ardía* (*Memory Where it Burned*). The main guerrilla group of those years was the September 23 Communist League. In the fall of 1973, the Marxist-inspired organization executed the two most radical actions of its brief existence: on September 17, beer factory owner Eugenio Garza Sada was killed in a kidnapping attempt in Monterrey by one of the cells of the guerrilla group. One month later, another guerrilla cell kidnapped British consul Anthony Duncan Williams and industrialist Fernando Aranguren Castiello in Guadalajara. Eugenio Garza Sada was a charismatic business leader in Nuevo León—the most industrialized state in Mexico at the time—while Aranguren Castiello was one of the most prominent entrepreneurs in western Mexico.

The League expressed its demands: in exchange for liberating Duncan Williams and Aranguren Castiello, they asked for $200,000 and the transfer of 51 imprisoned subversives to North Korea. The government rejected their demands via a message broadcast on national radio. One day later, the British consul was liberated, but Aranguren was not as lucky: he was executed in cold blood and his body was found in the trunk of an abandoned car.

It was war.

The industrialists of Monterrey and Guadalajara were enemies of president Luis Echeverría Álvarez due to his nationalistic discourse, the good relationship he had with Fidel Castro and the fact that he had launched a number of social programs that they viewed as pro-Communist. After the crimes against Garza Sada and Aranguren Castiello, the rift grew between corporate and government groups. Some trade association leaders in Monterrey did not trust the government, even to the point they suspected that Echeverría himself had ordered the killing of both businessmen and attempted to frame it as a guerrilla action.

The tension grew and the DFS received the order to find the material and intellectual authors of the crimes immediately, in order to curb corporate discontent and thus protect government executive power. The hunt for the two guerrillas began in the winter and did not take long: in the early days of February 1974, the two men who had planned the kidnappings, the national leaders of the Communist League, were found dead. The geography of the findings was no coincidence: José Ignacio Olivares Torres's body was dumped on the intersection of the streets Altos Hornos and Metalúrgica in Guadalajara, very near Aranguren's family home. The body of the other guerrilla leader, Salvador Corral García, was found in an abandoned plot of land in the Fuentes del Valle neighborhood of San Pedro Garza García, the Monterrey metropolitan area where the Garza Sada family lived.

The bodies of the two guerrillas had signs of having been heavily tortured before they were executed.

It was war.

Reading the declassified files of the DFS, it is apparent how the business world reacted to the murders of Garza Sada and Aranguren Castiello, and the urgency with which the guerrillas involved were hunted down.

The people who usually wrote the reports within the DFS were anonymous police officers with a high school level of studies. Some of them had literary aspirations and wrote a prose of extravagant precision, with infrarealist flourishes. In one of the reports, Salvador Corral García is described thus:

He is 26 years old. 1.63 meters tall. Slim build. Skin color white. Brown, semi-wavy and abundant hair (which he usually combs with a hard parting). Deep, vivacious black eyes. Large, Roman nose. Regular mouth. Thick lips. Closed beard. Sharp chin. The pinna of his left ear, more open than his right. Slightly hunched shoulders as though carrying a heavy load. Peculiar gait due to his flat feet. He swings his arms excessively when walking.

An internal document dated November 15, 1973, proves that Corral García was one of the main targets of the hunt, together with his brothers—one of whom, Luis Miguel, also died after one of the police shootouts, while the other, José de Jesús, was arrested by the DFS on March 8, 1976. Since then, José de Jesús has been disappeared. His absence is a quiet testimony of the truth: not all of those who died in the "Dirty War" have a grave.

Ciudad Juárez, Chihuahua. In view that Salvador Corral García, aged 26 years, born in Corrales, municipality of Tepehuanes, Durango, has been accused as one of the alleged assassins of Mr. Eugenio Garza Sada, and was believed to be in this city, officers of the DFS and the Judicial Police of Monterrey attempted to find him, locating only his brother Roberto Corral García, aged 28 years, who was arrested today at 1750 hours at his Industrial Hardware Store, located on the intersection of Ayuntamiento and Central streets, in the Industrial district of this city, and who is now being held at the First Infantry Battalion.

Very respectfully
THE FEDERAL SECURITY DIRECTOR
CAPT. LUIS DE LA BARREDA MORENO

Other files of the investigation on the murderers of Aranguren Castiello and Garza Sada contain only news reports riddled with euphemisms and lacking crucial information. However, there is a document that was secured by researcher Ángeles Magdaleno in 2000 via an appeal lodged "to prevent the mutilation of key documents in the works of our historical memory." It's file 11-235-L6. Pages 163 to 167 record the presence of guerrilla Salvador Corral García in Mexico City on February 1, 1974, where he was interrogated "by Mr. Julián Slim H., head of the Legal Department of the DFS."

This document reveals something that thirty years ago was considered a fact among the government opposition, despite the lack of official evidence to prove it: that Corral García was arrested in Sinaloa and taken to Mexico City to be interrogated; five days

later he was murdered and his body was dumped in Monterrey as
a blood tribute and sacrificial offering presented by the PRI government to the Mexican corporate elite.

In 2006, when the reports were published with the results of
the special investigations on the "Dirty War," by both the National
Human Rights Commission and the special prosecution's office,
they were brushed aside and criticized by everyone involved: on one
hand, the accused civil servants discredited the conclusions as "ten-
dentious." On the other, the victims' relatives and former guerillas
considered the reports to be insufficient, and the conclusions dis-
torted to cover up the facts. In short, the official memory of those
turbulent years received few positive comments.

Both reports contain internal documents and hundreds of testimonies collected thirty years after the facts. In that material there
are conclusive voices confirming, again and again, secrets that are
now undeniable: that torture was common practice at the DFS
during police investigations, and that the DFS was the main repressive mechanism of the powers that be. There were hundreds of
witnesses and victims of their atrocities. After being arrested—most
often without a court order—people were interrogated, blindfolded
and forced to sign declarations and confessions under threats, beat-
ings and torture through the application of electric shocks on the
genitals. Or they would be forcibly disappeared, never to be heard
from again. The cases are so many and the documentation on this
is so abundant that I would need 800 or 900 footnotes to include
each one of the victims in this book.

The reports also contain the names of almost a hundred police
officers who participated in this "Dirty War": Arturo Durazo
Moreno, Salomón Tanús, Jorge Obregón Lima, Francisco Sahagún
Baca, Luis de la Barreda Moreno, Francisco Quirós Hermosillo,
José Guadalupe Estrella, Florentino Ventura, Miguel Nazar Haro,
among many others. However, one name that is never mentioned in
the historical reports of the human rights commission or the special
prosecution's office is that of Julián Slim, who was not even called
to declare as a witness, as most DFS officers were.

After gaining possession of the official documents revealing that
Julián Slim Jr. interrogated Corral García before he was murdered

and dumped on a street in Monterrey, I asked several survivors of those years, such as former guerrillas Héctor Escamilla Lira, Elías Orozco, Alberto Sánchez and Manuel Saldaña, whether they had heard of officer Julián Slim. None of them could remember him well. All they managed to say was that he was perhaps a relative, "a cousin or distant uncle of Carlos Slim," who—it seems—had joined the PGR as a commanding officer after being in the DFS, and of whom nothing was known again.

On May 27, 2008, I submitted a request to the Federal Institute for Access to Information (IFAI), to obtain the PGR records of Julián Slim Helú, should they exist. On July 3, the PGR's Liaison Unit responded, saying that a file for a police officer with that name did exist, but it could not be delivered because it was classified as confidential. I appealed the decision, arguing that officer Slim Helú was no longer serving in any public position, and that the mandatory twenty years had passed, which is the time period specified in the regulations for maintaining under reserve any documents classified as confidential.

Convinced that that documentation should be made public, IFAI commissioner María Marván Laborde took over the case and helped me win the appeal one year later. The IFAI forced the PGR to deliver the file, which stated that Julián Slim Helú began work as a first commander of that department on the June 16, 1983, and handed in his notice on June 7, 1984, one week after the death of Manuel Buendía Tellezgirón, who was the most influential political columnist in Mexico at the time, and had been assassinated by a gunman hired by the DFS.

According to the file, Julián Slim Helú held the position of first commander of the Federal Judicial Police. He was assigned to work at the Mexico City International Airport and received a monthly salary of 21,240 pesos, plus a bonus salary of 7,343 pesos. Under the item "variable extraordinary income," it reads that he was also paid an "additional compensation for special services of 47,326 pesos"; that is, an amount greater than the sum of the salary and bonus he received. In total, his monthly salary was nearly 76,000 pesos—an exorbitant amount for a police officer in Mexico at the time. The checks he received were signed by Carlos Madrazo

Pintado, brother of the 2006 PRI presidential candidate, Roberto Madrazo Pintado. In addition, the commanding officer Slim Helú had life insurance for 1 million pesos.

The document I obtained through the Law of Transparency states that Julián Slim Helú received his military ID on March 18, 1952, after attending fifty sessions at the Mexican Army and being positively evaluated in conduct, dedication and academic progress. His professional license, n. 106050, certifies that he completed a law degree at the UNAM.

However, the precision of some of the documents is in stark contrast with the obscurity of others. His reasons for leaving the PGR are unclear. His file contains a letter of resignation written on June 7, 1984, addressed to the attorney-general of the republic, Sergio García Ramírez:

Dear Mr. Procurator and distinguished friend:

I would like to cordially greet you by expressing my deepest appreciation and gratitude for the honor that you were kind enough to bestow on me when I was designated, on June 16, 1983, first commander for the Federal Judicial Police.

As I carried out my duties, which I always deemed as a great responsibility, rather than a privilege, I was invariably encouraged by your continued expressions of trust, sympathy and esteem, which reaffirms once again the attributes of your human qualities which I have always considered to be of the highest order.

Considering that I have completed the sensitive assignment you decided to entrust me with, I would like to request, should there be no inconvenience, that you discharge me from this important position.

I take this opportunity to reiterate to you my solidarity, friendship and devotion.

JULIÁN SLIM HELÚ

The *Reforma* columnist Miguel Ángel Granados Chapa, a friend of Buendía Tellezgirón and one of the men who learned in detail, a few months before passing away, of the investigations of the crime against Mexico's most influential columnist, told me in an interview that Julián Slim Helú's resignation had nothing to do with Buendía Tellezgirón's assassination, despite it taking place within that context.

According to Granados Chapa, the journalist was killed by orders of José Antonio Zorrilla, who had come to the DFS in 1982, to replace Miguel Nazar Haro. Zorrilla was in collusion with drug lords, of which Buendía Tellezgirón was aware. During a meeting in Zorrilla's home, Buendía confronted him on the topic, which caused the all-powerful police chief to dictate a death sentence against him. The journalist was shot five times in the back by a gunman riding a motorcycle.

"Julián Slim Helú resigned five days after Buendía's murder. Did his resignation have anything to do with that case?"

"No."

"Don Miguel, why does nobody know anything about officer Julián Slim Helú? It's as if he never even existed."

"There are areas of crime that are not as glamorous and perhaps for that reason the name of Julián Slim was not heard of much. Perhaps he operated in one of those areas."

"What are those areas of crime that are not as well known?"

"Like archaeological crimes, or something like that, but, you're right, we don't know anything about Julián Slim Helú. It's one more of our mysteries."

Fructuoso Pérez Galicia, Carlos Slim's college friend, told me in 2009 that Julián and Carlos were very close as brothers, that Julián worked at a law firm during the 1990s and offered security assessments for the companies owned by his brother Carlos, and that, in addition, Julián owned a ranch in Veracruz where he spent extended periods.

"Do you know Julián Slim?"

"Yes, of course. I really value Julián."

"What is he like?"

"He's a lawyer. And well, Slim's whole family are very decent, very down-to-earth people. Extremely down to earth. Which is something that nobody believes, really."

"How do Julián and Carlos get on?"

"Perfectly. They get along really well."

"What does Julián do currently?"

"Julián has a firm, and in addition I think he has some... I'm going to say 'consultancies,' like that, in quotation marks, for his brother Carlos."

"What is Julián like physically? Does he look like Carlos?"

"They're very much alike. Julián's very quiet. Very highly educated."

"How do you think Julián handles the fact that his younger brother is more well-known than he is?"

"No, there's no jealousy or anything like that. There's a true understanding of who Carlos is."

"And what are Carlos's other siblings like?"

"The only one who's still alive is Julián."

"And is Julián involved in the businesses in any way?"

"I don't know to what extent, but I imagine he is somewhat involved. For example, Julián's son is Héctor Slim Seade, the current director of Telmex. And another one of Julián's sons, Beto Slim Seade, is the manager of the Calinda hotels."

"What does Carlos say about Julián's youth as a police officer for the DFS and PGR?"

"Carlos used to tell us that his brother was very restless and that he was in that environment because he liked it."

"But it was a world involving a lot of risks."

"True, the world is always a dangerous place for those swimming with sharks."

Gustavo Hirales Morán was one of the directors of the September 23 Communist League, along with Ignacio Salas Obregón, Ignacio Olivares and Salvador Corral García, who together directed what was one of the most prominent guerrilla organizations in the 1970s. Of all of them, he is the only one who is not dead or disappeared.

In 2009, writer Héctor Aguilar Camín introduced me to Hirales Morán at the Seps restaurant in Condesa, in Mexico City. I wanted to ask him about the EPR for an article I was writing for *Milenio* about a guerrilla's escape from a military base in the 1990s. Hirales Morán supported Aguilar Camín's critique regarding me taking the version of the EPR member at face value, as they both believed it be categorically false.

After that occasion, Gustavo Hirales and I corresponded a few times. In July 2011, I asked him for an appointment and we met again at the main plaza of Coyoacán, on the same weekend that the legendary café and bookshop El Parnaso shut down. We walked to another café, nearby. As we did, he spoke to me about his opinions on the War on Drugs, about some of the books he's written, and his controversies with former comrades. Despite being one of the historical directors of the guerrilla organization of the 1970s, Hirales does not have a good reputation within the Mexican left. The newspaper *La Jornada* called him a "repentant guerrilla and a sworn enemy of the cause he defended in his youth."

I had contacted Hirales not only because of his participation in and firsthand knowledge of the "Dirty War," but also because his analysis of the facts was widely considered to be impartial. Above all, I wanted to ask him a question that had been bugging me about commanding officer Julián Slim Helú, whose story I had been writing about at length for this book.

The question playing in my mind was: could anyone be a good police officer while working for the DFS?

I first asked Hirales about his memories of Salvador Corral García, the guerrilla leader found dead in Monterrey. Hirales told me that Corral García was short, stocky, serious and well-spoken: his mannerisms didn't fit the stereotype of a *Norteño*. He also told me that Corral García's death had been "an absolute motherfucker" because he was sacrificed for the northen Mexican corporate elite. To nail the issue down, I asked him whether he believed that the DFS killed Corral García.

"Who else?" he replied, somewhat agitated. "If I've got him and then he's found dead... if it wasn't me, then who?"

Then I mentioned Julián Slim Helú, and he said that the brother of "Don Carlos" was one of the Lebanese officers of the political police—others were Nazar Haro, Tanús—but that, as is the case today, in those years Julián was not very well-known.

"Why do you think he was not heard of much?"

"In hindsight, I think that Julián Slim took a lot of care not to affect his brother, who was already consolidating a business career."

"Was it possible to be a good police officer at the DFS?"

"Look, for instance, many say that Luis de la Barreda, director of the DFS, was a good police officer because he did not torture people personally. Meaning, he was the good cop you got to speak to after going through four different torture sessions conducted by other cops. I experienced that. It's not some story someone told me. There are plenty of cases that are widely known. For example, in front of Luis de la Barrera, they left José Luis Moreno hanging with a gunshot wound, until his arm rotted and they had to hack it off. If that's the measure of being a good cop, then he was a good cop, but in those years everyone working for the DFS was a torturer, at the very least."

"Could Julián have left the DFS being a good police officer?"

"The DFS was an academy for the drug kingpins. Miguel Félix Gallardo, Amado Carrillo, many drug lords worked there… Where are the good cops? I, for one, have no idea."

To date, there have been no official investigations into the alleged extrajudicial execution of guerrilla Salvador Corral García, who gave his declaration to officer Julián Slim Helú before being executed. His death is one of the dozens that took place during Mexico's dark years, which appear to be repeating themselves in recent times—within the context of the so-called War on Drugs, with the cases of Tlatlaya, Tanhuato, Apatzingán and Ayotzinapa, among others.

Despite being the closest brother of one of the richest men in history, Julián died the way he lived: in the shadows of anonymity.

Carlos Slim does not elaborate much when he speaks of his brother's role in Mexico's recent political history:

No one in the family liked him being in the government. There's some things I can't tell you, but what I can tell you is that if we're talking about values, and considering the powerful positions he was in—in the airport where smuggled goods are coming in, for instance—he was a very honest person, because he had to sell some of the properties he inherited from the family, for his livelihood. Whenever one of us got married, my mom would give us a house, you know. And afterward we divided up the properties, and he had to sell some of his properties in order to make a reasonable living. Which means that he is one of the few people working in government, well, I don't know, there's many, but who instead of earning something from what he does, it costs him money. But I insist, nobody liked him being involved in that.

20

Security

Jean Paul Getty's family history is tempestuous. After his death, it became known that he'd installed coin-operated telephones in his mansions to prevent staff, guests and family from making calls for free.

The most well-known story about his stinginess revolves around an ear. Getty's grandson, John Paul Getty, was kidnapped in Rome when he was sixteen years old, and the Calabrian mafia demanded $17 million in exchange for his liberation. The multimillionaire, known for being icily imperturbable, thought that it could all be a ploy cooked up by his own grandson to extract money from him. For several weeks he ignored the warning of the 'Ndrangheta, which led the kidnappers to cut off one of the captive's ears and send it to him. Getty only agreed to pay $2 million, which he would then charge his grandson for, as a loan, with a prime interest rate of 4 percent.

John Paul Getty never managed to pay his debt to his grandfather. At the age of twenty-five he took a cocktail of methadone, Valium and alcohol that left him paralyzed, mute and almost blind until his death twenty years later. He didn't get much of an opportunity to enjoy the inheritance his grandfather had left him.

Although Carlos Slim has never had to put a price on the life of anyone in his family, his generosity with other kidnapping victims places him in a more flattering light than Getty. A year after the magnate entered the *Forbes* list in 1994, his cousin, banker Alfredo Harp Helú, was kidnapped by a Mexican guerrilla group and liberated after nine months of negotiations during which Slim kept in contact with his nieces and nephews, even though in the years leading up to the kidnapping, his relationship with his cousin had been strained due to business competition.

Harp Helú was held for 106 days by a unit of the clandestine EPR, which, for a period, had alliances with other guerrilla groups in other countries. A couple of years prior, plans to kidnap several Mexican celebrities had been found in Nicaragua regarding Central American combatants working with the Basque ETA (an armed separatist organization). One of those planned kidnappings was Slim, who, in the early 1990s, was garnering fame in Mexico and Latin America.

Managua's Fifth Criminal Trial Court investigation file 83/93 comprises 6,000 pages distributed over forty-five volumes and includes documents confiscated from subversive groups. In June 1993, the journalist Gerardo Galarza gained access to the security file that the guerrillas wrote on Slim after closely following his movements in Mexico City. Although it contains several inaccuracies, it is interesting because to a certain extent it shows the apparently austere life of the man who would become, a little over a decade later, the richest in the world:

CARLOS SLIM HELÚ

He is of Lebanese descent. The media describes him as a prominent member of the Lebanese community in Mexico (together with Alfredo Harp Helú, of the Mexican Stock Exchange and association of brokerage houses).

CS lives on Reforma street, between Rocallosas and Apalaches streets, in the third house from the end.

Every day, at 10 a.m., the garbage truck passes by the corner of Rocallosas and Reforma. An employee exits the residence to dump the garbage. The doorman closes the gate after exiting. He has a gardener (cash-in-hand, hired per hour) and at least one housekeeper (aged around 40–45 years).

Opposite the house there is a bus stop for city bus 100. On the corner there is a public telephone. On the opposite corner of Reforma and Rocallosas there is a flower stall occupied by one, two men (watchmen?). Opposite it, there is a public telephone.

The CS household owns two red cars (one of them with plate number ASA380); sometimes only one of them is in. Next to the house there is an adjacent plot of land, where there are building works. The garden of the house reaches up to Virreyes.

CS owns the brokerage house Inversora Bursátil (office Paseo de Las Palmas).

According to *La Jornada* he also owns Probursa. This has not been confirmed. In relation to CS's businesses, *Excélsior* ("Portafolios," October 1987) mentions that he was skillful in his activities. While everyone was doing badly, the value of CS's shares was higher than before the crash. CS bought FUD off the Breners. He sold Bicicletas de México to a company he also owns (mentioned in the media as a not very transparent transaction).

Other companies owned by him include Sanborns (stores), Lampazo, S.A., Aluminio, S.A., Peña Pobre y Loreto (paper factory), Seguros América. A photo of his appears in *Proceso* (Sept., 1988)

Faced with this kind of threat, and given the kidnapping of his cousin Harp Helú, pressure was building within Slim's empire to develop a program of corporate security. In 1994, the year Mexico witnessed, in addition to the Zapatista uprising, the murder of PRI presidential candidate Luis Donaldo Colosio and a host of other political crimes, a group of specialists carried out studies in the main offices, houses and warehouses of Grupo Carso and created a security force equipped with very powerful counterespionage technology, according to testimonies and internal documents collected pertaining to that period. Slim, his children and his main partners were deemed to be facing an elevated criminal risk. Most were provided with intensive courses on crisis management and bomb threats, special guards trained in criminal surveillance and countersurveillance measures, as well as bulletproof vehicles.

To coordinate the efforts, security consultant Eric Lamar Haney, born in Rome, Georgia, began working at the Telmex offices. Haney was commanding sergeant major in the Fifth Battalion of the Eighty-Seventh Infantry, and in Infantry Brigade 193, stationed in Panama by the US Army. According to his CV:

He worked as a human resources manager of a workforce of over 600 men; he was responsible for the development and implementation of their individual training. He supervised the administration and management of an 85-strong security force. He developed, trained and led the most successful sniper organization of the American army. Between March 1988 and March 1990 he participated in and guided combat operations in Panama. He collaborated as an examiner and expert in counter guerrilla and counter terrorism operations, and in combat simulation military drills conducted as part of the training of different armies in Central and South America. He speaks fluent Spanish.

In 1992, before working for Telmex, Haney was in charge of the security and structure of the guard corps that covered the state visit of the prince of Saudi Arabia, Khaled Abdulaziz, to London. He was also chief-of-firearms instructor for the royal military police of Saudi Arabia and was shift supervisor for the protection operations for Prince Khaled and the Saudi royal family during trips to Europe, the United States and Bermuda. He was in charge of the security of the royal yacht during port operations. He also directed audits at Salomón Brothers petrochemical companies, and designed programs to increase their security. Other prominent actions include the liberation in 1990 of an oil businessman captured by the National Liberation Army in Bogotá, Colombia. A further notable feat is that after the US invasion, he "organized and trained the 60 men who comprise the Presidential Guard in the 'new' Republic of Panama."

Most of the heads of Slim's security team are specialists with similar CVs, as well as being extremely discreet. Of all of those who have worked in corporate areas, the only one with a high public profile is Wilfrido Robledo Rincón, an old acquaintance of the Mexican social movements known for being responsible, as the director of the Federal Preventive Police, for breaking the UNAM student strike in 1999 and persecuting students of the Rural Teachers' College of El Mexe in Pachuca, Hidalgo, in 2000. Both of these cases are emblematic of the police repression viewed by some as admirable and by others as characteristic of the prevailing authoritarian regime.

Robledo registered in the naval infantry in his native Oaxaca and, during the government of Luis Echeverría, rose through the ranks until he became presidential assistant. Later he worked on the presidential campaign of Miguel de la Madrid, another PRI candidate. Not very accustomed to giving interviews about his life, Robledo gave one to journalist Andrés Becerril for the newspaper *Excélsior*, in which he candidly claims that he was the mentor of Genaro García Luna, secretary of public security in the federal cabinet during the government of Felipe Calderón. García Luna had recently been accused of corruption, and of creating television montages like the false capture of Florence Cassez, a French woman accused of kidnapping, who was then freed by a Mexican Supreme Court of Justice ruling that there had been serious irregularities in the legal proceedings. "It was within the Protection Directorate that all these little angels were trained, such as Genaro García Luna, Facundo Rosas, and all the other little angels who are now devoted to the country's security," said Robledo to the *Excélsior* journalist.

Both García Luna and Robledo have publicly declared their admiration for and closeness to Slim. Sources who are close to both state that their relationship was consolidated in the 1990s, during their years at the CISEN, the intelligence agency that worked with Telmex for telephone interception purposes.

Robledo was the state security agent who directed the violent San Salvador Atenco crackdown in 2006, under the orders of then-state governor Enrique Peña Nieto, in the term leading up to his presidency. The human rights abuses committed by the police in Atenco against the *comuneros* and activists, who were blockading the construction of an international airport on their collectively owned land, were met with impunity and had no repercussions on either Peña Nieto or Robledo's careers. Three thousand police officers were deployed and over 200 people arrested during the raid. Dozens of women filed criminal complaints for rape and sexual abuse against police officers under Robledo's command, and two young people were killed, hit by police projectiles. In addition, around a hundred activists were brutally beaten by the police.

During this operation, which I witnessed and covered as a journalist, a Telmex worker—Jorge Salinas—became a symbol of the disproportionate repression tactics employed by the government to advance corporate and neoliberal interests. Salinas sympathized with the Other Campaign of the Zapatistas and had decided to go to the village near the capital to support the *comuneros*, when he was detained and beaten at least thirty-four times by a group of police officers. The cameras of Denise Maerker's program *Punto de Partida* captured part of this beating and broadcast it on Televisa. Salinas was incapacitated for several months of work due to the injuries he sustained, and afterward upheld his accusations of corruption within the telephone union led by Francisco Hernández Juárez, one of Slim's close associates. In contrast, in 2014, with Enrique Peña Nieto as president, Robledo retired with honors during a public ceremony hosted by the secretary of the Navy, Vidal Francisco Soberón.

As for the airport, in August 2014, Peña Nieto announced the reactivation of the project with an investment of 169 billion pesos. And the person appointed to develop it was an architect called Fernando Romero, husband of Soumaya Slim Domit, one of the magnate's daughters, in partnership with the prestigious Norman Foster. The announcement did not cause any major public opinion controversies, which would have probably been otherwise had it been any other businessman. "What would have happened if a son-in-law of Emilio Azcárraga [owner of Televisa] had been designated as architect for the project?" asked a commentator of the widely read Mexican website www.SDPnoticias.com.

Larry King interviewed Slim in Los Angeles during the 2013 global conference of the Milken Institute, a think tank created to develop what is known as "human capitalism." In the conversation, King asked Slim about security in the context of the so-called War on Drugs during the government of Felipe Calderón.

"What about security? Do you have a lot of security?"

"Yes, for some reasons that we have, we use security. But it's important to say I have never had problems of insecurity in my life. Never."

"You ever worry about it?"

"Do I worry that I never have insecurity?" Slim laughs, sarcastic.

"No. We read about the problems in Mexico, do you ever worry about your physical safety?"

"We are having a difficult time with crime and drugs. But they are mostly fighting among themselves and with the police."

"You don't think it affects you at all?"

"Not until now. I suppose it's the same thing that happened here, in Chicago, and in other cities in the Prohibition era, that the violence was not against society or against the people, but between the criminals and the police."

"You don't worry about it?"

"Well, we worry that the United States sells weapons to the criminals. There is a war, and drugs and the dollars stay here, while the weapons and the violence stay there, in Mexico. Like in Colombia."

But Slim's apparent lack of concern for security has not prevented him from profiting from the Mexico's security crisis. A little-known company of Slim's called Scitum partnered with Verint Systems Inc. in 2015 to provide cybersecurity to the private and public sectors. A press release outlines their plan to develop a "Threat Protection System," operated from a Scitum Security Operations Center located in Monterrey, which employs around 200 analysts and engineers. According to an investigation by journalist Emilio Godoy for the magazine *Proceso*, Scitum also has offices in Costa Rica, Colombia, Peru, Chile and Spain. Verint, on the other hand, is a global company with headquarters in New York, which openly offers espionage services. One of its most famous products is Engage, an app that allows for real-time geolocalization of mobile targets, as well as geographic alerts to monitor areas of interest, proximity of the target and suspicious activity. This kind of technology has been used by the Mexican government for specific espionage and tracking projects, both in the Attorney General's Office and in the defunct Federal Security Secretariat (now part of the interior ministry), which was directed by powerful former police chief Genaro García Luna, who was prominent during Calderón's War on Drugs between 2006 and 2012. García Luna is a close friend of the Slim family, especially Héctor Slim Seade, director of Telmex and son of Julián, who, as detailed, worked for the infamous DFS. In political circles, legislators and mayors have told me, asking for anonymity, that this relative of Slim is responsible for some espionage actions, however this has never been confirmed. What we do know is that Héctor Slim Seade has actively participated in projects such as Ciudad Segura, a network of 15,000 CCTV cameras, 10,000 panic buttons and 10,000 loudspeakers that were installed in Mexico City by the local government in recent years.

Another of Slim Seade's activities consists of protecting the Slim family empire, which until now has not suffered directly from the security crisis that Mexico has been experiencing in recent years.

21

Close

Carlos Slim is known for having a very relaxed sense of humor and for maintaining strong relationships with those closest to him. One of his best friends, businessman Ignacio Cobo, playfully refers to Slim as "a certain pain in the neck" when he phones officials to invite them for lunch to discuss legislation. Cobo also often tells entertaining stories about Slim and himself. One day they were traveling by car with a group of congressmen in the historical center of Mexico City. Slim was driving along one of the busiest streets and at some point he gently bumped the taxi in front of them. Slim was worried about the potential press scandal, so his friend Cobo promptly got out of the car and went to talk to the furious taxi driver. After a couple of minutes he returned to the car and told Slim to keep driving.

"What did you say?" the magnate asked his friend.

"I said my chauffeur was an idiot and asked him to please forgive us," replied Cobo, laughing.

It seems absurd that someone with so much money should drive his own car, especially in Mexico City's unbearable traffic. But an endless list could be made of the contradictions around Slim: the richest man in the world shares financial strategies with Fidel Castro to combat developing countries' debt through swaps, a system of foreign debt exchange for shares in state-owned companies. In 2000, with the governmental turnover in Mexico, a group of Mexican intellectuals proposed that Slim finance a newspaper that would be called *El Independiente*. The multimillionaire responded that his business remit did not include projects linked with the media. A decade later, in addition to his shares in the *New York Times* and Grupo Prisa, he has purchased dozens of print, radio and television networks in Latin America.

In the 1990s, Slim maintained a very close relationship with businessman Juan Antonio Pérez Simón, who was the first director general of Telmex and Slim's main partner at Grupo Carso, as well as Inbursa. In general, Slim's former associate tends to say that the world of politics is full of pride, arrogance and haughtiness, in which people can turn on a dime from flattery to defamation and from loyalty to ruin. He also shares Slim's wariness of foreign investors who arrive in Mexico, as they tend to have exclusively economic goals, and pay no attention to other business responsibilities. People close to Pérez Simón say that during his time as director general of Telmex he had several disagreements with the government of Salinas de Gortari, which always took place in the corridors of power.

"Salinas unleashed the forces of evil, muddied positions and changed up the signs several times," Pérez Simón has said at our various meetings. In particular, Slim's partner asserts that in 1994, during his last year in power, Salinas de Gortari named two presidential candidates—Donaldo Colosio (who was assassinated) and Zedillo—and made political maneuvers through characters as contrasting as Manuel Camacho Solís and Emilio Gamboa. However, Pérez Simón tends to conclude his reflections saying that Salinas de Gortari, unlike many presidents, will reach historical transcendence.

Pérez Simón had an enormous amount of power at the time, and managed to orchestrate a private and unimaginable meeting between enemy former presidents José López Portillo and Luis Echeverría in his home in late 1994. During the encounter, when faced with the mediation efforts of Pérez Simón and other guests, Echeverría said something like: "For us, all that's left to do is die." Soon afterward López Portillo died, while Echeverría celebrated his ninety-third birthday in 2015. Both ex-presidents, together with Miguel de la Madrid—all from the PRI—form part of the spectrum of relationships that Slim and his employees have maintained since the 1980s.

In 1995, Pérez Simón resigned as director general of Telmex and left most of the operations to Slim, although he is still involved in some administrative boards of the empire and a large portion of his own financial investments are in the magnate's businesses. Some of Pérez Simón's critics claim that there was a rift due to some of his refined and extravagant tastes, which annoyed Slim. However, the most widely accepted version is that Slim was making room for his sons in the consortium.

Pérez Simón has maintained a good relationship with Slim, although he has also led his own agenda: he has become one of the greatest Mexican art collectors, is board member for several museums around the world, and in the year 2000, after Andrés Manuel López Obrador won the elections for governor of Mexico City, he organized a citizens' group that sought to support López Obrador's administration. In December of that year, they held the first meeting at Pérez Simón's mansion in front of the plaza Río de Janeiro, in the Roma district. Combatting corruption in the Mexico City government was the main objective of the group, which was comprised of banker Rubén Aguilar Monteverde, economist David Ibarra, writer Germán Dehesa, analyst Fernando Solana and journalists Ricardo Rocha, Carmen Aristegui, Javier Solórzano and Miguel Ángel Granados Chapa—who, not long before passing away, told me about the consolidation of this group:

> Pérez Simón's house is extremely elegant. Out of three properties, two of them from the Porfiriato era, he made one and it has two entrances: one off Jalapa street and the other off Río de Janeiro. We used to meet in the dining hall, which has its own kitchen and staff of cooks. It's clear that business lunches are held there daily. And the food is amazing. We used to wish for the meetings to be weekly so that we could eat all that delicious food. The group met at least once a month. The meetings were attended by functionaries of the government of Mexico City and sometimes Andrés Manuel himself would chat to us. They gave reports on what was being done against corruption. The finance secretary, Gustavo Ponce, was at one of the meetings one day, and a week later we saw him on TV betting in Las Vegas with public funds. We hoped Andrés

Manuel would give us his version, but there was never another meeting.

Granados Chapa told me that he met Slim in 1965, when he worked for a news agency owned by Fernando Solana, who was a professor in the Faculty of Political Sciences at the UNAM. One of the services provided by the agency was a weekly dossier of financial information. It was called *Semana Económica*. Because of that responsibility, Granados Chapa used to visit the stock exchange regularly, which in those years was one of the main sources of information, even though it was new. In that period, Slim and Onésimo Cepeda, who was also the Bishop of Ecatepec, were great stock traders. And over time, the former became known for buying failed businesses, which he then turned around, such as the Galas printers, according to Granados Chapa. The next company he turned around was Sanborns, which, before being bought by the businessman, had a reputation for being a dirty and declining place. When Slim purchased it in 1985, the chain had thirty-five branches and 6,500 staff. Thirty years later he had multiplied its size and value by five.

"During all those years I saw him frequently and we were close," says Granados Chapa, who never believed that Slim was a front man for Salinas de Gortari. "I don't know whether Salinas received a cut, but what I do know is that Slim is not a front man for Salinas."

As for Pérez Simón, Granados Chapa described him as passionate about Asturias, Spain:

"He visits his country twice a year and he has the look of a Spanish dandy. He likes to live well, he's elegant. I don't think he's an enemy of Slim because, for example, he has acted as mediator between many intellectuals and Slim, like with what happened with the kidnapping of Julio Scherer's son."

The last time Granados Chapa saw Slim was in November 2009, during economist David Ibarra's eightieth birthday party, which Ignacio Cobo had organized at Hotel Geneve, on Génova street, in the Zona Rosa of Mexico City, where Cobo has an office through which he handles affairs for the magnate.

Granados Chapa also remembered a gigantic all-expenses-paid trip to Villahermosa, Tabasco, to attend a ceremony for the award of an *honoris causa* degree to former PRI governor Enrique González Pedrero, who was a friend of Cobo and had helped him learn the art of politics together with his father-in-law, Mario Trujillo, also a former governor. Of Cobo, Slim's main operator since the late 1990s, Granados Chapa said he was "a very vulgar friend, who was extremely popular and entertaining. He doesn't come across as one of the people most important to the richest man in the world."

"Do you think Ignacio Cobo is Slim's best friend?" I ask Fructuoso Pérez, Slim's college friend.

"I don't know if he's his best friend, but he is one of the best. There's no doubt about that."

"And it's a rough-and-tumble kind of friendship?"

"Yes, Nachito is very strong. He and Carlos are always play fighting."

"They lived together or something like that, didn't they? When they were in college."

"They started out doing business together in the sixties. I think they built some apartments where actually Carlos lived when he was just married. Nacho is a very close friend of his, very pleasant."

"How would you define Carlos Slim with his friends?"

"He's an extremely kind person, very down to earth, very caring..."

"Can you tell me something that shows his down-to-earth quality?"

"On one occasion he did us the favor of inviting a small group of us to a talk in his home with the former president of Spain, Felipe González, and Carlos got up, went into the kitchen, and came back carrying sodas and glasses. He put them on the table, started taking the tops off and started pouring us all glasses of soda. Can you imagine a man of that level, that category, doing that kind of thing? And he does it all the time, totally naturally. He's also a man who doesn't wear watches or any of those luxury items."

"And how does he get on with Felipe González?"

"They get on great."

"What did they chat about during that meeting?"

"Well, that time we chatted about experiences he, Felipe, had during his government. Or from when I was part of the union, at one time, of the CFE (Federal Electricity Company)."

"Were you a union leader?"

"Yes. Carlos told Felipe that I had been the union leader at the CFE [Federal Electricity Company] and he started talking to us about that subject. About the unions in Spain that he was part of and how they were run. We talked about different topics regarding different people and the conversation with Felipe was always very interesting, very enjoyable."

"Is Felipe González a friend or partner of Carlos Slim?"

"As far as I know, he's just a friend. I'm sure they speak about many international issues, for obvious reasons, but to say that he calls himself partner of this or that company, I don't know."

"And is Bill Clinton also his friend?"

"Once he brought ex-president Clinton to a conference here, which he organizes every year for the students. I've had the chance to be at those conferences in the auditorium, and he brings renowned, world-class speakers. And once he brought Bill Clinton to a conference and well, he, I imagine they must be on somewhat familiar terms. He has visited him over there, or when Clinton comes to Mexico... Well, we go back to the same thing: Clinton has sent baseball-related gifts to Carlos. One of them was a ball that belonged to Hank Aaron, one of the best baseball players in history, I reckon, after Babe Ruth. A super player. And he's also sent baseballs that belonged to several other players."

"And does he also follow Mexican baseballers like Fernando Valenzuela?"

"I haven't seen him have a baseball of his or a photograph. I haven't noticed."

"Is he not as interested in Mexican baseball as his former partner, Alfredo Harp?"

"No, the local league not so much, although he does know the history of Mexican baseball and he talks about when Babe Ruth came here and he asks you, "So, do you know who punched out Babe Ruth?" And he tells you it was Ramón Bragaña, things like that. Once we went to a baseball game. We went to see the

Mexico-Tigres because Alfredo Harp invited him and we were there for the game."

"Who are your best friends?" I ask Carlos Slim.

"My children."

"How do you choose your business partners? As far as I understand, Juan Antonio Pérez Simón and Ignacio Cobo are your partners."

"No, Ignacio Cobo is not a partner."

"Is Juan Antonio Pérez Simón a partner?"

"He owns shares."

"How do you choose a partner?"

"Look, the company is public. So any person can buy and sell shares."

"I'm talking about a partner at a more important level, like Pérez Simón."

"No, that was a one off. Often it's circumstantial. For example, at that time there was a partner for the stock exchange, [so] we merged with his, Juan Antonio Chico Pardo, but I don't know if he still owns shares or not. He hasn't been with us for some time. But Pérez Simón started working with me at some point when we started a company and there were several partners who were involved at the time."

"Do you mean that your partners are circumstantial?"

"No, I don't have partners in the new companies."

"Why?"

"Well, they're the partners of the market. Does that make sense? All right, I do have partners. When we entered in Telmex, France Telecom had 5 percent, AT&T and Southwestern had 10 percent, with five and five, we had 3.8 percent and others bought 8 and 5 percent. So, there, that's how we got in. Now that we're investing in a Spanish company, we have 26 percent, but there are partners with 2 percent and other partners. And there are other times we had partners, who were... let's call them 'techie' partners."

"Specialists that you needed for certain businesses?"

"Yes, for example—"

"Bill Gates with Prodigy, right?"

"No, no. I see, no, what we did was form a partnership for Hotmail in Mexico, MSN it's called, and the T-1, which is Telmex. What I mean is partnerships with other companies where we do invest, and in the end we have partners in the health or telecom business."

"So what role does Nacho Cobo play in the structure? Is he known for being your political operator...?"

"No, no, no."

"He tells jokes about you..."

"He does his thing. Actually, that puts quite a damper on our relationship."

"So, how would you define your relationship? Many claim that he's your operator."

"No, he's like a very friendly guy who gets it into his head that he can wander around getting involved in everything. How do I define him? On the job, people who are on the payroll hold clearly defined positions. We don't have political operators, we don't have political representatives on our boards or anything like that. We don't have political operators. And we do things ourselves, openly."

"But there are things that need lobbying."

"No, what do you mean lobbying?"

"I'm guessing there are some government initiatives that go against your position."

"Well, we bring our arguments to the table and negotiate."

22

Heirs

The engineer who can earn a million dollars in an hour has six children: three male and three female. Carlos, Marco Antonio and Patrick Slim are directors of his main companies; Soumaya, Vanessa and Johanna participate in cultural activities, while their husbands occupy leading positions in other businesses of the Slim empire. Unlike Warren Buffett—who has announced his plans to give back most of his fortune to society and has given his children only 20 percent of it—Carlos Slim has not said what will happen with his money when he dies. If he wanted to distribute it among his over 100 million Mexican compatriots, as some Twitter and Facebook users have asked him to do—each one would receive around $500 and everyone in the planet's eleventh most populated country could own an iPad.

When they were little, Slim's children slept for many years in two rooms: one for the three boys and another for the three girls. Their father is proud to have brought them up to be responsible. It seems true: none of the six has garnered a reputation for reckless spending. The one who has come closest to that is Carlos Slim Jr., the eldest sibling, who in 2010 celebrated his wedding with María Elena, daughter of businessman Miguel Torruco Márquez, who is a sympathizer of Andrés Manuel López Obrador, the recently elected left-wing president of Mexico, and former secretary of tourism during the administration of Miguel Mancera (of the Democratic Revolution Party, PRD). Over 1,500 guests attended the ceremony, among them several presidents and one Nobel Prize winner. The menu included over 100 desserts, but the food served at dawn, following the banquet and the night-long party, was Sanborns's dishes. The guests who remained until the end of a gigantic and lavish wedding ate food from a cafeteria, where a breakfast costs less than $10.

Veteran Mexican journalist Julio Scherer García, considered the celebration to be a "singular wedding":

Aided by newspaper articles and photographs in tabloid magazines, I imagined what the wedding must have been like. To my memory came, arbitrary and inevitable, the news articles that described in detail the celebrations of the court of Versailles, with Mary Antoinette and Louis XVI oblivious to the misery that loomed threateningly on the outside... As if a bolt of lightning were frozen into a spotlight, I saw a new powerful class making its presence felt. It was a consolidated society, an aristocracy formed of the outstanding men and women in politics and business, each one of them in their place. They may not agree on minor issues, but they probably agree on the essence, support each other, walk together; communicating vessels with those below definitely broken. To borrow a phrase from Coetzee, the South African Nobel Prize-winning author: "Power only speaks to power."

Two years before they were married, the young Carlos Slim Jr. went into the operating room to have one of his kidneys removed. His organ's recipient was his younger brother, Patrick, who had suffered renal failure, the disease their mother, Soumaya, died of. Before receiving Carlos's kidney, Patrick's associates remember how his face, legs and hands used to swell, as well as his complaints about the fatigue caused by his disease. As a result of their affection for Soumaya Domit, the Slim family focused a significant portion of their philanthropic efforts on health. Marco Antonio, the brother between Carlos and Patrick, instigated the creation of a national organ transplant foundation, directed by Gerardo Mendoza Valles. For the donors' campaign, Carlos and Patrick recorded some videos talking about their experience. The latter talks about how he coped with the disease:

I remembered everything that had happened to my mother and it was really hard... I had almost constant dermatitis, especially here, on my forehead. Just after operation it was as if I had my skin was moisturized, as if by magic. Carlos, with much love and total dedication, gifted me a kidney. Not only the greatness of what he did, but how much love he did it with. The truth is that the greatest wealth, we don't realize, but we have it right here in our families, and it's a blessing to be able to receive a transplant. The quality of life is extraordinary and it is an extremely simple operation; it's considered similar to having your appendix removed.

Meanwhile, in his audiovisual testimony, the magnate's eldest son says calmly:

I thought the recovery was going to be more complicated and it was astounding to see that on the same day you're already walking; three days later you're out of the hospital and almost going about your normal life within just a few days, without medication or special diets; I mean, no consequences. One of every 500 people is born with just one kidney and they don't even notice it their whole life. My quality of life is the same, practically as if I hadn't needed to donate, as if I still had my two kidneys, and both the procedure and the recovery were a lot simpler than I'd imagined. The kidney is one of the few organs you can donate while you're still alive and, well, be able to enjoy life, to be able to feel that experience, is incomparable.

Later, both were filmed in a conversation together, remembering the experience. Carlos emphasizes that it was one of the most important things that they have experienced together and claims that he always knew that, among the members of the family, he would be the one to donate the kidney: "I used to tell to Patrick not to worry, because I was sure of what I wanted to do, because for him as well, the person receiving the kidney, their family relationship might not be easy, feeling that someone is making a sacrifice for them." In response, Patrick says: "And what is essential is that, well, there are people like Carlos, who are so generously willing to donate the organ to that loved one."

VI

Not long before undergoing the kidney transplant, the youngest of Slim's sons undertook a political battle that even received the attention and response of then-president Felipe Calderón's team.

During the toughest periods of his disease, Patrick—known by those close to the family, together with Soumaya, as the most religious in Slim's family—had several mystical experiences and completed various pilgrimages. One of the most intense, according to what he has told his friends, was his pilgrimage to Lourdes, a village in the high Pyrenees of France, where there is a grotto in which the Catholic Church recorded an apparition of the Virgin Mary and erected the Church of Our Lady of Lourdes, considered the patron of the sick. Patrick was one of almost eight million pilgrims a year who go to her to be cured of their ailments.

Slim's son told part of this experience to a small group of PAN senators, with whom he met privately in 2007 to ask them not to approve the decriminalization of abortion in the country's capital. After several months of discussions, the PRD and the rest of the political parties represented in Mexico City, with the exception of the PAN, voted against incarcerating women who terminated their pregnancies. During the discussion process there was much debate and threats of excommunication of the legislators who supported the decriminalization initiative put forward by the government of Marcelo Ebrard. There was even a letter from Pope Benedict XVI being circulated, and some groups took to the streets of the city center with Catholic banners protesting against the members of congress. Activists such as the anthropologist María Lamas saw this reform as progressive and, citing the specialist Richard Hare, questioned "the attitude of those who pursue the affirmation of their own moral principles over the real interests of flesh-and-bone people, all the while remaining indifferent to the enormous damage that their actions cause to millions of human beings."

At the private meeting with the PAN representatives, in addition to recounting his experience in Lourdes, Patrick Slim told a story that surprised some of those present. He told them that he had witnessed an apparition of the Virgin of Cleveland, who asked him to help defend the unborn children of Mexico City. The cult of the Virgin located in Cleveland, Ohio, far from being recognized by the

Catholic Church, has even been condemned by it. At the end of the meeting, during which the senators said their hands were tied as the PRD has a strong legislative majority in Mexico City, the son of the richest Mexican in the world declared that he would continue with his mission.

That same year, in July 2007, two months after abortion was decriminalized in Mexico City, Slim's youngest brother started to have regular private meetings with members of the National Synarchist Union, a far-right extremist Catholic group, as well as radical members of the PAN and the founder of the transnational bakery manufacturing company Bimbo, Lorenzo Servitje, in the private area of a popular restaurant called Hacienda de los Morales. The objective was to try to do something about the PRD government, which, since 1998, had initiated several reforms considered too liberal by Patrick Slim, the Synarchists and some PAN members.

These meetings did not come to the public eye until late 2007, when Patrick and his allies decided to apply at the Federal Elections Institute to create a new party that would represent their interests. To that end, they organized dozens of assemblies and meetings, several of them in the Iztapalapa district, the main bastion of the PRD in Mexico City.

However, Patrick's political crusade worried the Mexican president more than it did the PRD. Then-president Felipe Calderón ordered some of his closest associates, such as Germán Martínez Cázares, to prevent Slim's youngest son and the Synarchists from being able to register as a party. Had this happened, it would have meant the immediate exodus of the most conservative faction of the PAN toward the new political organization, which would weaken Calderón's government and the party in power during the 2009 legislative elections.

The name planned for the organization of Patrick Slim and the Synarchists, had they succeeded in registering, was Partido Solidaridad—a word that in Mexico is immediately reminiscent of the government of Carlos Salinas de Gortari, as it was the name of the social justice program that became the symbol of his political project. This increased suspicions that Slim—forever suspected of being in collusion with Salinas de Gortari for the acquisition of Telmex during his administration, although it was not necessarily the case—was interested in possessing his own political party to represent his interests in Congress. However, according to research conducted, the initiative was taken by Patrick Slim without the full backing of his father, who was understandably more interested in Patrick's renal failure than his political crusade.

In June 2008, the elections institute rejected the registration of the National Synarchist Union. When he received the news, a PAN politician close to Calderón celebrated in front of me: "We nipped that in the bud!" When I ask Slim Sr. about this story, told by several of its protagonists, he's irritated: "I haven't asked him. I don't think so. He's extremely sensible. I'm going to ask him. Maybe he was invited. I have no idea, but I've said it many times: political vocation is very different from entrepreneurial vocation and I see in my sons that their vocation is entrepreneurial. So I don't see them getting involved in politics. The three of them are working, and so are my daughters. Now, if someone invites you to participate in something, I don't know."

After his defeat, Patrick Slim started the process of preparing to receive the kidney transplant from his older brother. His health improved considerably following the transplant and since then, although he has maintained his close ties to the Catholic Church, participating in several meetings with Vatican emissaries, he has also made incursions into the film world. He financed the motion picture *Cristiada*, the most expensive production in the history of Mexico, with Hollywood stars such as Andy García and Eva Longoria, who recorded in Puebla the scenes in which they defend the guerrilla groups of the 1940s made up of priests and devout Catholics fighting the anticlerical government of Plutarco Elías Calles.

In contrast, Carlos, his older brother, often sends people a copy of *El hombre que amaba los perros* (*The Man Who Loved Dogs*), the biographical novel of Leon Trotsky by Cuban writer Leonardo Padura, as a personal gift. And in early 2013, he and his wife María Elena Torruco named their second son after Zapata, hero of the Mexican Revolution. One of the grandsons of the richest Mexican in the world is called Emiliano Slim.

Of Slim's three sons, the one who thus far has kept the lowest profile is Marco Antonio, president of the administrative board of Grupo Inbursa. During the interviews he gave me, Slim Sr. often praised Marco Antonio's knowledge, and according to some of his closest associates, Marco Antonio is the son who most takes after his father. On one occasion he gave me a copy of an article of his, published on July 26, 2004, in *Reforma*. Titled "Public accounts: a strait jacket," it poses the question of what would happen if a company's actions were based on public accounts.

Slim's second-born son begins thus:

> The first thing we do when we are going to invest in, purchase or finance a company is we look at their financial accounts (statement and balance sheets). These documents give us the bird's-eye view of their history, a snapshot of their present and a fairly precise preview of their future; however, a country's public accounts are not done on an accruals basis, including the assets that are not in the accounts, such as non-recorded liabilities (i.e., pensions and Pidiregas).

During our interviews, Slim also highlighted how family-centric the vocation of his companies is. This is palpable and is linked to a business vision, according to various specialists: Slim himself and his children usually control 80 percent of the social capital of Grupo Carso companies—for example, América Móvil or Minera Frisco. To researcher Omar Rodrigo Escamilla Haro, of the NGO Poder, this is done for two reasons: the first is to avoid companies going bankrupt as a result of any "hostile" share-buying processes, and the second is in connection with the interdependence of the companies in which Slim is a majority shareholder. "This means," explains Escamilla Haro, "if any of his companies needs financing, they go to Grupo Financiero Inbursa, which is property of the Slim family; if they need to build, they go to IDEAL; if they need transportation, Grupo Carso owns over 20 percent of Infraestructura y Transportes de México, a company that controls a significant portion of our country's railways."

At age thirty-one, after the birth of his daughter, Mark Zuckerberg announced that over his lifetime he will donate, together with his wife Priscilla Chan, 99 percent of his shares in Facebook—valued at around $45 billion. The main objective of his philanthropy will be to promote equality between children. The creator of Facebook named this project the Zuckerberg-Chan Initiative.

A few days later, Slim appeared in public together with the minister of education in Mexico, Aurelio Nuño, an inexperienced functionary who was nevertheless tipped as the presidential candidate for the PRI for the forthcoming elections. At the end of the event, when asked by the reporters whether he would transfer the shares from his family to his foundations, Slim replied: "Foundations do not solve poverty... We shouldn't be donating companies, but creating companies." According to Slim, governments already have sufficient resources to tend to poverty and education. "What we are seeing is a problem of management and efficiency." Slim used a colloquial Mexican expression to assert that his philanthropic actions do not have budget restrictions: "We look at projects and results, we are not counting chilies."

"How do you believe a child should be educated?" I ask the magnate.

"I believe that they should be educated and brought up with freedom, with values; not domesticated, which is different. The values remain very firm. My dad died when he was very young and left us values of honesty and many things that remained deeply ingrained."

"Do you give your children any special advice?"

"It's not that you give them advice. You just speak with them regularly."

"And when it comes to the subject of business strategy?"

"No, they're already responsible for their things."

"But, what special things did you raise them with?"

"The first thing is that I talked to them when they were twelve."

"Did you give them account notebooks like your dad gave you?"

"No, I just talked to them. I told them that if they liked business, they should get involved; if they didn't like it, they shouldn't, because they would mess up their own life and mess up the business.

And they did, they got involved. I remember once I said to them, 'What do you think, should I get into this line of business?' Patrick, the youngest, said: 'Well, if we're going to get to see you, yes; otherwise, no.' They have always been very clear, very involved. There are times when you feel like being more irresponsible. Maybe there was a period when I should have been more irresponsible, like during my gap year. But at that age one of my sons had already taken on the management of a company. They've been able to combine responsibility and duty."

"Would you have liked any of your daughters to be the director of one of your companies?"

"Yes. Well, one of them is a board member and has her own business: Lomas Estudio. It's an early-years and karate school. And she's on the board of Sanborns and she enjoys going to meetings. The thing is, Vanessa studied engineering for a few years."

"Warren Buffet announced that his children will only inherit $500 million. How much are you planning to leave them?"

"My children are not going to inherit money. They're going to inherit shares in companies that they have to manage. So they inherit responsibility and commitment."

"And how can you guarantee that the consortiums will continue to be strong?"

"They are prepared and there is a trust in which they must vote 80 percent if they have to change or sell."

"Will this trust be collegial?"

"Yes, they'll have to reach an agreement."

VII

23

Philanthropy

Bill and Melinda Gates are the main promoters of "The Giving Pledge," an initiative for the richest people in the world to give philanthropically at least half of what they've accumulated in their lifetime. Mexican journalist Katia Dartigues asked Melinda Gates in 2015 whether she thought Carlos Slim would join this crusade. "There are people who start giving and then join the Pledge," Gates replied. "I don't know if Carlos will decide to do that in the future, but there is no doubt that he gives a lot (through his foundations) in Mexico. And he has done it for twenty years. I have a lot of respect for him because of that."

"Yes, he has done so, but there aren't any Mexicans on this list," said the journalist.

"Well, there may be one day. I hope there will," Gates responded, smiling faintly.

When Slim announced that he would donate $40 million to health research, he spoke about his ideas regarding altruism: "Our concept focuses on realizing and resolving things, rather than giving. We don't go around like Santa Claus." The money he donated that day has allowed his Instituto Carso to send doctors to indigenous communities in the Sierra Tarahumara and in Chiapas to help with women giving birth. Or to oversee 6,500 transplants and research kidney diseases such as the one his wife had.

"When it comes to philanthropy," Slim says with enthusiasm, "what I'm most interested in is education and health, and I see it more or less like this: we start with the mother's nutrition during pregnancy, then perinatal care, supporting the child through the birth, preventing hypoxia; the child's nutrition during those two years when their brain grows, child malnutrition and school-ing, including early education. Then, you won't have solved the problem, but here and there you have social spending or social investment, however you want to call it, it's the same, it can be done by the state or it can be done privately. At the end of the day, to end poverty, you need to create the jobs for that person to have a job in the future. To make sure that child will have a job when he grows up. And that job should be important, not only for society, but for the dignity of the person. The reality is that work is not just a social responsibility; it is an emotional necessity. Sometimes you work because you need to, because you feel the need to be active. Work gives you an identity, and dignity. It forms a part of the vital interests of human beings."

Slim's money has also been used to train 5,000 staff in addiction treatment facilities and to create psychosocial care teams for the terminally ill at public hospitals. His health institute has financed the study of the genetic basis of diabetes and several kinds of cancer, in addition to research on vaccines against Chagas disease and Leishmaniasis. But while Slim is not interested in the work of full-time giving, Warren Buffett, the businessman who competes with him on the *Forbes* list, investor in endless companies, from Nike to Coca-Cola, believes in philanthropy on another scale and has signed up to Gates's "Giving Pledge." Buffett has donated $31 billion, more than a third of his fortune. While Buffet stopped administering his businesses to dedicate himself to philanthropy, the Mexican magnate takes a completely different perspective. "Slim doesn't even like the word 'philanthropy.' He prefers to call it 'social investment,'" a former Telmex executive told me, saying that from his point of view, Slim "is not generous even toward himself."

The main criticism of Slim has been that he has turned his philan-thropy into a pastime, unlike other wealthy people in the world who take the radical action of donating a significant portion of their fortunes, such as Ted Turner, David Rockefeller, George Soros, Michael Bloomberg, Mark Zuckerberg and Oprah Winfrey.

These ultrarich people believe they can save Western civilization from its demise. Moreover, they want the members of the new generation who earn more than $1 billion to be radical philanthropists and to share their earnings during their lifetime. "I don't know anyone who can't live on just $500 million," Buffett often jokes, with a wink to the Occupy protesters, who took over a square in Wall Street as spokespeople for the demands of the 99 percent of the population of the United States who are not multimillionaires. In New Delhi, during the presentation of their campaign addressing Indian millionaires, Warren Buffett, next to Bill Gates, who accompanies him in the crusade, said, with a lot of conviction: "You can create jobs at the same time as being Santa Claus." Slim still denies his place in the ranks of the global philanthropic revolution.

A hundred years ago, Santa Claus didn't have that much money. At the end of the nineteenth century, the richest man in the world had accumulated $30 million, barely a morsel if we compare it to what Slim now owns. Andrew Carnegie, the Scottish immigrant who created a steel empire in the United States, published in 1889 *The Gospel of Wealth*, an essay that founded modern philanthropy. Carnegie defended the existence of a new species of rich people: the first multimillionaires of the industrialized world. He said that it was essential to the progress of the species for the homes of some men to also be the homes of the greatest examples of literature, the arts, and all the refinements of civilization. "Much better this great irregularity than universal squalor," wrote Carnegie. "Without wealth there can be no Maecenas," or patrons of the arts. In the vision of the father of philanthropy, the poor of the nineteenth century enjoyed what the richest of the past could not afford. What used to be luxury, according to him, had become items of basic necessity: "The laborer has now more comforts than the landlord had a few generations ago. The farmer has more luxuries than the landlord had, and is more richly clad and better housed. The landlord has books and pictures rarer, and appointments more artistic, than the King could then obtain."

The name Carnegie is now a synonym of art and knowledge. The best musicians in the world perform at Carnegie Hall. Artists such as Andy Warhol have had residencies at the Carnegie Museum of Art. Andrew Carnegie, a man who started as a telegraphist, frequently went to productions of Shakespeare's plays.

For his part, paying bail for poor Mexican prisoners has been one of Slim's most praised charitable initiatives: up to 2010, over the course of a decade and a half, Slim financed the liberation of over 100,000 people accused of petty crimes. He has also donated 416,000 bicycles to workers in remote villages, 87,833 wheelchairs to convalescents, 127,000 pairs of glasses, and 15 million bags of nutritional sweets, while a million pregnant women have received care through his special health networks. Among the foundation's most publicized initiatives is Aldea Digital, an event that holds the Guinness world record for gathering 258,896 participants in 2014. Slim also gifted a lifetime pension of $500 per month to twenty-two retired world boxing champions. Other donations that Slim's PR team publicize are those made to the foundations of Bill Clinton and Shakira, who invest in health and education. All in all, according to his own reports, Slim's philanthropy has benefited over 36.2 million people around the world. Slim's most interesting public initiative since he became one of the wealthiest in the world, although it has more to do with work than philanthropy, has been well received in some social circles. Slim has spoken at a number of international forums about the need to reduce the current work week, which is between five and six days, to only three or four days per week. We are facing a new civilization that needs to change certain paradigms, including retirement age, according to the magnate. However, to building his arguments in favour of the reduced working week, Slim explains that in the mid twentieth century, retirement age was sixty-five years, while life expectancy was between fifty-five and sixty. Now that life expectancy is between eighty-five and ninety years, despite pensions being reduced, there is a great debt. In an interview with Larry King, he stated:

I think it's a bad solution to problems; they are using only political and fiscal policies that were used in the '20s and '30s that don't work now. In the past, for underdeveloped countries, they used a very strong fiscal policy. That means that the crisis was paid by the consumers, decreasing consumption. And in developed countries the crisis was paid by the savers, reducing the interest rates. Now they are affecting both, with negative interests and restrictions in economic policies, mainly in Europe. I think they are making many mistakes.

With this diagnosis, Slim supports further privatization of public resources as well as the reduction of the working day. According to the magnate, governments should sell assets such as highways and airports for them to be administered privately.

"You think government should sell its assets to private initiative?" asked King.

"Yes, that's one point, and the other is that the public investment that they are not doing because they have a big deficit, they should look for the private initiative to make those investment through public-private partnership or other kinds of concession. There are many concessions, let's say in highways, for twenty years. Well, it is private during twenty years, and every day it is an asset for the government. In twenty years, it is 100 percent owned by the government. I think it's the best formula. And what is not acceptable is to have this high unemployment."

In addition to more radical privatizations, Slim proposes that the age of retirement should be seventy-five and the normal working week should be three days with eleven hours per day, so as to allow others to work the remaining three days.

"Machines must work twenty-four hours and people should work fewer hours." Slim explains that in the past it was necessary to have slaves and more people working long days to achieve efficiency, but now people need money and the time to spend it, "so that they can be part of the economy that helps feed back into countries' development and growth."

———

"I am going to ask you a simple question. In your life so far, who has been the most generous person toward you?"

"What do you mean by generous?"

"Well, that they've given you something that's important to you."

"My dad, of course. My family, my dad, my mom. Generous? Giving me what? It's just that you enrich yourself from everyone.

We are talking about people, because material things are secondary. You learn from everyone, but not just people, also from what you read, what you see. Then you often learn from the bad experiences or bad examples."

"You even learn from enemies?"

"Yes, of course. For example, a year and a half ago I was with the kids, with the interns at Telmex, in the auditorium, and they asked me something about education. I wanted to tell them that the marvelous thing, the most important thing, is that human beings can discern when a person's a good teacher, we recognize them, we learn from them, we love them, etcetera, and the bad teachers remain as an anecdote, as an example of what we should not do. Even bad teachers don't damage you. I'm not sure if I'm being clear."

"Yes."

"I mean: you lose out in terms of the subject they taught, because you lost interest, but at the same time you learn from those people, because you say: blimey, this dude never even showed up to teach, or was always late, he had a drinking problem, he couldn't communicate, he was no good at explaining things."

"My son was complaining to me this morning about a terrible and unfair Spanish teacher…"

"That's where he learns he shouldn't be like that in life. I was very close, for a large part of my life, to older people. I learned from them: people with certain capabilities as businesspeople or politicians I admire. I really admire these presidents: Sanguinetti, Cardoso. I admire Cardoso, but I also believe that Lula did very well in many senses. Lagos, Felipe González…"

"And what do you think of the ex-president of Uruguay, José Mujica?"

"I've never had anything to do with him, I don't really know him."

"Of all your philanthropy, what's your favorite thing you've done?"

"Whatever we do next," he jokes. "No, I think we have huge potential to do more things."

"Do you remember your first act of philanthropy?"

"The foundation began formally in '86, but look, perhaps the first thing I did was when I started teaching. I was getting paid and I didn't need that money. I was in third year and I gave out two scholarships."

"To whom?"

"Two kids at the Faculty of Engineering."

"And how did you choose those students to benefit?"

"I asked someone to choose them. I don't choose the 18,000 kids we have. That was in '59."

"Can you remember who they were?"

"No, there were two of them."

"You don't know who are all the people who get your money?"

"I don't do it for them to get it. Did I tell you about Khalil Gibran? Shall I read you the poem that talks about giving?"

"Thank you, you already read it to me."

24

Press

In the early hours one day in the '90s, a phone call woke up journalist Julio Scherer García, the patriarch of Mexican journalism: "If you don't deliver 300,000 pesos by dawn, we will kill your son." The founder of *Proceso*, the most important left-wing weekly magazine in Mexico, only had 4,000 pesos at home. At 4 a.m., he called Slim asking for help. Around that time Soumaya Domit was already being treated for renal failure.

"I'll get everything I have in my safe right now. Also, Sumi and I will get in touch with some friends in case you need anything else. I'm sorry, and so is Sumi. As you know, she's very fond of you," Slim told Scherer. Moments later, one of Slim's messengers arrived to Scherer's house with the money in cash and the instruction to remain by Scherer's side. The money was delivered to the kidnappers and Scherer's son was freed.

Scherer himself tells this story in his book *Secuestrados* (*Kidnapped*):

Carlos Slim's messenger arrived and delivered a small plastic box.

"How much is it?" Elena Guerra demanded.

"I don't know. Mr. Slim gave me this and instructed me to stay to help with whatever was needed."

Without any further explanation I went with him to get his car, parked in the square opposite the development where he lived, in the borough of Contreras. What I wanted, more than anything, was to look at the sky, scrutinize it. I watched the blackness of the stifling night slowly giving way. Dawn was closing in, inexorable. I returned to the library at the same time as my mobile phone rang. I listened to Pedro's dry words:

"Tell him yes, that we have the money."

Together with Elena Guerra I had counted the pesos, dollars, and gold bullion coins that Carlos Slim had sent us. The price of the rescue had been covered by everyone.

The flirtation between journalism and power has always been a story of pacts, hidden interests and betrayals. The story of Scherer and Slim has been, additionally, a turbulent one. In that same decade the main criticisms against Slim for the purchase of the telephone monopoly during president Salinas de Gortari's term were penned by journalists working for Scherer's magazine. One of them, Rafael Rodríguez Castañeda—today editor-in-chief of *Proceso*—wrote *Operación Telmex: contacto en el poder* (*Operation Telmex: Contact in Power*), a book in which Slim is scrutinized for benefiting from government corruption when the Mexican economy was opening up to the foreign market. Around those years the businessman Juan Antonio Pérez Simón, a friend of Slim's and Scherer's, intervened to reconcile them. It was during that period when Scherer made that phone call in the middle of the night. In recent years the relationship between the magnate and the journalist has deteriorated further, though, over a series of articles criticizing Slim for buying so many properties in the historical center of Mexico City that it seemed as if he were playing Monopoly with the capital.

Slim has also been generous toward other independent intellectuals and Mexican writers. He gave Carlos Monsiváis four stories and the terrace of the Esmeralda, a building in the city center that was the most exclusive jewelry store in the nineteenth century and which, before it became Slim's property, was at some point also a nightclub called La Opulencia. Monsiváis housed some 12,000 objects there: paintings, comics, indigenous toys and *lucha libre* masks, among other rare objects and personal belongings collected over decades. The museum is managed by a trust: its name is El Estanquillo, which is what the erstwhile corner stores used to be called.

However, Slim is in no way a gratuitous man. After journalist

Miguel Ángel Granados Chapa launched the magazine *Mira* in 1990, he was never able to convince Slim to place adverts for his businesses. "We had a cordial relationship that was not contaminated by business relations, since I never succeeded in my intention to get him to advertize in my publication," Granados Chapa told me. Slim's fortune gives him the opportunity to become the cover star in the newspapers we still care about in the world. In two of them, one in Europe and another in America, he holds a percentage of shares that he does not use to influence their editorial lines. Granados Chapa confirmed to me that the man who rescued the *New York Times* by providing a loan to recover its liquidity is an invisible sponsor of a significant share of the newspapers and print magazines in his country. When journalist Federico Arreola was about to launch the now-defunct magazine *Milenio Semanal*, he says he went to the owner of Telmex to offer publicity. Although the publication was just about to come out, when he saw the authors' list, composed of renowned journalists, Slim accepted immediately and bought an advertising package for two years, at a special rate. Slim's assistance eventually became a hurdle for Arreola and the owners of the weekly magazine, however, due to the fact that *Milenio Semanal* fast became a success and the businessman had bought publicity spreads at rates that were far below what they were worth within less than one year.

Although he is a member of the editorial board of *El Universal*, Slim has a better relationship with Alejandro Junco de la Vega, owner of Grupo Reforma, which owns three leading newspapers: *El Norte* in Monterrey, *Mural* in Guadalajara and *Reforma* in Mexico City. Granados Chapa and other leading writers I interviewed mentioned different meetings organized by Junco himself in the house Slim owns on Julio Verne street in the Polanco district in Mexico City. "At those meetings, we saw more than once how Slim told Junco off in front of us. Well, he didn't tell him off, he corrected him," says Granados Chapa.

In contrast, Ramón Alberto Garza, the journalist who helped Junco de la Vega found *Reforma*, had a negative experience with Slim. Garza was named director of *El Universal* as part of a sales arrangement when it was about to be bought by the Spanish company Grupo Prisa. However, on December 17 of that year, the sale fell through when the owner of *El Universal*, Juan Francisco Ealy Ortiz, decided to keep the newspaper and was able to secure the funds needed.

The following day, Garza attended a lunch meeting at Slim's house in Mexico City's Palmas district. There with the two of them, according to Garza, were Juan Antonio Pérez Simón and Ignacio Cobo, the men closest to the magnate. The meeting lasted from 2 until 8 p.m., and at some point Slim told Garza to leave the Prisa Spaniards and go with him.

"Here's $100 million for you to fund a media group," Slim said.

"No, Carlos, this is not about checkbooks."

"Well then, tell me, what do you need to stay afloat?"

In addition to directing *El Universal*, Garza was one of the main shareholders of the Colombian magazine *Cambio*, whose Mexican edition had been created by him and Gabriel García Márquez, in partnership with Televisa.

"The first half of next year is going to be very difficult for *Cambio*. It's always the way. Could you pay your advertising for the whole year with the magazine?" Garza requested.

"Is that it? You're going to work out very cheap."

"Neither cheap nor expensive. I just don't want to let García Márquez down."

"Can you wait till January, because I already closed the tax year," Slim responded.

Garza said that, based on that verbal agreement with Slim, that month he spent $1 million paying bonuses, and paper and editorial production matters. The critical date was February 20, 2003, because the solidarity agreement between the magazine and Televisa would expire if the magazine were to close, in which case both parties would absorb the losses. Alfonso de Angoitia, vice president of Televisa, reminded Garza they needed to close before that date for the agreement to be valid. The date was getting dangerously near and they still had no news of Slim's advance payment. Garza told García Márquez about it and the Colombian writer phoned Slim to ask. After that, Ignacio Cobo invited Garza to lunch at the Angus restaurant.

"How could you doubt Mr. Slim's word?" was one of the first things Cobo said to him, somewhat resentfully, Garza remembers.

They spoke about the subject for ten minutes and then continued to have lunch and chat about politics. The businessman and editor Antonio Navalón was present.

Next morning, Cobo called Garza to ask him to meet again, this time at Hotel Geneve, his center of operations. There Cobo announced that something had happened, and that there was no check.

"What do you mean there's no check? There's no check now or there'll be no check ever?"

"Ever."

"What do you mean? Had I been told that sooner, I would've closed the magazine and would've been the end of it."

"Well I don't know what happened, but there's no check. Someone screwed you over."

"If somebody screwed me over, it must have been one of the candidates for members of congress who come here to pick up their campaign check."

"I have no idea who it was."

Garza believes that those who conspired against him with Slim were some old PRI politicians with whom he had become enemies during the time when he was director of *Reforma*; it may also have been the ex-president himself, Salinas de Gortari, with whom Garza initially had a privileged relationship that then deteriorated.

On March 3, 2003, Garza phoned Televisa to tell de Angoitia what had happened. "I'm sorry, Ramón, but my hands are tied. The shareholders would not agree to it," the executive responded. Garza claims he had to spend $2 million of his own funds.

Years later, Garza founded *Reporte Índigo*, a print and online journal that has been hugely successful. The journalist, who was born in Monterrey, says that the richest Mexican in the world does not do philanthropy, just atonement for guilt.

Another journalist who has openly criticized Slim in recent years is Denise Dresser, a columnist and political analyst for *Reforma* and *Proceso*, precisely the media accused by some sectors of Televisa of protecting Slim's image. In March 2005, Dresser published an article entitled "The true unnameable," in which she states:

> Today, Carlos Slim's power in Mexico is an unnameable power. A power of which almost no one dares speak; which almost no media looks at; which no journalist writes about; which no intellectual talks of; and which no Mexican legislator dares touch. At least he is a Mexican businessman, they say. At least he invests in Mexico. At least he is concerned with the development of the country and delivers speeches about it. But there's a serious problem with this reasoning. It circumvents the undeniable fact that this is a zero-sum game: what enters Carlos Slim's pocket comes out of the pocket of Mexican consumers. And the portion he keeps is greater than what should be his share. More than what the government should allow.

Years later, in 2009, Dresser analyzed an interview Slim gave to the celebrity magazine *Quién* and wrote a column entitled "Yo soy Carlos Slim," where she said:

> There are only a handful of people in Mexico willing to publicly criticize Mr. Slim, to speak on the record, to say what so many whisper in private but dare not vent openly. And it's crucial that Mexicans understand why the fear, why the silence. The answer is in the dysfunctional political system from which Mr. Slim has benefited and that now, due to his weight in the Mexican economy, he has managed to put at his service. A system characterized by weak institutions, corrupt courts, functionaries who abide and abet, broken legislators, consumers unaware of their rights or without the legal capacity to collectively organize, and a media that is largely silenced because they depend on his publicity or financial backing.

Perhaps the most well-known article that Dresser has dedicated to Slim is an open letter published in *Proceso* magazine and for which she received the National Journalism Award in 2010. Almost at the end of the missive, the journalist says to the magnate:

Of course you have the right to promote your interests, but the problem is that you do so at the expense of the country. You have a right to express your ideas, but given your behavior it's difficult to see you as an altruistic and uninterested party whose sole interest is the development of Mexico. Of course you possess a singular and laudable talent: you know when, how and where to invest. But you also display another less attractive trait: you know when, how and where to pressure and blackmail legislators, the media, judges, journalists, the left-wing intelligentsia, those who allow themselves to be guided by a poorly understood nationalism and accept being plundered by a Mexican because at least he is not a foreigner.

In contrast, one of the journalists nearest to Slim is José Martínez, to whom the magnate gave several interviews for him to write *Carlos Slim: Retrato inédito* (*Carlos Slim: Unpublished Portrait*), a book that is very well positioned in Sanborns book stores. Martínez is an experienced and discreet journalist who has written a series of books about powerful people in Mexico. Before Slim, he wrote about two other key figures in the PRI system: Carlos Hank González and Elba Esther Gordillo. Some of his colleagues consider him to be one of the disciples of Manuel Buendía Tellezgirón, who was the most influential political journalist in the 1980s, until he was assassinated.

"When did you first hear of Carlos Slim?" I ask Martínez in our interview.

"It was at the newspaper *El Financiero*, where I worked for several years. My job there was very rewarding because it allowed me to learn the nitty-gritty aspects of journalism specializing in economy and finance. After working in different editorial positions, I founded and edited the area of political analysis. I have always been very careful when managing my journalism archives. I properly understood who Carlos Slim was when he donated a seven-figure sum to Mexico City rescue efforts after the earthquake of 1985. I started to dig and I discovered he was a successful businessman. The teacher Froylán López Narváez, who was one of his peers at Preparatoria número 1, had told me about Slim at some point."

"What motivated you to research and write about him, alongside or after writing profiles of Carlos Hank González and Elba Esther Gordillo?"

"His talent for business, his power of seduction over intellectuals and politicians, as well as his immeasurable economic and political power."

"When was the first time you saw him in person? Could you tell me about that moment?"

"I was working for the newspaper *El Universal*, editing *Gráfico*. I published, in a magazine that was called *La Crisis,* an article about Carlos Slim and that's how, in the year 2000, he invited me to lunch at his home, the house that had been his parents' home on Calderón de la Barca street, in Polanco. He was surprised by the accuracy of my information. The next day he invited me again to have coffee at his office, on Paseo de las Palmas, in Lomas de Chapultepec. A dialogue was established that then carried on for several years. He was very respectful towards me, which I'm grateful for, and my access to him at times led to long encounters, always in my role as a journalist."

"Why do you think Slim is so influential in the world of Mexican journalism?"

"It really amazes me that this magnate is very present in the media. I have seen how people of all social classes ask him for an autograph or to take a picture, as if he were a rock star. Photos here, selfies there, with athletes, intellectuals, politicians from all over the world, artists and all kinds of characters. As for the media, I have seen how swarms of journalists form around him at events; he appears on the front pages every other day, and when he talks about business a silence falls: everyone wants to listen to him, because everyone dreams of success and thinks that Carlos Slim is going to give them his secrets to becoming rich."

Christie's and Sotheby's art magazines abound in Slim's office, but I've never seen a printed newspaper there. It's said that he tends to read the daily news in a Grupo Carso internal bulletin and that when he does flip through a newspaper directly his favorite is *Reforma*, the newspaper considered to be closest to the political center, or from time to time *Excélsior*, considered right wing, or *La Jornada*, which is left. Among his sources of information he does not mention Uno TV, the online television channel with a politically moderate editorial line directed by his son-in-law, Arturo Elías Ayub.

Slim gives the impression of being a reader who is also up to date with what happens in the media. "When you live off other people's opinions, you're dead," is a phrase Slim often repeats to those close to him; however, he speaks in detail about publications, managing boards and journalists. Some of the opinion writers he claims to read regularly are Federico Reyes Heroles ("he's very good"), René Delgado ("a brilliant guy") and Jesús Silva-Herzog Márquez ("brilliant as hell, although sometimes I don't understand him").

"Look," Slim says to me when I bring up the subject of journalists who have questioned him, "what Ramón Alberto said is dishonest and vindictive and it was because of something he arranged with Nacho Cobo—I don't know what. Those are issues between him and Nacho, because I've had information from several different people. And Denise Dresser, that's what she's like, but sometimes she says things that are not true. It's all well and good to take someone like that and say that you are very intelligent and very brave and very fierce because you lay into people, right? Once, as I was giving a lecture at ITAM [Autonomous Technological Institute of Mexico], there were attendees she'd sent to attack me. I argued with them and with their people. I've only ever talked to her once."

"And she wrote a very harsh article after you spoke."

"Yes, but what I'm interested in is being criticized by serious people."

"Like who?"

"From time to time they write things about me, but you can't respond because you're busy with other things and so on, a repeated lie, which is what has happened to us—that we're the most expensive [telecommunications provider] in the world! And I say, alright, if you're my competitor of course you'll be glad to hear that your competitor has the most expensive market in the world and the worst service. But these are lies that get repeated and believed."

"And the journalists you get on best with, like Larry King and José Martínez?"

"José Martínez I see very seldom, unfortunately. He tells me a lot about the Universidad de Puebla. Larry King, well, I'm very fond of him. The other day I was with Charlie Rose. He interviewed me over dinner, a very aggressive interview. It was private, but there were about 500 people. I think what I'm interested in is journalists who are going to tell the truth, not blindly believe everything they read, because it turns out that many journalists take just one source… for example, these idiots of *Why Nations Fail*."

"Did you sue them?"

"Yes, they've removed it now, but I wanted to sue them so they'd make it public. But they've removed it now. Rogozinski also sued because he was making sure the things about government corruption wouldn't come out." Slim looks for the book and some letters from the trial, which he shows me.

Julio Scherer, founder of the magazine *Proceso* and winner of the Maria Moors Cabot Award given by Columbia University, is perhaps the journalist with whom Slim had the most intense relationship. Despite several fallouts over the course of their friendship, one of Slim's favorite anecdotes about Scherer has to do with the journalist's chivalry toward the actor María Félix, considered *the* diva of Mexican cinema until her death.

"I remember a meeting with Julio Scherer. He was with Juan Antonio Pérez Simón and he called me to say that he wanted to deliver a book, and I told them: 'Come over, I'm having dinner with María Félix,' and it was very pleasant. I remember suddenly María drops her napkin and Julio picks it up. Then María drops it again and Julio picks it up again, and says: 'For you I would do that a thousand times, María.' And María says to him: 'No, Julio, I'll give you a more interesting occupation.' Beautiful, beautiful! I've been at lots of gatherings with Julio, also with my wife. Did we have any disagreements? Of course. You know what it's like at *Proceso*."

"Did you help create Proceso.com?"

"Maybe I did, I don't know. Huh, maybe."

"Did you not help *Reforma* in the crisis of 2010?"

"We bought some advertising with them at quite a high price. Was it in a crisis in 2010, 2011?"

"Did you pay up front for advertising in *Reforma* for one, two or three years?"

"No, for one year, although I wish it had been three. In 2011 we raised our advertising rates everywhere."

"Miguel Ángel Granados Chapa told me you were the invisible sponsor of the Mexican press, that almost all the media came to you to ask for money."

"No, that's not true."

"Don Miguel Ángel said that even he asked you."

"Yes, he asked me for money for the magazine *Mira*."

"But you didn't give him any."

"Yes, I did."

"He said you didn't."

"I gave him advertising, because in terms of media partners I'm only part of the *New York Times*. Wasn't it Federico Reyes Heroles who was at *Mira*? Yes… yes, we did give him money. Maybe he wanted us to give him more, that might be true. I'm going to check, but I think we did. I really valued Granados Chapa."

"Do you pay for advertising up front to media for them to survive certain crises?"

"No, it's not that. Thirty years ago Televisa invented the 'French plan'—instead of selling the advertising and you paying by installments, they sell you an advertising package in advance at a special rate. So what we do, I think, is that we negotiate advertising deals for our companies for the whole year, but it's not that we give them an advance when they're in a crisis."

"Televisa journalists have said that you control *Reforma* and Carmen Aristegui, as well as *Proceso*. What's your opinion of *Reforma*, Carmen Aristegui and *Proceso*?"

"What I think is that Televisa has to say that because it can't control them. Everything Televisa can't control is blamed on me. They've come up with a very interesting scheme. They have their people and then they put them on weird programs, on some channel that nobody watches, co-opting them. So, if you notice, almost everyone is on certain programs, including Denise Dresser, she was there for a while, but then she escaped… So they keep them co-opted and then they also have others, but those are the ones they use as hitmen of sorts, like the people on *Alebrijes* [a financial commentators program]. Did they tell you that *La Jornada* was mine too, by any chance?"

"That too, but these are the ones that Televisa claims especially."

"They used to say I had bought *La Jornada*. And there it's individual partners. Carlos Payán [founder of the newspaper and then senator] was indeed a good friend. I really value Payán, I hold him in great esteem, but anyway, they also say that *Reforma* is mine. They're sure of it."

"Granados Chapa told me that there were some editorial meetings at *Reforma* with you and Alejandro Junco, owner of the newspaper."

"That's true."

"And Granados Chapa and another of the assistant editors said that sometimes you told Junco off in front of them."

"No, I just say what I think. I didn't tell him off. I contradicted him and maybe they weren't contradicting him. But I didn't tell him off, let alone there. What I do is: I confront people. And I did that with Payán at the time. I used to sit down with his people at *La Jornada* to discuss things. For example, there's Demetrio Sodi, who's closely linked with Roberto Hernández [Slim's banker rival] and he started to bust people's balls and then we had a meeting and I took papers. I've also done that with people at *Proceso* and other media. I like to confront people."

Slim has an open conflict with Televisa, the main TV chain in Mexico, one of the most important in Latin America and one of the business consortiums nearest to the government of president Enrique Peña Nieto. The level of confrontation is such that in 2011, Televisa stopped showing commercials paid for by the billionaire's companies, citing a disagreement regarding the prices. The version of the story from Slim's team is that this was due to Televisa wanting to damage the Telcel brand, since the broadcaster had entered the mobile telephony market with their own brand, Iusacell, through a partnership with TV Azteca, the second largest Mexican TV chain. TV Azteca joined the boycott denounced by Slim. However, during the 2015 Oscar awards ceremony, Telcel commercials were shown on the screen owned by Ricardo Salinas Pliego, who, shortly after terminating his partnership at Iusacell with Emilio Azcárraga Jean, obtained huge earnings by selling AT&T at over triple what it initially cost him. Slim's conflict with the main television broadcasters in the country benefited several Mexican newspapers and magazines, because Grupo Carso companies' spending on advertising was significantly reassigned from Televisa and TV Azteca to the printed press, radio and cinemas. In the midst of this battle, many influential journalists have been seen as picking sides between Slim and Televisa.

"The thing is that television chains prohibited our advertising. They blocked the advertising to tear us down. In order to take over the telecom business they've done a thousand things. Did you know that? Among other things they stopped selling us advertising. I think they made a weird agreement with the past government—Calderón's—and those friends of yours who tell you those stories about me supporting Andrés Manuel López Obrador, or that I wanted a change of government. But that's what happened: because they stopped our advertising on the TV channels, we slowly increased our advertising in other media. And because we no longer invest in television, we got into cinemas, for example. But it was them who blocked it."

Years ago, at Slim's request, journalist José Martínez organized a dinner for the billionaire with some of the columnists who write daily in the main national newspapers. According to Martínez, the political journalists were captivated by the magnate, and one of them, it being the first time they spoke to the owner of Telmex, said in front of everyone that if the billionaire had managed his businesses so well that he became the richest man in the world, then he should become president of Mexico as he would surely manage the country equally well. Some people blushed. Slim responded saying that he would never get involved in politics.

"I'm curious about the way in which Julio Scherer developed his friendship with you. How do you think an independent journalist can become friends with such a powerful public figure?" I ask.

"What powerful figure?"

"You, of course."

"No, the ones who have power are the media and the government."

"Do you believe yourself to be less powerful than the media and the government?"

"Less powerful than the president? Of course I do. And the media? Which? The television companies? The television companies are the ones who control everything, you know that. Haven't you seen the way they've attacked us?"

"In fact I have several questions about that."

"Well, I might not answer everything you ask me on that subject..."

25

Telecommunications

When Carlos Slim took control of Telmex he obtained a monopoly —it was the only business with the legal right to offer local and long distance national and international telephone services for six years. The power he accumulated with that operation became so entrenched that his majority shareholders, Southwestern Bell and France Telecom, were legally unable to seek administrative control of the company.

One of the few legal obligations to which the magnate was forced to agree pertained to a prohibition from participating in the television sector, dominated by the company Televisa. The last paragraph of Term 1.9 of the modification to the concession of Teléfonos de México, S.A. de C.V, of August 10, 1990, states that "Telmex may not make use of, whether directly or indirectly, any concession of television services to the Mexican public." Likewise, Televisa was also prevented from participating in the telecommunications sector. This was the way in which the PRI regime was able to maintain a certain balance between two of the private conglomerates that were most strategic to the country's national security. Mexico's television monopoly had long been held by Televisa, a company that experienced rapid growth under the management of Emilio Azcárraga Milmo, nicknamed "El Tigre," who openly declared himself to be a PRI soldier and ordered his news programs to only broadcast information generated or approved by that system. In their superb biography of Azcárraga Milmo, Claudia Fernández and Andrew Paxman describe several key events that illustrate the collusion between this broadcaster and the PRI. One of these occurred during the legislative elections of 1991, the first held after Carlos Salinas de Gortari won the presidency in the midst of fraud accusations. Fernández and Paxman write:

> Three weeks before the elections, a reporter cornered Azcárraga at the Guelaguetza, the cultural festival held annually in Oaxaca, and asked him about Televisa's biased coverage of the campaigns. Azcárraga responded: "Televisa considers itself part of the government system and, as such, it supports the campaigns of the PRI candidates. The president of the Republic, Carlos Salinas de Gortari, is our ultimate leader and we are very happy for that to be the case."

In the 1990s, Televisa saw the emergence of a competitor, TV Azteca, the former state television broadcaster privatized by the government of Salinas de Gortari and sold to businessman Ricardo Salinas Pliego. However, over the years Televisa and TV Azteca would sometimes form strategic alliances in order to preserve a television duopoly. They even did so formally by means of the telephone company Iusacell, with which they attempted to challenge Slim's monopoly. As for paid television, another company with which Televisa should have competed was Multivisión, property of businessman Joaquín Vargas, who in that same decade managed to win over a significant amount of Cablevisión clients. If in the long term Emilio Azcárraga Jean—son of El Tigre—and Salinas Pliego became allies of Televisa and TV Azteca, Slim and Vargas made their own alliance with Telmex and Multivisión.

In that period, though, Slim did not seem concerned about the restrictions on doing business in television, especially seeing the enormous advantages he obtained with the purchase of Telmex. In 1995, attorney Guillermo Hamdan, as part of a lawsuit against Telmex, offered an analogy about the advantageous purchase of the state telephone company. In a document delivered to the media, Hamdan equated the sale of Telmex with that of a taxi leased for under half its price and, in addition, with the privilege of circulating on the streets without any competitors.

When selling Telmex, the government, comparatively, sold a taxi worth 28,000 pesos at the price of 12,000. For good measure, it threw in receipts, license plates, road tax, route permissions, repairs workshops, the profits of the whole year in which the purchase was made, and a six-month term to finish paying for the vehicle. For six years he would be given official protection for his monopoly. He would be the sole provider of taxi services in Mexico, and this already has an intrinsic value, which was not taken into account when calculating the sale price for the unit. Likewise, a circulation permit was handed to him for fifty years, plus fifteen years' grace, plus the possibility of renewing it for another fifty years. These 115 years also represent a value, which we presume was not included in the price, either. And in addition, to guarantee juicy earnings, the taxi was sold to him along with a market demand that was growing day by day, in perfect conditions and with public tariffs established with substantial increments. Furthermore, the government accepted that the users needing scheduled services should pay the owner of the taxi up front and if for any reason they no longer required the service they paid for, the remaining balance would not be reimbursed.

Milenio financial columnist Jesús Rangel, who has followed Slim's career since the 1970s, is one of the many analysts convinced that before purchasing Telmex, the magnate was already a consolidated businessman after several important purchases, such as that of the advertising company Galas in 1976, the tobacco manufacturer Cigarrera La Tabacalera Mexicana—owner of Marlboro and other brands—in 1981 and Seguros de México in 1984, for the sum of $55 million from the legendary Mexican banker Manuel Espinosa Yglesias. He also explains that the dizzying growth of Slim's fortune in the 1990s was framed by a global opening of international markets to Mexican companies and, in general, to countries with emerging economies, as they are called in financial parlance.

In the long interview he gave the magazine *Proceso* in 1995, Slim argued:

Thirty or forty years ago there would be maybe one Mexican company registered in the New York Stock Exchange, if any. But in the '90s they went en masse to those markets. And when a company trades in those markets, it can make significant gains under favorable conditions. That's what happened in the '90s. There's nothing mysterious about the growth and development of the groups.

Slim maintained a solid alliance with Televisa before competing against it. During the last years of Azcárraga Milmo's life, Slim purchased up to 49 percent of the shares of Cablevisión (property of Televisa) with the purpose of bolstering the company's finances, despite the fact that this action violated the concession given to Telmex. The government of Ernesto Zedillo, who took over and confronted his predecessor, Salinas de Gortari, maintained the status quo of Televisa and Telmex as the favorite companies of the PRI regime. During the December economic crash of 1994, both Televisa and Grupo Carso were anonymously accused by other businesspeople of having received privileged information to change any debts they had in dollars into pesos before the drastic devaluation of the Mexican currency was announced. When Azcárraga Milmo died, Slim, in agreement with President Zedillo, helped El Tigre's son, Azcárraga Jean, maintain control of the television network. He did this through the purchase of shares from the Alemán and Díez Barroso families, who tried to gain control over the most powerful television network in Mexico after Azcárraga Milmo passed away, according to sources. Slim thus became a key player in keeping El Tigre's son as a Televisa director, while also showing his loyalty to the new president, after having been very close to Zedillo's predecessor and adversary, Salinas de Gortari.

The alliance between Azcárraga Jean and Carlos Slim began to deteriorate after Zedillo completed his term of government and Vicente Fox took up office as the first PAN candidate ever elected president. It was then that Televisa asked the regulators to force Slim to sell his 49 percent of the shares of Cablevisión, as Slim's ownership impeded the expansion of the company created to offer paid television. That was how, in 2002, Slim left Cablevisión for good.

There were other reasons for the rift between Azcárraga and Slim, in addition to the necessary preparations for the inevitable fusion between telephony and television services that each one offered. Jenaro Villamil, a journalist specializing in the subject of telecommunications in Mexico and one of the harshest critics of the political role of the TV broadcaster, claims that bad Televisa content was what caused the end of the alliance between Televisa and Carso. According to Villamil, Slim chastised Azcárraga Jean, as well as his three main partners—Bernardo Gómez, Alfonso de Angoitia and José Bastón—for the low quality of Televisa programs. "You are producing trash. That is not acceptable television content," he said to them at a meeting held on February 3, 2006, in Valle de Bravo, during which the alliance was definitively dissolved, says Villamil.

In 2006, Televisa and TV Azteca succeeded in lobbying the Mexican Congress to approve a series of reforms to the Radio and Television Law, as well as the Telecommunications Law, with which both broadcasters secured the use, free of charge, of the digital spectrum of frequencies, considered a public resource. The fast-track approval on the part of legislators from all political parties, with a handful of exceptions, became known as the Televisa Law.

In the heat of the 2006 post-electoral conflict, during which left-wing candidate López Obrador claimed the elections had been rigged, the government of Vicente Fox promoted a convergence agreement in favor of fusing landline telephony, cable television and broadband Internet services. With this maneuver, which benefited Slim's business, the PAN administration was trying to balance the scales after passing the Televisa Law. It was not the only nod that Fox's government made to Slim, who, during the presidential elections, had financially supported Fox's campaign. In another major gesture symbolic of their alliance, Fox named a former Grupo Carso employee, Pedro Cerisola, as minister of communications and transport.

However, Fox's successor, Felipe Calderón, also of the PAN, invalidated Fox's convergence agreement through the Federal Telecommunications Commission, which in turn announced the creation of a Fundamental Technical Plan for Interconnection and Interoperability, which impeded the participation of Telmex. That same year, the Supreme Court of Justice declared key articles of Televisa Law as partially unconstitutional, as they fostered "monopolistic practices and prejudice to the public interest, to free competition, and to the stewardship of the State." Slim, Televisa and TV Azteca were thus back to square one in their dispute, albeit in a different technological era, in which companies were able to offer "Triple Play" service: Internet, fixed telephony and cable TV.

Purificación Carpynteiro, undersecretary of communications and transport during Calderón's government, claimed that when deciding whether to support Slim or Azcárraga, the ex-president opted for the latter. In her book *El fin de los medios* (*The End of the Media*), the former public servant writes:

> In that same term of government, Grupo Televisa purchased Cablemás and TVI, who were added to their subsidiary Cablevisión. It won the bids to provide fiber optics to the CFE [the state-owned electric utility] and the public bidding process to enter the mobile telephony market in partnership with Nextel. This partnership was later dissolved, when the merger of Grupo Televisa and Grupo Salinas was announced, the latter owned by Slim's alleged competitor, Ricardo Salinas Pliego, in order to purchase Grupo Iusacell. The Federal Competition Commission authorized the merger of Televisa and Iusacell in June 2012, one month before the presidential elections. The pressure from the outgoing president, Felipe Calderón, was clear and explicit about the instruction that Azcárraga Jean's company was to be granted this additional privilege.

This dispute increased in 2007, the year in which Slim appeared for the first time at the top of the *Forbes* list. International attention on Slim increased and he began to make much-discussed financial transactions, such as buying shares in the *New York Times,* a maneuver that caused an enormous amount of curiosity around him in the world financial capital, where everything that happens ends up becoming a global phenomenon.

Lawrence Wright—who won the Pulitzer with his book, *The Looming Tower*, about the Al Qaeda attack on the Twin Towers, and who became scriptwriter for films such as *The Siege*—visited Mexico in late 2008 and early 2009 to ask about Slim and write about him. In the article published in *The New Yorker*, Wright describes a meeting held in March 2008 at the official presidential residency of Los Pinos, during Calderón's term. The meeting was called by the then-minister of communications and transport, Luis Téllez, aiming to introduce competition into the telecom sector dominated by Slim. In exchange, Slim would be allowed to participate in television.

According to Wright's description, the meeting took place around a large U-shaped table. On one side was Slim, his eldest son Carlos, his nephew Héctor Slim Seade and his sons-in-law Daniel Hajj and Arturo Elías Ayub. On the other side of the table were Luis Téllez, commissioner Rafael del Villar and two experts not identified by the American journalist. President Calderón presided over the meeting, sitting at the curve of the table. "We're going to let you into TV, Carlos Slim, but first we have to agree on a set of terms," Del Villar said, according to the article in *The New Yorker*. The terms that the Mexican civil servants requested of Slim were "reasonable" fees in telephony interconnection, reducing national long distance rates, sharing Telmex infrastructure, and eliminating the rounding up in minutes for cell phone calls. Slim's team responded that the interconnection rates were competitive compared to those of other countries and the discussion went on for over two hours. Three of the assistants told Wright that Slim was so enraged that he threatened to sell Telmex; however, when speaking to the writer, Slim denied having said that exactly: "I said, 'Tell me what you want. If you want me to sell, OK. If you want us to divide it into two parts, three parts, OK. The only thing we will not do is destroy Telmex.'"

The meeting concluded without an agreement being reached. Months later, Luis Téllez resigned from the Ministry of Communications and Transport following the scandal unleashed when journalist Carmen Aristegui broadcast on MVS Radio some of Téllez's private phone calls, where he makes disparaging remarks about a number of figures in national politics, especially former president Carlos Salinas de Gortari.

In late 2008, former undersecretary Purificación Carpynteiro sent president Calderón a long diagnostic document and proposed solutions for the confrontation between Televisa and Slim. The private document, which Carpynteiro made public years later, when she was on her way to being voted in as a left-wing federal member of Congress, described the crisis that was to come:

The sector is at war. There are more than forty-five lawsuits, injunctions, administrative appeals, and even criminal complaints against civil servants and individuals by people from both blocks of influence. Should this progress in the same fashion, lawsuits that should be settled in court will not be resolved until three or four years later; and the legal uncertainty around the applicable rules will keep the sector paralyzed and with low investments, and the war will become a lot more aggressive even against the government, which will suffer the onslaughts from either side for their actions or inaction. In the best of cases, if the government does not change its strategy, the next four years will be like the first two. But this war could be advantageous and lay the foundations to change the result of the history that you are writing, Mr. President. As a character in this narrative, I dare to alert you to the fact that it is not necessary for the conclusion of this chapter to be a mere continuation of the failures of previous governments. The technological opportunity opens up the possibility of writing in a surprising twist that would revolutionize the sector. We are not destined to remain in the hands of the powerful players who currently manipulate political forces to exclusively defend their interests. We have sufficient weapons at our disposal to impose bargaining conditions that [could] result in a peaceful telecommunications revolution in Mexico without needing a battle that will be to the detriment of the country's political needs (on the contrary, it could support the improvement of the current position of tendencies during 2009). The Minister (of Communications and Transport) is aware of this strategy, which consists in four actions (presentation attached), and he is in agreement. However, we require coordination with several departments at the highest levels and the evaluation of potential political consequences during the process. If that coordination does not take place, even the players themselves will lose confidence that the government is firm in its position. This strategy does not guarantee success, but it is the only alternative to all-out war and divestment. But if this proves successful, how would this chapter in history read?

Calderón's government did not resolve this dispute. The only war Calderón seemed interested in was the War on Drugs. Faced with Calderón's inaction, Slim sustained what some specialists and civil servants define as a low-intensity war with Televisa. The battle became more fervent in 2011, as the new presidential elections drew near. An article published in *Reforma* about the delays incurred by Bestel, a subsidiary of Televisa, in the installation and operation of a telephony network for the state workers' social security institute ISSSTE, detonated one of the first open confrontations. After that publication, Televisa paid for spreads in various national newspapers, in which it accused Telmex of being the cause of the delay and claimed that *Reforma* was twisting reality to serve Slim's economic interests. The statement, signed by Manuel Compeán, communications director of Televisa, also questioned Granados Chapa, who had revealed that Televisa and TV Azteca had formed an alliance to buy Iusacell—a claim furiously denied by both companies, although over time it was revealed that the journalist had been right. But at the time, Televisa opened fire directly: "We now realize," says the article, "that this is not just the position of one writer at *Reforma*, but also that of the owner and directors of the newspaper. What better proof of this than the malicious lies propagated from the 'Templo Mayor,' according to which the authorities were hysterically called in to intervene and 'save' Grupo Carso."

The spread continued to reference old internal disputes in the family of Alejandro Junco de la Vega, owner of *Reforma*, who I contacted to give his version, but he declined, saying it was a very old rumor.

In addition to *Reforma*, as mentioned earlier, Televisa has accused Carmen Aristegui of working for Slim. A newspaper spread published and signed by Alejandro Puente Córdiba—president of the National Chamber of the Cable Telecommunications Industry, a trade union controlled by Televisa—openly questions Slim and Aristegui: "You, Carmen Aristegui, want to make Slim the owner of all of us, the way he already owns you. You help him annihilate his competitors and continue to fatten an empire he already owns." That was Televisa's reaction after Aristegui interviewed PRI presidential candidate Enrique Peña Nieto, asking about his close relationship with Televisa.

———

On December 1, 2012, the day he took office as president, Enrique Peña Nieto seemed to send a message of mediation to the protagonists of the Triple Play war. During the official ceremony at the Palacio Nacional, Slim, Emilio Azcárraga Jean and Ricardo Salinas Pliego were seated together. In the majority of the photographs that were published, Azcárraga Jean and Salinas Pliego are smiling, while, beside them, Carlos Slim is scowling in contempt. Politicians who were nearby claim that the owner of Telmex said only hello and goodbye without speaking to his competitors during entire event.

Beyond the apparent message of mediation, those close to Slim claim that the telecom magnate has been sailing against the wind during the government of Peña Nieto, due to the special alliance between the president and Televisa; the latter's widespread support was fundamental for the politician to bring the presidency of the country back into the hands of the PRI. Meanwhile, a politician close to Peña Nieto says that, beyond the favoritism that the president might hold for the broadcasting company, which successfully promoted his public political image, the new government sought to "hit everyone equally, but they needed to start with the biggest one." According to *Forbes* magazine, Slim's fortune is thirty times that of Azcárraga Jean's.

In March 2014, president Peña Nieto presented an initiative to reform the telecom and radio broadcasting industries. The proposal particularly affected Slim's monopolistic interests. América Móvil, his leading company and the administrator of Telmex and Telcel, was hardest hit as it was forced to offer connection services for free. Conversely, there were very few new measures against the television duopoly. After the presidential initiative was submitted to Congress, a series of protests and criticisms were levied against the new reform. In an action organized by Cuauhtémoc Cárdenas, the moral leader of the left, and PAN senator Javier Corral, the telephony union took part in a human chain that stretched from Televisa's headquarters to the presidential house of Los Pinos; the move was criticized as one of Slim's attempts to sabotage the reform. "Slim takes to the streets," was the title given by Carlos Loret de Mola, one of Televisa's most important journalists, to one of several articles he wrote in his column for the newspaper *El Universal*. Loret de Mola claimed that Slim had prepared a special strategy to maintain his monopoly: he first created a group of legislators at his service, "the so-called Telcel-nators and Dish-putees," in reference to Telcel and Dish, the latter a cable company in which he is partnered with Multivisión. Afterward, according to Loret de Mola, Slim took control of the media and journalists by means of advertising contracts, and later brainwashed intellectuals and artists, financing protests such as the human chain organized by Cárdenas Solórzano.

Saturday was the agreed date to form the human chain from Los Pinos to Televisa Chapultepec, as a protest against the secondary telecommunications law promoted by PRI and PAN. Characters who are close to Slim were there, in addition to some who hate the television duopoly (but don't mind being allies to the telecommunications monopoly). And others arrived who were seduced by them, perhaps without realizing who they ended up supporting. The invitation said 11 a.m. They needed six kilometers of people. It was noon and the chain still wasn't formed because there were only enough people for five non-continuous blocks: one near Los Pinos, two around the Ángel, two near Televisa. Just then the contingent from the Telmex union arrived, which is under total control of Mr. Slim through the figure of Francisco Hernández Juárez, who has been the union leader for forty years. Although there were not enough people to create a chain across the entire route planned, Slim's workers—identified with baseball caps and T-shirts—fed the protest with banners demanding all the things the multimillionaire wants in the secondary telecommunications law. These were professionally printed banners and placards with texts as technical as: "Telmex and its workers must not be punished for complying with the concession title and declaring it preponderant." And right next to it: "Peña puppet of Televisa." If the richest man defies the president of his country this way, challenging the State, defying the institutions and financing a protest, this should be making international headlines.

At the end of his article, the Televisa journalist opined that there should be greater competition in the world of television, but the most harmful company to the national economy and the pockets of Mexicans was Telmex-Telcel.

Peña Nieto's initiative was approved practically as he sent it. The legislators who voted against called it the Peña-Televisa Law. After the approval, in a surprising move, Slim ordered América Móvil—the main company affected by the reform—to be diminished through divestiture and sales to operators that were not Televisa or TV Azteca; thus, he abandoned his post-reform position as preponderant economic agent and maintained the tension with his main competitors in Mexico. Slim had turned the victory of his direct competitors into a Pyrrhic one.

"Are Televisa and TV Azteca your main adversaries in Mexico?" I ask Slim in an interview.

"Well, they conspired together and did all this to screw things up, but they've now separated from the partnership they had with Iusacell. One sold to the other, and the seller made a mistake. But our true competitor is Telefónica de España."

"And your adversary?"

"What do you mean by 'adversary'?"

"The group with which the dispute goes beyond the economic aspect, to include politics."

"All the other terrains often move in the economic aspect, but that is their problem. Look, as long as it's a business where those who decide are 100 million people, we don't care what they do."

26

Sharks

At 9:30 p.m. on Sunday, August 19, 2012, the Nicaraguan National Police received a telephone call alerting them to an illegal operation being carried out in their country by a group of Mexicans. Shortly before 10 a.m. the following morning, eighteen people who purported to be Televisa employees and were traveling in six SUVs sporting the broadcaster's blue logos were stopped at a border crossing between Nicaragua and Honduras. During the interrogations, the police heard contradictory versions regarding these individuals' activities in Central America: some claimed they had been working on a travel show about Nicaraguan tourism destinations, and others just said they were en route to Costa Rica, where they were planning to shoot a special report on money laundering.

The arrest was kept secret for three days, during which the Mexican embassy in Nicaragua informed the Nicaraguan government that Televisa claimed no responsibility for the individuals arrested, or their vehicles, in which $9.2 million in cash had been found hidden in secret compartments. Finally, on August 23, the news was made known and spread like wildfire over the following weeks, during which several accusations were made against Emilio Azcárraga Jean's company. According to Nicaraguan records, Raquel Alatorre, the purported leader of the group (some of whose members were ex-police officers from the Mexican states of Durango and Tamaulipas), had crossed the country forty-five times in recent years. The names of some directors of the Mexican television broadcasting company were found stored in her cell phone. Soon the facts became a scandal and even Sandinist president Daniel Ortega addressed the police officers involved in the arrest, stoking the fire: "I want to congratulate all the institutions, and especially all of you, brothers of the police, and commissioner Ms. Alatorre, for your success in uncovering the secret of Televisa, which is proper soap opera material: the secret of Televisa revealed."

A few hours before these arrests were made public, according to Televisa, its prime-time news anchor Joaquín López-Dóriga received a phone call from Arturo Elías Ayub, América Móvil's director of Strategic Alliances and Content. Elías Ayub, who is Carlos Slim's son-in-law, said he had a message from the "*Ingeniero*"—the honorary title used by Slim's associates instead of his name, as a sign of reverence. López-Dórriga was not wholly surprised that Slim, with whom he'd been close since the 1980s, would send a message through Elías Ayub, with whom he had an even closer, familial relationship, but he was surprised by the urgency and haste. He asked Ayub to give him the message by phone, but Ayub responded that they'd best meet in person, immediately. The journalist was about to appear on his morning show on Radio Fórmula, so they agreed to meet at a Starbucks along the way.

There, according to Televisa, Elías Ayub dropped the bomb: "The Ingeniero is very worried because he has been informed that you had sent a team of six remote control units to Central America to investigate some supposed money laundering operations of his."

López-Dóriga could not believe what he'd just heard and asked him to repeat it. When Ayub said it again, the journalist remonstrated: "Is this some sort of joke? I can't believe Carlos would suspect that of me!"

Elías Ayub said Slim had obtained the information from a Central American president, but refused to say exactly who. Later it would become known that it had been Ortega. López-Dóriga told Ayub it was "a ludicrous claim," because Televisa News in Mexico City did not have seven remote control units available to send anywhere, which would include seven reporters, seven cameramen, seven helpers, seven technicians, seven producers, seven chauffeurs and seven assistants. The journalist said he was outraged, offended and disappointed that Slim would believe such a story.

That same afternoon, López-Dóriga discussed the claim with Bernardo Gómez, executive vice president of Televisa. Gómez was surprised at the story and said it was nonsense. That night, the Attorney General's Office issued a press release stating that it had begun an investigation because of the finding in Nicaragua of some Televisa SUVs with money in cash and traces of cocaine. López-Dóriga once again contacted the executive vice president: "I call Bernardo and say to him: 'I'm going to send you a statement from the PGR.' At this point it was 9:20 p.m. He sees it and says: 'What? So the story was true?' A few minutes later I call him again and say to him: 'Hey, I now have a statement from the Ministry of Foreign Affairs too.' Then came the complaint from the United States government to the government of Mexico, and after that, the Nicaraguans saying they were going to investigate."

In an interview with Gómez, he told me that he considered this fact the greatest public attack Televisa had received from Slim: "That's in the public forum, because from the business side he's done everything in his power: he's brought down our systems, he's contaminated us, but that's how it is. We're tough and we defend ourselves, and we're going to keep moving forward, but in the public arena that has been—the thing with the SUVs—the most grievous thing he's done. And if at least they'd done it well, it would be a different story. But drug trafficking? I don't get it. Watch where you're going, don't get lost. Look at the kind of power Slim has. No one touches him, and instead Televisa gets criticized all the time. Is that power? I give up. If that's power, I give up. Power is Carlos Slim. He's sacrosanct. That's power, Diego, don't get confused."

When I interviewed him for this book, Elías Ayub told me the first he heard about the SUVs was in the news, although he later remembered, without going into details, that he'd had a prior conversation with López-Dóriga, in which he told him they had information that the supposed Televisa employees were investigating Slim's business in the area. The Telmex director told me he would give no further comment.

In the end, the eighteen members of the money laundering network arrested in Nicaragua were extradited to Mexico in December 2013 without it ever being publicly clarified to which organization they belonged. The Attorney General's Office made no further statements on the case, despite my requests, while the National Security Commission of the Interior Ministry has still not divulged, as this book goes to print, at which penitentiary facility the eighteen arrested individuals were located.

———

Bernardo Gómez and Alfonso de Angoitia, Televisa's vice presidents, met me at the network's office in Las Lomas, Mexico City. It does not seem like a coincidence that there are four of Damien Hirst's dissected sharks in the entrance to the place where the four men in charge of Televisa hold their meetings—the president of the administration council, Emilio Azcárraga Jean, and vice presidents de Angoitia, Gómez and José Bastón.

In 1997, after the death of Azcárraga Milmo, "El Tigre," these four sharks took control of the television broadcaster when their average age was twenty-eight. Among them, Gómez oversees the company's news department and is in charge of political relations.

"To say that Televisa has no power would be disingenuous," says Gómez. "But that doesn't mean the power is down to any one person. It's a company and a logo. When Don Emilio Azcárraga Milmo, El Tigre, left, everyone said: 'That will be the end of Televisa.' And El Tigre left and it kept going, and we're all going to leave and you know what's going to happen? Televisa will keep going, because the company, the institution, is more powerful."

When Azcárraga Milmo died in his home in Miami, Florida, Televisa owed $1.4 billion and the holding company, Grupo Televicentro, owed another $1.4 billion. As if this were not enough, El Tigre had a personal debt of $500 million toward different creditors, among them Inbursa, the bank owned by Slim. In addition, the way in which his will was made left the door open to various disputes among his children and partners. It was a terrible scenario for twenty-eight-year-old heir Azcárraga Jean, who had only received 10 percent of the Televicentro holdings, which at the time elicited doubts within the business world regarding the heir's ability to control Televisa.

"People were right when they said: 'These guys aren't going to manage,' because if you looked at the panorama of the debts and what Emilio had at the time, it was quite complicated," recalls de Angoitia, who was also president of its financial committee. Alongside Gómez, Bastón and de Angoitia, Azcárraga Jean restructured the company's liabilities by offering additional guarantees. Furthermore, the new administrators eliminated several expenses that were viewed as excessive, including the three private airplanes available for Televisa executives.

"There were many things that were allowed in the past, because for a long time it was a monopoly, and when the competition arrived, it was very difficult for them to understand and adapt," says de Angoitia.

During that process, businessman and politician Miguel Alemán, who owned 14 percent of the company, ran out of patience and asked to leave Televisa precisely when Azcárraga Jean and his team were about to invite him to buy the shares of another investor called Fernando Díez Barroso, who had capitalized some liabilities. Alemán responded that not only did he not want to buy, but he wanted to immediately sell his own shares, since he was about to start his campaign as the PRI candidate for governor of Veracruz. The Televisa quartet tried to convince him to stay, offering him a special share package for his son that would provide his son with corporate rights. Negotiations began, but were stalled when Alemán's lawyers demanded that any operation over $1.5 million be approved by Alemán. De Angoitia explains that yielding on this point would have made the company's operations impossible. This was the equation into which Slim was brought.

"That's when we said to Miguel Alemán: 'We can't seem to reach an agreement here and we both think we are right. You want to protect your son with all these rights, and we think that's not how the company is going to operate, and if we go down that route we are going to cause the company to fail. So, why don't we name Carlos Slim as an arbiter and have him say what's reasonable and what isn't? What protections you need and what the company needs to operate freely? That is, with protections, but freely.'"

Slim got involved as a mediator between Alemán's family and Azcárraga Jean's team, remembers de Angoitia. After several sessions, he gave his verdict: "With all these protections you're requesting, the company is not going to be able to operate and an agreement will not be reached, because one wants to overprotect and the other wants freedom." With this dilemma, Alemán again insisted that he would sell and asked Azcárraga Jean to pledge the control of the company as collateral in case his parcel of shares was not sold. A decision like that would have put at risk the leadership that Azcárraga Jean and his team had only recently consolidated at Televisa. Finally, Alemán offered to sell Slim his shares. Slim responded: "Miguel, you're my friend, and I'd be buying too cheap because this company has a future. So I won't be able to buy now." Alemán insisted, and in this way Slim managed to become a non-voting partner at Televisa, through purchasing that parcel of shares of Grupo Televicentro.

"Was there no legal impediment due to the Telmex concession title clause?" I ask de Angoitia.

"It's what he did through Sinca Inbursa and not through Telmex or América Móvil. He thought 'Well, where I have certain restrictions is in the area of telecommunications, so I'll just do it through my bank.'"

According to Televisa's assessment, in that moment there was no legal impediment for Slim to be a partner. The only existing restriction in Telmex's concession title was that the company would not be allowed video, a key factor that in the long term would unleash a battle between the television company and Slim, who in that moment already owned 49 percent of Cablevisión, Televisa's cable company, which meant that in some way in some way he was already a partner of the Azcárraga family, remembers de Angoitia.

"Was there no legal regulation on this?" I ask Gómez.

Gómez explains that Televisa was a very important company for the Mexican state, and that Azcárraga Milmo had built a very important network of friends and allies, both in the business world and in government. "President Zedillo was very clear when he spoke to us. He said: 'You have an opportunity, and that opportunity is there because of the relationship I had with your father, but if you fail, I will not hesitate to do whatever is needed, because this company cannot fail.' And the truth is that Emilio Jr., with incredible courage, said: 'Look, I don't have much to lose.' At the time he was twenty-eight years old and he said: 'You know what? I have a small percentage, and if I fail, I'll be failing at age twenty-eight. I can start over.' Normally the advice given when it comes to funds would be to sell your share, as with $30 million you'll have your life set up. But Emilio said: 'No, I want to take a chance.' Alfonso [de Angoitia] and I spoke with him at the time and said: 'It's OK if you decide not to go for it,' but his response was: 'No, I want to take a chance, I want us to take a chance together.' And as Alfonso said, it was a very, very complicated operation, because of all the things it entailed. Because Televisa is not a normal company. And the partners were family, partners that I know personally: the Díez Barrosos, the Burrillos, the Alemáns, who managed to get Slim out, but above them there were many people from the company wanting to control Televisa. Everyone wanted a hand in Televisa. Slim didn't. When Don Emilio died, people came out of the wood-work, like the Monterrey businessman Alfonso Romo, who said: 'I'll buy it.' Why? Because Televisa was very appetizing. Not many people trusted Emilio Jr. and because the image of Don Emilio was so well-known and carried so much weight, they thought that his son was going to fail: 99 percent believed that."

The eldest of the four young men who took control over Televisa in 1997 was Alfonso de Angoitia, who was just thirty-four. Azcárraga Jean, Gómez and Bastón were all twenty-eight. When reminiscing on those times, Gómez reflects on why they decided to enter the dispute over the control for Televisa: "I think it was absolute irresponsibility and that we didn't think the consequences through. When we talk sometimes, we say: 'What were we think-ing?' If we were asked again whether we would take the risks we took then, I wouldn't do it." Gómez considers that they were also lucky: 'God was behind us, there was a run of luck, a lot of good energy, because everything fell into place. That we worked our-selves to the bone is clear. And there were days... every Friday we said: 'That's the end of it.' I don't know how many times Alfonso [de Angoitia] stood up from the table and said: 'It's all gone to shit,' and Emilio [Azcárraga Jean] too: 'Everything's gone to shit.' And we would stand up and start the weekend with that idea. But then we'd arrive on Monday morning and say: 'Let's see, it seems that the patient's pinky finger moved, let's take him into the operating room again, and again, and again.' But they were difficult days. I think it's been the hardest we've experienced. It was like that in '97, '98, '99 and 2000."

The situation was such that Goldman Sachs foresaw a catastrophic panorama for the television company, and in 1998, together with other banks, it modified the expiry of the credits that had been arranged by Azcárraga Milmo. After buying his shares from Miguel Alemán, Slim was part of Televisa, and during those critical days he might have been able to take control of the television company.

"Had Emilio failed, he would have said, 'All right, since I'm already here, now that I'm a part and it didn't work out: you didn't pay, I'll pick up the mess.' This is what Slim has done systematically with other companies and he's very good at it. Nobody would have been able to recriminate absolutely anything," explains de Angoitia. "From that time they have nothing to recriminate Slim nor María Asunción Aramburuzabala, the other shareholder who also entered Televisa in that difficult moment, after buying Alejandro Burillo's share."

According to Televisa's financial team's assessments, Slim tripled his investment.

"It would be bad manners not to be grateful," says Gómez, "to each character who believed in the project, from the actress who said: 'Hey, we can't earn the same salaries we used to,' and the actors who said: 'I used to earn 10 pesos and now I'm going to earn less.' [They should] feel as grateful to Slim as they do to López-Dóriga, because they both believed in the project even though they had very little to hold onto. López-Dóriga had a very well-established career in radio and he used to say: 'But why, why, if I am doing so well in radio? I'm the most important presenter.' He believed in us, and, if you think about it, what credentials did we have? None. He looked us in the eye and with an open heart he said: 'I'm in.' And here he is. To date, López-Dóriga does not have any signed contract with Televisa. He's worked for eighteen years perhaps in the most important public position of the consortium, based on a verbal agreement made in December 1997."

Loyalty is something that de Angoitia also recognizes in Slim, who in those years met with Paula Cusi, widow of Azcárraga Milmo who was at loggerheads with Azcárraga Jean, and who offered to give Slim her share so he could gain control of the company, but she found that the magnate responded, cuttingly, that he would never do anything of the sort.

"How did Slim benefit from being a non-voting shareholder in Televisa?"

"What Mr. Slim has done very well is that he woos businesses, particularly telecom, the way Juan Villalonga, who was king of media, did in Spain," says de Angoitia, explaining that with his near-unlimited budget, Slim buys advertising while setting guidelines of behavior. Case in point: the newspaper *Reforma*, which according to de Angoitia hits Televisa hardest when Slim is injecting the most cash. "I can show you the graphs. It's very obvious and it's fine. But let's leave *Reforma* aside and look at *La Jornada*. A left-wing newspaper treating a magnate such as Slim as sacrosanct. How can that be? Why? Because money talks."

"Slim didn't give any opinions or participate in the financial operations of Televisa?"

"He never said to me: 'Hey Poncho, did our sales go down?' He never asked how sales were going. We used to have lunch with him and look at general things. On the other hand, when Televisa said: 'Hey, we're thinking about going into this business,' Slim's associates used to say, 'Oops! The Ingeniero will not be very pleased about that.' Slim used to say: 'You're fine, but you're on your own.'"

De Angoitia summarizes Slim's participation in Televisa's critical moment: "He would have wanted to buy Televisa, but that would have been impossible. But if it had been the other way around: 'I wasn't paid, what do you want me to do? I had no choice but to keep the company.' This was the scenario if it went badly for Azcárraga and his team. And if it went well for us, well he would just earn a lot of money, which fortunately is what happened. I think that's the way he saw it. And he was helping Emilio at the same time."

Despite the age difference, Slim built a very close relationship with Azcárraga Jean, and his children also played a part.

"Why did the disagreement happen?" asks de Angoitia rhetorically. He then explainss: "Because of technology, which nobody controls, and it keeps moving."

Since its beginning, Televisa has focused its business on two aspects: content and distribution. The first in the dynasty, Emilio Azcárraga Vidaurreta, owned XEW, the most important radio station in the country and which featured legends such as Pedro Infante. When television emerged as a new distribution channel, he had to learn to project his content through the so-called "magic box." Azcárraga Milmo, second in the dynasty, saw the emergence of satellites and ventured to buy Panamsat, both to make an alliance with a direct-to-home service such as Sky, and to create an ephemeral pager called Skytel.

"Why did El Tigre get involved? Because these were communication channels. The reason he didn't enter telephony sooner was because he was never allowed."

However, with the inevitable digital convergence, cell phones became massive and instant content distributors. Herein lies the crux of the battle against Slim, who owns the greatest mobile phone distribution channel.

In 2009, the Televisa quartet met with the owner of América Móvil to explain the situation: "We didn't show up one day out of the blue, knock on the Ingeniero's door, and say: 'We have a bank and we want to compete against you.' We are not bankers. We only know how to do one thing and Joaquín López-Dóriga is not going to let me lie, his proposal to Slim was: 'You set out the conditions.' Gómez told Slim during that lunch meeting: 'Ingeniero, this is everyone's ship, please stand at the helm. You're the captain, we're the crew,' to which Slim replied: 'No, I'm tired, I'm old and I'm devoted to the foundations now. Speak to my children.'"

Around the same time, the Televicentro holding had dissolved due to a Televisa contract with Aramburuzabala, to liquidate her investment. De Angoitia coordinated a very complicated operation in which at the end of the day all partners had direct shares in Televisa and Azcárraga Jean took direct control of the company.

When this happened, Slim took market shares and he had the same standing as any other investor, so when the Cablevisión convergence came to offer telephony, Slim said, "I don't agree."

"Another version of the rift between Televisa and Slim is that he did not agree with the content. Is that true? Was that an issue?" I ask Gómez.

"Joaquín López-Dóriga has a long personal friendship with Carlos Slim. When did he say anything to him? Never. He wasn't even interested. Zero. Do you think he gets into the editorial content of the *New York Times*? Of course not. What he wants is not to be spoken about."

"Yet another version spread by some of his associates is about your ungratefulness after he had helped you."

"It's normal for that story to be told and I think he is in that dynamic: 'Seriously? I helped you, and now you're attacking me?' No. The only difference was, and Alfonso and I explained it thoroughly at the time: 'What better ally for your children, Ingeniero? What are you going to leave your children apart from money? Relationships. Because when you are no longer here, they are going to swoop down on them and Emilio Azcárraga Jean has something that others do not: Emilio does not want to be you, he does not want to be the richest man in the world. He wants to have a prosperous business and that's it. El Tigre of course wanted to be El Tigre. But Emilio is not like that. The only thing Emilio wants is to be able to have his business and to do well.' Joaquín López-Dóriga was there and was listening. He heard what we said."

"Did the separation between Televisa and Slim happen strictly because of the digital convergence issue?"

"In that moment," De Angoitita replies, "Televisa had to do what it had to do in order to survive. Then it started to get into telecommunications and the Ingeniero started getting more and more annoyed, until he started to tighten his grip and said: "Why should I give you money? I'm providing the funds for them to buy cable companies and compete against me. Schmuck if I do.' Then he says: 'No, the truth is you are treating me very unfairly and Telmex will no longer advertize.'"

The face-off became more apparent in 2014 during the approval of the telecommunications reform. At the time Slim was pushing for Telmex to receive the official authorization to distribute video, but he did not succeed. Televisa favored the entry of two new television chains, but in return it asked to "level the telecommunications playing field, because it's uneven and it's impossible to compete this way." The main objection was that the rates were regulated by Telmex. De Angoitia explains: "When the avenues are regulated by just one person who says: 'The signal has to go through my antennas, and I will decide how much it costs,' then it's not on. That's where the confrontation begins in earnest. The Ingeniero did all he could in politics to get what he needed and Televisa responded for one reason: for survival, not for anything else, right? Because let's be clear, if the Ingeniero was given video, Televisa would instantly disappear. Why? Because he'd dump the price of video and say: 'I'll give you video for free and voice will cost you this much.' If he applies his tactic here, you go down."

Slim has sought to obtain the permission to distribute video since 2007, and from the point of view of Televisa his lobbying has been intense.

"He is brutally astute, because he invites the journalists, he invites the party leaders, and because he invites them, these dudes go: 'The Ingeniero invited me!' He obviously dazzles them. López-Dóriga usually tells me that if Slim grants you an appointment, it's almost the equivalent of getting one with Queen Elizabeth or the Pope."

In 2011, three years before the approval of the telecommunications reform, Grupo Carso made it known that it would stop advertising on Televisa and TV Azteca, claiming that he had been vetoed by the television companies.

"The veto is from him, never from us, because we would be shooting ourselves in the foot if we did that. Imagine us saying to him: 'No, we won't take your advertising money,'" Gómez explains.

"It's absurd. It makes no sense. Our main business is selling advertising," concludes de Angoitia.

By spring of 2015, Grupo Carso decided to advertise again through Televisa and TV Azteca, seeing the new entry into the Mexican telephony market of AT&T, the main telecommunications company worldwide—of which, by the way, Slim owns 8.2 percent in preferred stock.

VII

During the years the magnate didn't advertise on Televisa and TV Azteca, these companies came together to participate in the telecommunications market through the telephone company Iusacell. That partnership was terminated in 2014, when Televisa agreed to sell to TV Azteca its half of the company for $717 million. However, sixty days later, TV Azteca sold the entire company for $2.5 billion to AT&T, minus $800 million in debt and contingencies, with which it obtained millions of dollars in earnings over just a handful of days.

"In business," explains de Angoitia, "some come out well and others don't. The issue is the average. Televisa was at some point worth $3.7 billion and today it's worth $22 billion. Maybe in some businesses you make mistakes."

Gómez adds and de Angoitia nods: "We don't have the Ingeniero's intelligence. Of course we don't. But neither do we have his ambition. That's what I say about us: we don't have his ambition. All Emilio Azcárraga wants is to run a successful company and he is in telecommunications because the technology has led him there. He didn't say: 'I'm going to compete against Slim.' He didn't say: 'I'm going to open a Sanborns.' What other line of business is Emilio Azcárraga in? What he has, what he's involved in, is because technology lead him there, while the Ingeniero also bought football teams. What for? To get into football and fight against us. He's very good, but that's life. We're in his bad books now and we just have to put up with what we get from his allies in the media, we understand this and accept it, because we are defending this company. We're not going to open a bank tomorrow. We're not going to open a cafeteria. On the contrary, we're going to be grateful to the Ingeniero, but being grateful doesn't mean we're going to sit here twiddling our thumbs. We already asked him to steer the ship. Even last year, with the subject of the telecommunications law, we said to him: 'Please understand, what we want is to be in this business and you are the leader in this. We want a part in the sector, but we don't want to take the whole cake for ourselves, nor do we have those ambitions.' If Televisa takes on a fight, it's always head on. It fights directly. It's too transparent. It's a glass screen, while the Ingeniero has a tremendous ability, because he keeps the media hostage with something that is very simple: advertising."

"But that includes Televisa. I can't remember any analysis or criticisms of Slim when he was a partner of yours."

"Of course you have a point, but I'm going to say one thing: the Ingeniero, if there was anything minor, the slightest thing against Telmex..."

"And that's where we get fed up with this thing about 'the Ingeniero.' I think not even in the presidency of the Republic will they throw the president at you the way they did with the Ingeniero. They don't call him Carlos or Carlos Slim: 'It's just that the Ingeniero is very confused, quite taken aback, very disappointed.' And you'd say: 'What is it this time?' 'It's just that they pulled out a Sanborns logo.' If you asked me what the difference between you and them is, it's that we get hit so often that our skin gets this thick," he says, making a gap between his fingers. "You can't lay a finger on him," says de Angoitia.

In the narrative of the quartet of youngsters that took over Televisa in 1997, beyond the battles with Slim, there is the pride of having kept the television company afloat and then multiplied its worth seven-fold as compared to when Azcárraga Jean inherited 10 percent of the shares, recalls de Angoitia. At some point it was rumored that president Zedillo had not only operated in favor of Azcárraga Jean, but that he was even a partner of the company.

"That's nonsense and time has shown that Zedillo doesn't own even half a share of Televisa. He's an honest person," says Gómez, who remembers when Zedillo's personal secretary Liébano Sáenz, as well as the head of the presidential office, Luis Téllez, warned him that if they didn't stabilize the company soon, the government would take over, because they couldn't allow Televisa to fall, especially because of the financial impact it would have represented internationally. Mexico was only just recovering from the financial crash, and a crisis in a company with global reach such as Televisa, would have been a tremendous setback for the country."

Gómez continues, "Everyone had interests here, and whatever they told me, they were guaranteed with shares. But the president of the Republic did not."

Another thing they both agree on is that the battle between Slim and Televisa is sure to continue.

"When people say: 'It's a battle of Titans,' you think 'That's cute! What do you mean Titans? Haven't you noticed the man is worth $70 or $80 billion and Emilio is worth $2 billion? One day we were joking and said: 'No, *Forbes* should bring out a second volume because Emilio doesn't even show up in the first one.' I mean, but there's the perception that Televisa is extremely powerful. I can tell you, man, you have no idea what power is. Power is being able to say: 'Hey, Bill Clinton, here's $50 million for your foundation.' That man," Gómez points at de Angoitia, "gives $50 million and Televisa's sales drop 10 percent. It's totally out of proportion, but we have this stigma that Televisa is a giant. It's huge, but when you compare the value of the companies... And that's cute."

Although we'd agreed for the interview to be only be about the history of Televisa's relationship with Slim, before concluding I ask them their opinion of businessmen, politicians and journalists who consider Televisa to be the most powerful company in Mexico.

"Do you really believe that?" Gómez tells me as de Angoitia nods. "Haven't you seen the criticisms we receive every single day? Does that happen when someone has power? When you truly have power, you're sacrosanct, like Carlos Slim."

VIII

27

The Left

Carlos Slim's generosity has at times put politicians in a tight spot. One day the magnate traveled to Buenos Aires and met with president Cristina Fernández de Kirchner. At the end of his appointment he gifted her a MacBook Air in front of the cameras. It was not the first computer that Slim had given the president, but it was the first time he'd done it in front of journalists, who were of the opinion that the aerodynamic computer was far too expensive a gift for a head of state, according to the local etiquette.

The relationship between Slim and the Argentinian president began during the administration of her predecessor, her deceased husband Néstor Kirchner, who was head of state in that country between 2003 and 2007. One of the key characters in Slim's relationship with the left-wing president is Juan Manuel Abal Medina, an ex-guerilla leader who, after his exile in Mexico, became an important political shadow operator. Abal Medina is known in his country for having organized a special operation so that former president Perón, overthrown by a military coup in 1955, would abandon his forced exile and return to Buenos Aires in 1973 to govern the country again until his death not long after. His wife, María Estela Martínez de Perón, known as Isabelita, succeeded him during a brief period until the imposition of a new military dictatorship.

In that context, Abal Medina moved into clandestine circles and formed part of the Montoneros, one of the most notable guerilla groups that have existed in Latin America. Abal Medina in the end took advantage of Mexico's open-border policy at that time, which allowed entry to guerilla leaders from other countries while also brutally repressing its own guerrilla movements. Medina collaborated with Mexican national security agencies and met Julián Slim, Carlos Slim's older brother, who was in charge of persecuting "subversive elements." The ex-guerilla leader became a friend of both brothers, and when Carlos Slim entered the Argentinian market, Abal Medina participated, although never though his law firm or in any official capacity.

Medina's importance is such that his son, who bears the same name, reached the position of head of the cabinet office for Cristina Fernández de Kirchner and was even tipped as the presidential candidate to replace her. Grupo Clarín—owner of the most important newspaper of that country and other media companies—has constantly questioned Abal Medina during its confrontation with Cristina's government. Behind these allegations is also Clarín's owners' concern regarding Slim's incursion in Argentina. Slim, in addition to purchasing the telephony company Claro and a percentage of the oil company YPF, has acquired radio and television chains. In the eyes of Clarín, Slim is a competitor, while the government of Fernández, often criticized by her political rivals for her management of the economy, showed off Slim's investments: if the richest man in the world is investing in the country it proves that the national economy is healthy.

In Cuba there was no scandal whatsoever when Fidel Castro said that Slim visited Havana in the '90s and gifted him a modern television that Castro kept in his living room until 2009. Slim is seen by those who led the revolution as "an intelligent man who knows all the secrets of the stock exchange and the mechanisms of the capitalist system." In April 2010, the official newspaper, *Granma* published an article entitled "The giant of the seven tongues," where Castro does an extensive review of the book *La mafia que se adueñó de México* (*The Mafia that Took Over Mexico*), in which the author, Andrés Manuel López Obrador, criticizes the Mexican business elite while avoiding questioning Slim, the richest of them all. Castro writes:

López Obrador's opinion on Carlos Slim is one I also share. I know him too. He visited me whenever I went to Mexico and he once visited me in Cuba. He gave me a television—the most modern kind at the time—which I kept in my home until just a year ago. He did not do so with the intention of bribing me. I never asked him any favors. Despite being the world's richest, with a fortune of over $60 billion, he is an intelligent man who knows all the secrets of the stock exchange and the mechanisms of the capitalist system.

Slim and Castro met on December 2, 1988, after that year's hugely controversial election of Salinas de Gortari, in the midst of serious allegations of electoral fraud by Cárdenas and thousands of his followers. Castro was in Mexico during those days to participate in the swearing-in ceremony of Salinas de Gortari, who organized a dinner for the Cuban head of state and a select group of businesspeople, including Claudio X. González, Jorge Kahwagi and Carlos Slim.

According to an article by journalist Fernando Ortega and the testimony of a politician who collaborated with the government of Salinas de Gortari, the meeting between Castro and the Mexican magnates took place at 22 Sierra Negra street, in Lomas de Chapultepec, at a mansion owned by Enrique Madero Bracho.

"If you were in Mexico, you'd be a great businessman. You have the talent for it," Antonio Madero Bracho said to Castro.

"Kid, I *am* a businessman, but for the state," Fidel replied. The presence of Castro in Mexico at that time signified his important and controversial support for Salinas de Gortari, especially after the home secretary, Manuel Bartlett, halfway through the count, had pronounced the sad words burned into every Mexican's memory: "We had a system crash." The presence of Fidel Castro helped legitimize Salinas de Gortari and the "perfect dictatorship" of the PRI for six more years in government.

According to Ortega, during the dinner party, Slim brought up the topic of foreign debt, saying that Mexico needed to preserve its exterior credit to guarantee the modernization of the country. Castro replied that what Mexico should do is stop paying the debt, as it was unpayable. Then they spoke about swaps—the exchange of external debt for shares in Mexican businesses—as a solution to partially resolve the country's debt, and although Castro praised that measure, he still recommended the debt not be paid, because Mexico had already given its due to "Yankee imperialism." According to Ortega, Castro asked Slim about the meaning and scope of the country's modernization, to which the businessman replied that that task was important not only for the industry, but also for education, politics, social life and democracy. "It's a modernization in all senses."

The good relationship between Salinas de Gortari and Castro continued. In the years that followed, during the crisis that took hold of the island after the fall of the USSR, Cuba received a series of economic support measures. Among the group of businessmen who traveled to Havana to try to participate in different economic projects was Slim, but the first ones to do so in any significant measure were Luis Niño de Rivera, in mobile telephony, and Mauricio Fernández Garza, from Monterrey, who made an investment in conjunction with the Cuban government to reactivate fifteen Cuban textile factories, which were paralyzed due to the lack of funds.

Twenty years after that meeting, Castro, from an honorific but still powerful position, continued to be in charge of Cuba, while the previously little-known Slim was among the richest on the planet.

"I know Fidel has a very good relationship with you. So good that he did something he does not do with almost any businessman —he publicly praised you, in a 2008 article where he says that you gave him the only television he has ever used. Could you tell me a bit about your relationship with him?" I ask Slim.

"I saw him in person for the first time at Salinas's swearing-in ceremony."

"And what did you both speak about?"

"I didn't speak. There were around thirty of us there, although we did all give our opinions. It was an open conversation. In reality, I went to Cuba for the first time in '94 and one evening he invited me to dinner quite late. We'd already eaten but we went with him to dinner and it was all very pleasant. It was very cordial, and that's where we chatted."

"Why did you visit Cuba in '94?"

"For many reasons."

"Business?"

"Well, that I'd rather not comment on."

"Did you have dinner at Fidel's house?"

"No, at an office. There we chatted first and then he, who hadn't had dinner yet, ate with us."

"Did you arrive to a protocol house?"

"Yes."

"And what was your impression of Fidel?"

"Oh, he was interested in everything, very inquisitive. He'd already been informed about everything we'd speak about. I thought Cuba was about to change, wanting to change, and I felt that was possible. We sounded out something about investment in telecommunications and the truth is there were many ways in which Cuba could have started doing what it's doing now. I'm talking more than twenty years ago. It has started opening up, little by little. There was already Spanish private investment in hospitality and all that. I went that time and then twice again, too. Vicente Fox invited me on a trip to accompany him regarding Cuba's historical center. We were already working on Mexico City's historical center."

"And did you participate in the renovation of the historical center of Havana?"

"No, I just went twice to see Old Havana and chat about what it was like, what they had done, etc. With the guy who's doing it, Eusebio Leal… In fact, in 2002, when I went to Cuba for the last time, with President Fox, for some reason Fidel and Fox went to the house of Eusebio Leal's mom, an elderly woman. So I think it's always been important for Cuba to transform and modernize. Cuba has one advantage: it has good health and education, although their education is a little deformed due to the kinds of things they learned."

"When you say 'deformed,' do you mean ideology?"

"It was not because of the ideology, because Fidel himself asked for them to be prepared to see more computers and change history. When Russia lost influence, the Soviet Union, after '89–90, then it changed to learning about Cuba's history, English and other things. So the education level is good."

"With that level of education and the recent opening, what do you expect will happen in Cuba?"

"I hope they accelerate it. I hope they accelerate it…"

"Wouldn't you be interested in investing in Cuba?"

"The thing is, I'm not looking for more activities. I already have lots on my plate."

"What do you mean? Last time you told me about a lot of activities that you were doing."

"Well, that's what we're doing."

"OK, back to Fidel, why do you believe Fidel and you got on so well?"

"Look, I believe in diversity, plurality, freedom. To be honest, since childhood I've always sought that potential. I don't know if I told you last time that I went to a school that was almost a boarding school. I couldn't bear it. There are certain activities I've never had a vocation for. So, speaking to interesting people, with leaders such as Fidel, as it could be any other, well, it's a privilege to be able to converse with those people."

"Someone in Cuba told me that you and Fidel used to speak a lot about countries' foreign debt."

"No, some of the conversations were very long, not only with me. In some of them there were other people present. The first time I went I was with several high-up people. And I used to ask the guy from Cuba's Central Bank, the vice president [Carlos Lage]: "How much money in circulation do you have?" I remember the price of the dollar that the government handled at the time was 130 Cuban pesos, which meant that the highest salary was four or five dollars, because people were paid 500 pesos… So what I used to tell them was that all the money in circulation at market price was $100 million. Afterward, what Fidel thought about was a VAT [value-added tax], and I told them that they should have a shop where the products could be sold in dollars. Then, with those dollars they could clean what there was. Anyway, we did discuss economics, but not with him. With him we spoke about other things, about possible situations. For example, we spoke about Cuban tobacco.

He gave me a box of cigars, which people used to say did not exist: the Trinidad cigars. I'd read about them in a magazine and he did me the favor, at the end of the trip, of sending me a box of Trinidad cigars, which I still have."

"And you gave him a TV because of that?"

"Yes, I gave him a television. I said: 'A television can be interesting for you to use or to donate to a space where people use it.' I had a similar one at home and it was a product we used to sell in Sanborns stores."

"And what was it like or what was special about it?"

"It was a big Sony TV."

"I'm sorry, but I find a gift like that a bit disconcerting."

"Why? If you're going there you need to bring a gift, what other gift can you bring? I'm not going to bring medicine or aspirins. What do you bring?"

———

One of the passions Carlos Slim and Fidel Castro share is baseball. Mark McGwire, one of the most impressive batters in the history of that sport, inspired Slim to write an article that was published in the magazine *Letras Libres* in the October 1999 issue. The piece begins thus:

> Baseball, whose fans seem to be awakening in Mexico after long seasons of half-empty grandstands, is a spectacular sport that leans largely on the physical prowess and technical skill of its players, but also on the deployment of their intelligence. That's why the best games are known as 'pitcher's duels,' closed games, with very low scores, which are usually decided by good fielding or a solitary home run. In baseball—as in any other team sport—numbers talk, memory comes to life, and legends are forged.

One of the legends forged about Slim is that his relationship with Andrés Manuel López Obrador, was owed precisely to their shared enthusiasm for baseball, which led them to consider the possibility of looking for a Major League team to have a permanent headquarters in Mexico City. That never happened; what did happen is that they made an alliance so that Slim, with the support of the left-wing government, would invest in the historical center of Mexico City.

With his sober personality and use of his enormous power, Slim has built a reputation as modest and restrained, despite being among the richest in the world and living in a country like Mexico, where there are few millionaires who manage to curb their desire to be noticed—it's enough to flick through the social magazines to see this is the case.

It would appear that the communication strategy Slim has chosen —which his son-in-law, Arturo Elías Ayub, is in charge of—lies precisely in appearing rarely in the media and in making public declarations that are so neutral that they never cause any controversy. The construction of that politically correct image—compared with Televisa's Emilio Azcárraga Jean, who has appeared in the media celebrating, euphoric and shirtless, the triumph of his football team, the América—has perhaps caused Slim to have fewer Mexican critics than Azcárraga. This image should also be added to the climate of fear around Slim. At least three reporters and editors told me in private of lawsuit threats received from Slim or his team just for passing mentions of his name in certain unflattering articles.

Slim tends to maintain a discreet image of himself and his companies, with the odd absurdity. Telcel, one of the jewels of his empire, launched an advertising campaign for the mobile telephony company that contrasted with the measured style expected of Slim. A private letter the businessman sent on November 6, 2009, to ex-presidential candidate López Obrador reveals the mystery that this campaign represented to many, whose tagline was "Todo México es territorio Telcel" ("All of Mexico is Telcel territory"). In the missive, the magnate responds to a criticism made by López Obrador after visiting communities in Oaxaca where there is no Telcel reception.

The letter, written by hand by Slim, and made known in López Obrador's book *The Mafia That Took Over Mexico*, is as follows:

Dear Andrés Manuel:
After almost four years I would like to thank you for your greeting, send you warm greetings back, and make the following comments:

1. It is true that Telcel delivered for some time the advertising campaign that said "All of Mexico is Telcel territory" to communicate the vast coverage of its reception, superior to our competitors, although you will have noticed that this does not represent my way of thinking or being, which is why it was changed despite being so successful that it continues to have a high level of memorability even after several years.

2. For Telcel and Telmex it has been a responsibility and a commitment to offer high quality telecommunication services, the most technologically advanced available, and with nationwide reception. However, the pressure and limitations that the regulating authorities impose on us have set the brakes on our investments, reception, and video and satellite services, whose authorization is denied to us despite more than three years of agreement and convergence, not to mention the importance of satellites for reception in the most remote areas.

3. When our competitors provide services only to our high-income clients, those of middle and low income are not of interest to them and are served one hundred percent by Telmex, which makes our participation in the market high by number of clients, and not by income and results. That gives them the pretext to accuse us of being dominant companies, with which they discourage us from providing reception in areas not served by the competition to avoid asymmetrical regulations that give even more advantages to competitors who do not intervene and use our networks for free, putting at risk the financial stability of Telmex and placing us under permanent pressure of substantially reducing our operations.

Not very accustomed to using a moderate tone toward the Mexican oligarchy, in the missive revealed by López Obrador, Slim also reveals the existence of a relationship that seems contradictory.

"What's your opinion of López Obrador's way of doing politics?" I ask Slim.

"It's his style."

"But your opinion. You've met many politicians, many heads of state. López Obrador is a controversial figure that many people love and many people hate. It seems as though there is no intermediate point. What's your opinion on his way of doing politics? Do you like it or not?"

"I think the way of doing politics... well, that is not something I'd know how to judge. What I think would be good is for him to travel more, to better understand how things are done abroad. The mentality that's needed now to understand the world and the new civilization implies traveling and understanding what is being done in other places, and to see what technology is causing and how it is transforming the world, to be able to understand and be a good politician and a good governor. I think one cannot stay in the past, with ideas from the past, thinking they still apply. Look, there is a comment by a person who for many years has been very advanced when it comes to many things, Alvin Toeffler.

"Alvin Toeffler, in one of his books, states that if there is a country that has been stable and advanced in its constitution, it's the United States. There, the founding fathers, as they are called, drew from Europe and created the most advanced laws in all fields. Franklin and Jefferson were in Europe, but even with all that... there is a moment when we have to bring things up to date. I would say that those who identify as left wing, and especially those who still have a mentality that is not modern, that they do not understand technology and its implications, the unemployment it is causing, I believe that is very important for us all, and in that I include López Obrador in particular."

———

On one of the occasions I visited Slim in his office, a few minutes after sitting at the table where he likes to work, the magnate asked me to look again at his library, in case there was anything new that was not there in my previous visit.

"What do you imagine is inside that satchel there?" he said, pointing at a green bag resting in the middle of a row of books.

"Because of the kind of bag I think it could be a weapon, but I imagine maybe it contains books."

The billionaire asked his secretary to hand him the satchel. He unfolded it on the table and then opened it to pull out a leaflet, a kind of German diary and a notebook where there were several notes made by hand. It was one of the facsimiles of the journal that

Ernesto "Che" Guevara wrote in Bolivia before he was murdered. The copies were so perfect that they even reproduced the stains of colors and cigarette burns that are found in the original diaries of the iconic guerrilla fighter. Slim explained that Evo Morales, president of Bolivia, had had some copies made to be given as gifts to several heads of state around the world and somehow that gift had reached his library.

"When we started chatting, you asked me if I was left or right wing. Now I ask you the same thing."

"I don't believe in those things. I don't believe in political geometry," says Slim.

"And how do you think others categorize you?"

"I don't know or care... I think a good governor, whether right or left wing, will do the same things. I mean, in the past maybe there were differences, but now I don't know. I've said this to several left-wing politicians and other kinds. A good governor will do the same things. There are policies that are neither left nor right wing, they are a fortiori. If someone believes that because they are left wing they can just set the machinery in motion and implement populist policies, they are wrong. For anyone, whether they are right or left wing, unless they are some kind of fanatic... but I'm talking about people who are up to a point sensible. If they are good, what are they going to do? They'll try to ensure people have good nutrition, good health, good education, economic activity, investment, jobs. It's the same thing. They're going to look for the same things. Nobody finds poverty advantageous. Poverty is an issue not only of social justice and ethics. The fight against poverty is an economic necessity. Why is China growing? Because it's getting 20 or 30 million [people] out of poverty every year. What did Mexico do from '33 to '82? It took [the country] out of peasant, rural, on-farm consumption to the urban and industrial. It's a process. Tell me, what difference is there between sensible governors, whether they are left or right wing, in their actions?"

"Well, their priorities."

"Let's see, what priorities?"

"For example, left-wing politics is more focused on social welfare and right-wing politics is more concerned with the economy."

VIII

"You need both. You need to think like a head of state. If they think three years into the future, I agree; six, maybe. They try things and see how they're doing. By then they've already become a kind of populist. They look at the surveys to see if it's popular or not popular. Look, Marco Antonio, my son, wrote an interesting piece that I'm going to give you about the difference between the interpretation of public accounts and trade balance that maybe corrects a discussion from before that was very silly: that first we needed to create wealth and then distribute it, do you remember? And others said no. What we have to do is this: wealth should be administrated thoughtfully, creating more wealth, and the fruit of wealth, which is income, should have better distribution, and the best distribution is through the combination of salary, work and taxes, because fiscal payment entails an efficient and honest management."

"It's what Adam Smith says, that first you have to generate wealth and then it spreads everywhere."

"The issue is not spreading wealth. Yes, but the problem is not about wealth, it's income. If you are a worker... Let's imagine that you, or any other worker who earns a good living... How much do you think a good income could be: 30,000 pesos or 40,000 pesos a month?"

"Yes."

"Okay, then 30,000 or 40,000 pesos. Fine, the shares are given to Pemex and distributed to all Mexicans. What are they going to do with their shares of Pemex?"

"They should work, right?"

"No, they're going to sell them. When 4.4 percent of the shares of Telmex were distributed to Telmex workers, who are well paid, 80 percent of them sold, because you want to have a better house, a car, a better quality of life. Because you're interested in having a good income, work, job security, health security, a pension, education, et cetera. So what you need is the income. Now, what makes societies better is the kind of income they have, the purchasing power to acquire a home and goods without needing to save up the money first and then buy things; that is, access to credit, job security, and obviously a situation that can become better over time."

"So you don't see much difference between the left and right?"

"I don't see much difference in the thinking and ideology and discussion. In dialectics there may well be a difference, even in the way of life, a modest lifestyle and an extravagant lifestyle, but that does not mean being right or left wing. The left can also overspend."

"Looking at your personal circle of public relations, it may seem that you lean more toward the left than the right," I show him a leaflet of an event that Telmex hosts each year, where different public figures from around the world are invited.

"Because of Hillary Clinton?"

"Felipe González."

"But there's also Greenspan… What I would tell you is that I don't exclude people. Neither do my children."

"You're a pragmatist?"

"No, why a pragmatist? I'm diverse, plural. We have to accept others' thinking. For me, I don't know, I might discuss different forms of thinking, but I'm not going to get annoyed at someone who thinks differently than I do. I respect different opinions. What I am very clear about is that one of my responsibilities as a business-man—when you realize that you know how to administer resources and you can do things, beyond business—is having an awareness of social issues. But having social awareness does not mean you are left wing. There are people who are right wing and have social awareness."

28

Kafka

On January 1, 2006, thousands of members of the Zapatista National Liberation Army marched, masked by their balaclavas, through the streets of San Cristóbal de las Casas, Chiapas. They were bidding farewell to Subcomandante Marcos—now Delegado Cero—who was preparing to travel around the country as part of a tour called the Other Campaign. The campaign, inspired by the Sixth Declaration of the Lacandon Jungle, a document that sets out the anticapitalist agenda of the organization that took up arms against neoliberalism in 1994, was set up to provide another perspective during the presidential elections. Despite the fact that the Zapatistas had lost visibility in national politics, on that occasion the media were very interested in hearing the Zapatista leader speak in the main square of the Chiapas town.

The possibility a left-wing candidate winning the elections for the first time was more real than ever. Andrés Manuel López Obrador—candidate of the PRD, the PT (Work Party) and Convergencia (later called Movimiento Ciudadano)—was ahead in the polls, which is why the opinion of Subcomandante Marcos, the other major figure in the Mexican left, had become relevant. Although the position of the Other Campaign was to question all political parties, the press statements that stood out the most were those directed against the faction represented by López Obrador.

However, according to what Marcos said that day in San Cristóbal and at dozens of other events I attended, the goal of his tour around the country was not to torpedo López Obrador's campaign, as he was accused of doing by the electoral left:

The main addressee of the Sixth Declaration of the Lacandon Jungle did not acknowledge receipt until a few months after it was received. The enormous power of money in Mexico signed what can be known as the Counter–Sixth Declaration and that is publicly known as the Pact of Chapultepec, which was signed in that castle. Previously, the Mexican political class had been invited, assembled and paraded in all its ridiculous appearance at the Palacio de Bellas Artes. Now they are asking us to forget everything, our needs, our struggles, and put everything at their service so that they can decide for us, making the decisions there, in the castles and palaces of this country.

The Pact of Chapultepec was the name Slim gave to an initiative launched from the old castle of Chapultepec, where emperor Maximilian had lived during the ephemeral Second Mexican Empire. The proposal was immediately compared to the Pacts of La Moncloa in Spain, which allowed socialist Felipe González to become head of government and carry out economic reforms in a country that was still reeling from Franco's long dictatorship. Although the former Spanish president—a friend of Slim's—was not the ideologist behind the Pact of Chapultepec, as was speculated in certain political circles, he did advise the magnate, according to some participants in the initiative. The pact brought together most of the economic and political elite in the country. The Zapatistas defined these elites as their main adversaries. Subcomandante Marcos said:

What we are forgetting is that in this country—as in all places in which the system we are fighting is the dominant one—we are not all equal. There are people who grow ever richer and there are those who become increasingly poor. And poverty among the majority of the population is not the product of bad luck or fate, nor has it been willed by some distant god: it is a product of precisely that system. And the misery that we are suffering is what fattens the elite, such as Carlos Slim here in Mexico, who is the person who truly governs—alongside the North Americans—the destiny of this nation. It is the members of this elite, such as Carlos Slim, who have decided on the lines of action that any party elected into government will have to follow: the so-called "Pact of Chapultepec." This pact or plan of government consists in the following: what we are going to do—say the rich—is to finally conquer this country, to finally seize possession of it, to parcel it all out, including its people, and sell it to the highest bidder.

Regardless of the ideology behind the initiative of the richest Mexican in the world, some of those closest to Slim claim that in practical terms the Pact of Chapultepec was a way of supporting the campaign of López Obrador. Through these kind of public commitments he sought to guarantee "stability" and "prevent authoritarian temptations such as that of Hugo Chávez in Venezuela" in the winner of the elections—who, at that moment, all polls indicated would be López Obrador. "The Ingeniero is giving a certain coverage to López Obrador with businesspeople, but the candidate downplayed the pact," says one of the employees who carried out activities in several states and helped gather more than a million supporter signatures.

The battle-hardened leader of the Barzón movement, Alfonso Ramírez Cuéllar, known for having barged—on horseback—into the assembly hall at Congress during a protest, was another one of the men on the ground during this pact of Slim's, alongside the telephony union leader, Francisco Hernández Juárez. "The pact was not that awful," says Ramírez Cuéllar, although he admits it was difficult to persuade the other members of his party to fully support it. Porfirio Muñoz Ledo, one of the historical leaders of PRD, called it "the Slim Pact" and said that its supporters were already "Telcel territory."

Ramírez Cuéllar met Slim during the 1994 Mexican peso crisis, for which the Zedillo government created a bailout fund for the affected banks. Slim was wary of this strategy, perhaps in part because one of the main beneficiaries was Roberto Hernández, then owner of Banamex, who turned from friend to foe after losing the Telmex bid. "Whether he's left wing or not, I think Slim really valued Andrés Manuel López Obrador, and I know that Andrés even took his children to some of the meetings he had with Slim."

The then-presidential candidate of the electoral left, who had just been head of government for Mexico City, declined signing the Pact of Chapultepec, which some initially theorized to have been a platform to prepare for Slim's presidential campaign. According to politicians close to López Obrador, Slim offered to financially support the politician, but he rejected Slim's donations, offered through indirect schemes. The left-wing candidate already felt victorious, but everything changed after an important part of the electoral machinery of the PRI worked last minute in favor of the PAN candidate, Felipe Calderón.

When faced with the victory of his right-wing opponent, López Obrador claimed the elections had been rigged, said "the institutions can go to hell" and demanded a vote recount. He led an enormous protest and the occupation of Paseo de la Reforma, one of the main arteries of the country's capital. While this was happening, at a ceremony for *Forbes* magazine, Slim claimed that the protest was an act of "Mexican, Kafkian madness," which was the first and only criticism that the magnate made publicly against López Obrador. The same day, Slim acknowledged Felipe Calderón as the winning candidate.

Despite this, Calderón's team were cautious around Slim due to the close relationship he'd had with López Obrador before his "Kafkian madness" remark. According to one of Calderón's closest associates, their alarm bells rang when they found out that while the Federal Electoral Tribunal was analyzing the contestation submitted by López Obrador, Slim had organized a couple of private meetings with other businessmen and religious and political leaders, in which he spoke about the existing situation and the danger of losing the country's governability.

According to the source consulted, during the meeting there was even mention of a potential legal scenario in which the Federal Electoral Tribunal annulled the elections and the presidency would remain unstable. The name of Juan Ramón de la Fuente, doctor of psychiatry and former rector of the UNAM, was given as the possible interim president, and de la Fuente and attorney Diego Valadés laid out the legal scenario of the annulment to electoral magistrates such as José de Jesús Orozco. The source, an associate of former president Calderón, said:

From the Law Research Institute at UNAM itself, they provided an assessor to each magistrate of the Federal Electoral Tribunal, trying to influence the final assessment of the elections. Around those days, Cardinal Norberto Rivera called businessman Olegario Vázquez Raña to ask him about a meeting that Slim was organizing. Olegario told him he would not attend because they might give the impression of trying to organize a coup. The Cardinal, following Olegario's lead, decided not to go either. In those days, Juan Ramón de la Fuente was spending 200,000 pesos a month at a corporate image office. That was in connection to a strategy that was underway to make him interim president in 2006. The one who put a stop to it from Spain was Dr. Jorge Carpizo, head of the Law Research team at UNAM.

In an interview, Diego Valadés denied this and referenced an academic essay written before the 2006 elections, in which he looks at the Mexican problem of the lack of legal clarity on the process of substitution of a president in extraordinary circumstances. The article begins thus:

> Democracy in Mexico includes numerous problems that are yet to be solved, several of them similar to those that have been resolved in other constitutional systems. One of them is essential for institutional stability: the substitution of head of State in extraordinary circumstances. Electoral instruments are in place to secure presidential succession through periodic, free, secret and effective vote. But exceptional circumstances should also be considered to avoid constitutional collapse when the absence of a head of State comes about before the normal conclusion of his term.

Juan Ramón de la Fuente was also contacted, but he decided not to comment.

To make matters more complex, Calderón's campaign committee claims that the government of the state of Mexico—which, at the time, was Enrique Peña Nieto's—was spying on the electoral magistrates while they prepared their deliberation. According to this associate of Calderón, although the Fox administration had evidence, they never used it. They decided instead to engage in negotiations with the PRI when Calderón was about to take up office. "We also had suspicions, which were never confirmed, that Slim did the same through his nephew Héctor Slim Seade, director of Telmex," explains the Calderón associate, who says that this direct relative of Slim wooed prominent PAN members, such as legislator César Nava and spokesperson Alejandra Sota, by inviting them on hunting trips to Tamaulipas and Estado de México soon after the post-election crisis.

The Tribunal finally ratified the triumph of Felipe Calderón and he was sworn into office on December 1, 2006, in the midst of chaos. However, President Calderón was afraid that López Obrador's protests would continue, as would corporate lobbying, preventing the start of his administration, so to strengthen his mandate he decided to increase the budget of the Army and the Navy, as well as giving them additional powers. One month later, he dressed in military attire and was photographed in front of 4,500 soldiers at a military base. That was the backdrop of what was later known as the War on Drugs, which has thus far produced more than 150,000 violent deaths and thousands of disappeared people.

Slim's maneuvers in 2006 affected his relationship with Calderón's government. Although the president never broke off contact, he didn't trust Slim, either. From his point of view, Slim had tried to give him "a technical blow adhering to the law," although in plain terms some of Calderón supporters also called what had happened an attempt at a coup to prevent the PAN candidate from taking up office.

Ignacio Cobo, Slim's friend, tried to ease the relationship between the two men, without ever fully succeeding, although Slim did not stop attending the public events he was invited to by the president nor he to those which Slim invited him. The magnate did not make any public criticisms against Calderón, though in private he often spoke in harsh terms. Those close to Calderón say that the relationship with Slim, paradoxically, improved after the Calderón left the presidency.

According to Purificación Carpinteyro, Calderón was on the offensive against Slim during his administration:

Felipe Calderón marked him in his list of adversaries, adopting as a crusade a direct battle against Telmex and Telcel. From early on in his government he created an informal group to discuss what should be demanded from Telmex to allow it to compete in paid television. The initial negotiations by the group of the president's advisers, including the Minister of Communications and Transport, Luis Téllez Kuenzler, who had designated as undersecretary Rafael del Villar, adopted as their own the list of conditions for the National Chamber of the Cable Telecommunications Industry provided the authorities as prerequisites to be met by Telefónica, before even considering the possibility of eliminating the prohibition from his concession title to offer paid television services.

Slim did not lose the presidential elections in 2006, as some of his critics say. The following year, in 2007, *Forbes* magazine named him for the first time the richest man in the world.

When I ask him about the supposed coup he attempted during the elections in 2006, Slim responds: "The competition was the most open of them all. All the candidates had television broadcasts, everyone participated. Now, it is true that there were groups who wanted to cancel the elections, but they were people close to López Obrador. Not me: that thing with [the coup] is foolish."

Minutes after ruling out his participation in the alleged coup attempt, Carlos Slim alludes to the history of the country to explain that, when Mexicans have become divided, they have lost national territory and time for development. He referenced "Mexico in a pine nut," a speech delivered by historian José Iturriaga on August 27, 1988, which focused on the presidential successions throughout Mexico's history.

The magnate reads me a fragment in relation to Mexico, after its Independence in the nineteenth century: "'There are amnesiacs or uninformed people who do not remember or do not know that in two bloody periods in our history that add up to fifty-five years (from 1821 to 1876) we Mexicans experienced a civil war, during which time our national territory was mutilated four times, we were attacked seven times by foreign powers, we registered ninety-five changes in head of the Executive Power, and we had ten different constitutions or fundamental laws'... Do you think I'm interested in the country being in that kind of situation?"

At the end of the interview, Slim gave me a copy of Iturriaga's speech. Later I noted that throughout the twenty-two pages, there were a series of notes and sentences underlined in black ink. Some of the things Slim marked when reading this historical essay include the following fragments. The emphases are Slim's:

When we consummated our independence from monarchical institutions in 1821, untrained as we were in the exercise of self-government, considering that Spain was not an excellent teacher in the field of political science and the art of governing, we did not perceive with *clarity* the *model of the country we wanted to build*, as it is said now. And that is why we *jumped from one constitution to another in lucid or short-sighted search of freedom and justice, of national sovereignty and inner peace.* An *egregious* minority—of course—did see that model with clarity. I shall not stop to describe the comings and goings of the nine constitutions or the fundamental laws referred to that appeared in the first phase analyzed.

The fourth war we had with a foreign superpower *was initiated in May 1846* by the United States, at the time governed by the *democrat James Polk*. He claimed that the Mexican army had invaded Texas, supposed North American territory, because *in December 1845 its annexation to* the United States *had been approved* by the Senate of that country. But that was without our Congress confirming or approving the handover of Texas, signed in a cowardly act by Santa Anna nine years earlier.

Weak and anaemic as we were in the face of the endless war among brothers, we were not able to resist the attack from an army as well trained as that of North America. *We were defeated by the United States and gave them in February 1848 more than half of our territory,* because of the threat that if we did not deliver such a gigantic extension *it was possible we might lose the whole of Mexico. ¡?*

A prudent patriotism guided president Peña y Peña and, especially our Congress—in the midst of explosive opposition—to preserve our national sovereignty even if it was in the middle of our sea.

The French invasion lasted five years: from early 1862 to mid-1867. Bloody and cruel encounters and wars of French-Mexican guerrillas took place on our soil until the courage of the *liberal troops, together with the diplomatic aid provided by presidents Lincoln and Andrew Johnson to Juárez, allowed us to win our second national independence.* And although our motherland did not lose at the time a single inch of soil, with that triumph the patrician *decided to re-establish the republican institutions in July in 1867.*

When one looks into that tumultuous period in our nineteenth century, one notices with embarrassment up to what point Mexico's survival appears miraculous. That's why it constitutes our moral and political duty to preserve the unity of Mexicans; only that way will we protect and preserve the sovereignty of the motherland inherited by our elders.

Porfirio Díaz opened the doors to foreign investment to cover the costly construction of railroads that would cross our territory, which was badly connected due to the numerous mountainous regions in our geography. *The railroads were drawn out* based on English and North American interests *linked to the extraction of mining wealth,* exploited by both capitals.

Had there been no victorious revolution, *the vitality of Porfirio Díaz*—despite his aches and pains—would have allowed him to complete not only his *tenth presidential term in 1916,* but, perhaps, he would have also *concluded another one in 1922,* considering he *lived in exile four years more.* That, without speaking French, and especially, with his nostalgia for the absolute power *he wielded for 30 years.* Yes, there is no question that Porfirio Díaz would have completed at least one more six-year term, accustomed as he was to governing *almost without speaking,* or with *silent fierceness,* or with a *pretend cough,* or with *a blink of an eye.* Surrounded during three decades by the unquestioning obedience of his associates, he should have had vital reserves for survival after his defeat four years later, not in his homeland, but *in a foreign nation,* until his death in Paris on July 9, 1915.

For the first time since we have become an independent nation, that is, since 1821, three heads of State have delivered in peace the power to their respective successor. Portes Gil to Ortiz Rubio and he to Abelardo Rodríguez—the three of them together governed for six years only—while eleven heads of state have completed their respective six-year terms: Cárdenas and Ávila Camacho, Alemán and Ruiz Cortines, López Mateos and Díaz Ordaz, Echeverría and López Portillo, De la Madrid and Salinas de Gortari [and added by Slim in the margins: "Zedillo and Fox"].

And Fox was followed by Calderón, after the tight election that he won by barely half a percentage point.

29

Virreyes

The initial symbol of the relationship between Carlos Slim and Andrés Manuel López Obrador was the historical center of Mexico City, which the businessman had had his eye on since 2000, aiming to invest in and boost the economy in the area. The left-wing leader was elected head of government that year, and together with then-president Vicente Fox, he named a commission of prominent figures including, in addition to Slim, the late pro-government journalist Jacobo Zabludovsky and writer Carlos Monsiváis. At that time, López Obrador's main enemy was former president Carlos Salinas de Gortari, who was operating on various fronts against his administration, claiming that national institutions could not rely on López Obrador. The relationship with Slim, together with his austerity policies, caused newspapers such as *El País* in Spain or the *Washington Post* to speak of López Obrador as the representative of a modern left.

However, this closeness between Slim and a left-wing governor such as López Obrador also raised questions from some critical reporters.

"You supported the formal accusation that triggered the investigation into the privatization of Telmex, during years when Salinas and Slim were almost synonymous. How did you overcome that?" the late journalist Antonio Jáquez asked López Obrador, who was then at the height of his popularity.

"The explanation has to do with my current responsibility. It's not the same to be leader of a political party as to be a head of government. I care a lot about the renovation of the historical center, and to achieve that objective I had to call people to help. This does not imply any illegality or weighty conscience."

What is known as the renovation of Mexico City's historical center could also be called the massive buyout of properties by Slim, with the commitment of a left-wing government to invest greater public resources in area infrastructure, as well as to evict groups of homeless people, indigenous people, street vendors, rag and bone men, improvised transport drivers and sex workers, who had been well established in those streets for decades. The evictions themselves would increase area property values. Ten years later, the properties Slim bought at low prices had skyrocketed.

Slim was very well acquainted with the historical center. His family owned shops there, and during his youth the magnate took his first financial baby steps in the area, when the stock exchange was located at 68 Urugual Street—in a building now occupied by Carso offices. Financial journalist Jesús Rangel remembers seeing Slim working for years as a stock broker and also, several times, playing dominoes at the Pico de Gallo barroom, which was between the streets of Venustiano Carranza and Bolívar. Among his regular opponents at dominoes were banker Roberto Hernández and his cousin, Alfredo Harp Helú, with whom he did business for years before distancing himself and, in the case of Hernández, even becoming enemies. According to Rangel, after the agreement with López Obrador, Slim went in person to sound out the purchase of properties in the historical center.

Among the hundred or so houses and buildings he purchased is the Virreyes, a hotel built in the 1960s where the best boxers in the country and other famous visitors used to stay, from world champion José Ángel Nápoles, *Mantequilla*, to Hollywood actor Rock Hudson. However, as social life declined in the historical center and moved to areas such as Zona Rosa and then to Condesa, the Virreyes hotel gradually transformed into a meeting point for furtive couples or patrons of cabarets and bars located in the surrounding areas. But Slim bought the Virreyes in 2003 and, after minimally refurbishing it, decided to turn it into a hostel for students or young people who had newly arrived in the city.

I was one of Slim's first tenants when the property was given a new lease on life. In 2003, after living abroad for nearly a year, I was sent to work in Mexico City in the newsroom of *Milenio*. I arrived in this city at age twenty-two, planning to stay only a few months. At the time my main project was to travel to Cuba to live there for three or four years and write about life under the Caribbean perestroika, or so I thought. I was inspired by Ryszard Kapuściński's *Imperium*, his great reportage about the Soviet transformation in the late twentieth century.

However, shortly after arriving in Mexico City I realized I would not be able to leave the city that easily. My home for one year was room 401 of Slim's hotel, located on Izazaga and Eje Central, two of the noisiest main streets in Mexico City. For someone searching for something that he hasn't the slightest inkling of what it might be, to walk around those streets, and especially to wander the historical center of their country's capital offered something hopeful and vital. History—with a capital H—and histories—in lower case—appeared everywhere; five senses constantly at work while facing the wealth of situations unfolding all around. The best part came later, though, when I started to look at the rest of the country from the vantage point of the capital. The perspective was blindingly bright. To an extent, the streets of Mexico City contain the distillation of that abstract and tremendously diverse entity we call Mexico. And that thing we call Mexico does not look the same when seen from the capital as it does from the northern municipality of San Nicolás de los Garza or from the southern San Cristóbal de las Casas. To a certain extent, by investing in the historical center of Mexico City, Slim had purchased a piece of the country's soul.

However, this aspect of his business has been considered by different people as philanthropy. Carmen Beatriz López Portillo, daughter of the former president and rector of a central city institution, the Universidad del Claustro de Sor Juana, awarded Slim the Sor Juana Inés de la Cruz medal for saving the historical center.

In the late summer of 2013, hundreds of teachers from Oaxaca began occupying the Zócalo in Mexico City for three weeks, protesting against an educational reform approved by Congress, which reduced their labor rights and opened the door to a possible immediate privatization of Mexico's mandatory, public and free education. Without ever mentioning Slim, the main investor in the area, civil servants and the media constantly highlighted the way in which the protest affected businesses in the center and insisted for that reason that the protesters should be forcibly evicted.

On September 13, several hundred federal police officers raided the protest site set up by teachers of Section 22 of the National Teachers' Union (SNTE). Nobody was seriously injured, but by 6:00 p.m., the authorities had destroyed the tarps and tents on the Zócalo and taken back control of the main square. Coincidence or not, that same day Slim announced his collaboration with the Khan Academy, a cutting-edge organization that promotes the education of children through online tutorials, without necessarily having in-person classes and teachers. In an interview given to Larry King, Slim claimed that this project represented the future:

> The Khan Academy has forty employees and in its network there are millions of people learning in short ten or fifteen-minute courses, and I understand that the number of exercises that have been completed through the Khan Academy is more than one billion—this with a staff only forty. The platform is growing, and I think it's a great way to go for massive education. And what are the numbers and concepts? First of all, the Internet is becoming very fast with broadband, in which you can have streaming and video nearly instantly. That's important. First to have connectivity; that's one of the parts of the equation, to provide connectivity, and the other part of the equation that is more important maybe, or as important as connectivity, is to provide content and applications. And to provide the courses or the training, to meet people through the network, to be educated without any cost. It's free education. The Khan Academy is free education for everyone, everywhere, every time. That is the future. The past, that's today.

Following this logic, teachers such as those from Oaxaca would represent the past.

Slim worked with López Obrador for economic reasons that had to do with the historical center, says Fructuoso Pérez.

"I'm sorry, I don't want to talk much about that, because I don't know if they liked each other or not. They must have had commercial relationships in the sense that Carlos was very concerned with the restructuring and renovation of Mexico City's historical center. Then, López Obrador being the city's head of government at the time, he had to negotiate all these kinds of things with Slim and that can be interpreted in different ways. Some might say he was a very good friend and others might say he wasn't. He says he supported López Obrador; others say he didn't. But it was true that Carlos got very involved in the renovation of the historical center. If it weren't for him, well, him and maybe other people, and another group, a group that he formed, the area would not have recovered."

"Why was the historical center be so important to Slim?"

"Oh well, because he lived there. He went to high school there. He lived... the businesses that his parents owned and everything. He's someone who loves the historical center."

"Is Slim a nationalist?"

"Totally. He is very much a nationalist. I don't doubt that at some point, given the situation of the businesses he owns, well, he has international relationships, but to what extent I don't know. Most of his investments are here in Mexico. So that speaks volumes of what he wants for Mexico and how he thinks things should be."

"And why do you think he is such a nationalist?"

"His father, despite coming from another country, was a person who loved Mexico very much, because it was the place that welcomed him and gave him shelter. And I think he instilled that love in his children. Another time he told us something about his father giving a speech in the Chamber of Deputies as president of a traders' association or something like that, where he showed how much he cared about Mexico. He taught that to his children and Carlos learned it."

In his belief in the future, Slim took advantage of the abandonment and deterioration of another area of Mexico City. Near Polanco, in a run-down area where there used to be a tire warehouse, he built an enormous development called Nuevo Polanco that includes luxury apartments, the Carso shopping center, and an aquarium—as a whole the place is known colloquially as "Slim City." As Slim says himself, he adopted the model for Mexico City's historical center for this project.

An icon of this new development is the Museo Soumaya, designed by Slim's son-in-law, architect Fernando Romero, the same man in charge of designing a new airport for Mexico City. The museum houses Slim's private collection of over 66,000 works of art, which includes pieces by Auguste Rodin, Salvador Dalí and Tintoretto. Before 2011, when the Carso shopping center was inaugurated, one part of this collection was exhibited in the museum of the same name at Plaza Loreto, on the other side of the city, in an area where the conquistador Hernán Cortés had settled.

However, most of the main art critics in the country were underwhelmed by the inauguration of Slim City's flagship museum. The consensus among many of the experts consulted seems to be that the owner of Telmex made an impulsive selection of the work based on economic rather than aesthetic criteria. Avelina Lesper, one of the most respected specialists, published an article entitled: "What is money for, Mr. Slim?" in *Milenio's* cultural supplement, *Laberinto*.

The building is pretentious and the exterior promises something that is not delivered within; we are put inside a concrete cylinder with badly designed ramps, with unfinished surfaces, a minute reception area and exhibition rooms with no organization or flow. There is no museuography, it's an assembly of things as if we were in someone's house—with their peculiar decorative tastes—someone who's taken poor advice from those antiquarians who filled up the Gallery of the National Palace. A panel by Il Sodoma, a José de Rivera, a Siqueiros mural, a drawing by O'Gorman and Rodin's bronze sculptures is all the museum offers; the rest is decoration. Works of very, very dubious originality and mismatched objects of no historical value. What hurts most is seeing that here there is neither a collection, nor a love for art.

Museo Soumaya was inaugurated by Slim himself. Guests at the ceremony included Larry King, Gabriel García Márquez and President

VIII

Calderón, who gave a speech highlighting that there were few collections that grouped together so many schools of art and "few venues that show works by the great maestros of Mexico alongside those from around the globe. I invite all Mexicans to come and take pleasure in this unprecedented collection." King, meanwhile, spoke of the "brilliant piece of architecture" that the cultural space represented.

In late 2013, in the days prior to receiving a homage, Raquel Tibol, the most respected art critic in Mexico, commented that the magnate phoned her after a conversation held on Carmen Aristegui's radio show. Slim sent a chauffeur in an old, dented Tsuru to collect the ninety-year-old specialist to take her to the headquarters of Inbursa, where, according to Tibol, she met with Slim and Alfonso Miranda, director of Museo Soumaya, who did not speak during the meeting.

Tibol said that the conversation was cordial and they shared tales of the art world, in addition to her criticisms of the space, which she reiterated. When Aristegui asked Tibol if Slim had taken her comments into account, the critic replied: "I have not visited [Museo Soumaya] since, but I think that in that aspect [Slim] is a stubborn man. He believes that if he arrives to a certain conclusion, he is right and he moves on. I don't think he even listens to anyone around him." For Slim, both the historical center and the Nuevo Polanco projects represent his personal interest in the urban regeneration of Mexico City.

"I think the best proof of how this model works is the historical center," he says to me. "These are projects to transform run-down areas into areas of intense economic activity, where people live nearby, work nearby, do their leisure activities nearby, go to school nearby, have hospitals nearby, et cetera.

"That way, when they leave their own neighborhood it's because they are exploring another place for leisure. So there are various run-down areas in the city where people could live, instead of having to commute for an hour and a half. Because commuting is costly, it reduces people's quality of life and it also generates transportation problems. Regenerating an area also creates a lot of employment. For example, there in Plaza Carso—in Nuevo Polanco—I believe there are 15,000 employees where previously there were only 400. Fifteen thousand people so far. And there will be more, as it develops, but it's not just Plaza Carso, there are lots of developments elsewhere. In the historical center, the Doctores district needs to be regenerated. That's where Mexico City's hospitals, courts and Attorney-General's office are. You see, if that run-down area was regenerated, if it went up, if it became more vertical and less horizontal, the nurses would not need to live an hour away, nor would the doctors or medical students or the secretaries or the judges or the lawyers. Then the idea is for these to be more like self-contained cities or neighborhoods, whatever you want to call them, but neighborhoods where all social classes can live, not just one."

"But the tragedy of this model is that people are being displaced."

"No, it's the other way around. Not in the historical center. It's the other way around. In the historical center there's an area that the government of the Mexico City expropriated and it is currently in limbo; that will hopefully be redeveloped as social housing. In the historical center, previously, 100 years ago, there were people living in mansions alongside people of very low income. There were some very working-class areas and some very affluent areas, and everything in between. What is lacking at Plaza Carso is more mid-income housing so that all the staff that works there can live there too."

"How will you do that in Nuevo Polanco? Because it's already very expensive to live there."

"Originally, the plan was to build mid-income housing in the Pensil district. Pensil is walking distance and is a degraded area that needs planning. Of course, there we need the authorities to create the housing schemes and the high-rises."

"Well, I imagine you need to use your political influence to be able to carry out those projects, because otherwise the plans may be abandoned."

"No, it's not political influence, because I'm not going to do everything myself."

"But what if the politicians don't do their part?"

"There, first of all, it's not the politicians: it's the governments. The government needs to create a plan of economic activity, city regeneration, urban infrastructure and facilities, and to develop a program for these areas. Not just a program, but regulations, to stimulate and develop the area and bring private money in to see it through. That's the good part: all of this can be done with private money. And we are talking about the Doctores district, Irrigación, but also Tlalnepantla, Naucalpan, Vallejo, Azcapotzalco, and more areas in the south. That's what needs to be done.

"And that is what brings in much more economic activity for this new society. What happens when there is that kind of investment? People have more jobs. And then, as activities develop, whether it's training or culture or education or health, there's more economic activity, and of course, construction, both temporary and permanent. That is a path. We're talking about real estate. The other part is infrastructure. Our country needs a lot of infrastructure, and we need to create it, but it cannot be done with public money, because there's not enough or it's being used mainly for matters of health or education. So we need to use private money. Private investment, with public-private partnerships."

"So, privatizing highways, airports...?"

"Look, one of the first public-private partnerships we created was there, in the historical center. It was the Ministry of Foreign Affairs. We did the construction, the association, and then it was auctioned and BBV won, and the Ministry of Foreign Affairs pays BBV a monthly fee, and after so many years it stops paying the monthly installments. We need to take advantage of all this now that money is very cheap, at negative cost due to inflation and in the long term. We need to take advantage of that situation. This can accelerate the process a great deal. And, in addition, private investment can be effective. I'm not talking about businesspeople, companies or large investors. It can be the workers themselves through their *Afores* [pension funds], which, instead of having 3 percent profit margins, can have yields of 10 or 12 percent, allowing them to have a better pension when they decide to retire."

"I would like to understand your logic around investing by looking at a particular case: why did you buy the Virreyes hotel?"

"When we entered the historical center, we got involved to improve the area, but there was a lot of skepticism. Some very prominent people said: 'This ain't gonna work.' Even at the first press conference, when the advisory board was introduced, some very esteemed people came with me and said: 'I want to see what you'll say.' The proposal was very straightforward: we wanted to revitalize the area. Then we got into the program to raise the socioeconomic level, the school networks. We created all the comprehensive programs at the foundations, the Cirugías Extramuros [providing surgery for low-income people with no access to medical care], Leer para aprender [education programs]... bam, bam—we did all of that. We had projects doing this thing here, and that thing there, and in that area, which was the famous cultural corridor that we were going to take all the way to Universidad del Claustro de Sor Juana; we created a real estate company to buy foreclosed properties and make use of them. So we gave them great property mobility, and they said that I was going to keep the historical center. And it's true that we bought a lot and then the properties were sold for this purpose and the other. So the group has 8,000 staff or more working in the historical center. Some were already there, at Central San Juan and elsewhere, but we took many of them to call centers, to Bancomer, and the stock exchange. And these hotels were being sold and we bought them to create the hostels program. I believe the rate was 120 pesos per night including breakfast. That was the objective. I was familiar with the place from many years ago. We bought it along with the Señorial hotel. These hotels, back in the day, were where young people went, and to inject life into a historical center you need there to be young people. We weren't able to keep going with the Vizcaínas theater. There's a theater there owned by Mexico City. So we wanted it to have more activity. There was a part of the Vizcaínas that had been demolished and we wanted there to be shopping malls and for it to be used for commercial as well as cultural activities, but we were no longer able to move forward."

"Was this whole project your idea or was it an existing project you got involved with?"

"It's an old idea that we came up with many years ago, with Guillermo Tovar and Teresa and also with Don Pepe Iturriaga. The initial concept for the protect and for the conservation of the historical center was Pepe Iturriaga's, and then Guillermo was one of the great defenders with his book *La ciudad de los palacios* (*The City of Mansions*). A writer friend of mine approached López Obrador when he was elected governor of Mexico City and invited me to invest in Avenida Reforma. And I said: "Not in Reforma; if you want me to invest, I'll invest in the historical center, and only if President Fox agrees." Then, when the president agreed and they spoke and began negotiations, we got the ball rolling. The project had support from everyone and we created an advisory board and a general board. The advisory board had three local government civil servants and three from the federal government, and four individuals from civil society, who were Guillermo Tovar, Jacobo Zabludovsky, the Cardinal and myself, but I designed the program."

"Is that where you met López Obrador?"

"I don't know if that's the first time I saw him."

"And did you become friends?"

"Well, we had some kind of issue with the project. In the first meeting (he didn't go to the meetings; he proposed the project and supported it and it was an important project for his government and for the federal government) they proposed holding a referendum on the projects, and I don't know, I said to them: "OK, you know what? You go ahead and do that and I'll do my thing." And also once the head of government proposed something and I said to him: "Hey, you go ahead and do that and I'll do my own thing, but the historical center will be a success."

"But, did you become friends?"

"Friends in what sense?"

IX

30

1 Percent

Carlos Slim does not always have a driver. Sometimes he drives his Mercedes Benz himself through the infuriating traffic of Mexico City. Many of his closest friends find him as normal as the next person. Alfonso Ramírez Cuéllar, a respected peasant leader who defends bank debtors, says that sometimes Slim invites him to talk about the economy and that he's a friendly, unassuming guy: "Slim is a dude who almost always walks around in socks in his office. In a suit and no shoes. Because of things like that, I like him," he says. "He does all his math by hand and sometimes uses a calculator."

Slim can be a fascinating character because he has so much money but doesn't show it off. When he travels outside Mexico, he stays at hotels or friends' houses, because he decided not to buy any mansions abroad for his own personal use. He's proud of the fact that he has lived in the same house for thirty years, and his PR team likes to publicize the fact that the clothes Slim wears come from any of his Sears stores and not the sophisticated Saks.

When he founded Inbursa he decided not to register it with the Mexican Banks Association because he thought the membership fee of $500,000, which included the use of facilities at an exclusive sports club, was too expensive. Intellectuals and influential journalists who have been invited to lunch at his offices in Lomas de Chapultepec say the food is sometimes brought in from the nearest Sanborns. All I saw was the distinctive blue and white Sanborns dinnerware hiding among some of his papers.

At important events, Slim tends to behave unpretentiously: he often chooses Diet Coke over red wine, and at public events I've spotted him munching on cracker nuts. He is an ex-smoker, although from time to time, on special occasions, he lights one of the cigars given to him by Fidel Castro.

Luis Maira met Slim when Maira was the Chilean ambassador in Mexico. When he tried to explain who Slim was, the Chilean sociologist defined the businessman as a child of the Mexican Revolution, which did away with the old aristocracy and allowed the emergence of the nouveau riche with no lineage. After meeting and talking in private with Slim, Maira made the observation that the magnate "speaks as though he were not rich."

His main home is in the Lomas de Chapultepec area and only has six bedrooms. Although there are paintings on the wall by El Greco, Pizarro, Monet and Renoir, the furniture looks like it hasn't been replaced since the 1980s, when Slim and Soumaya moved in. In an unusual decision, in 2007 the multimillionaire opened the doors of his home to be filmed by María Celeste Arrarás, host of a Telemundo show whose title is a faithful description of its content: *Al rojo vivo* (*Red Hot*). During the tour, Slim explained that he and his wife chose a house like this one because another larger place would have prevented greater family interaction. He said that his three daughters slept in one room and his three sons in another.

That tour through Slim's favorite mansion ended with a playful dialogue between him and the TV host:

"Your wife died eight years ago. I know it was painful. Have you thought about starting a new life? About marrying again?"

"Starting a new life? Well, you start that from..."

"Romantically."

"Getting married? No."

"Not getting married."

"I mean, starting another family, no."

"But going out and enjoying the opposite sex?"

"Of course. What do I look like? Why do you ask that?"

"Because these things must be asked. How do you meet your potential candidates?"

"I meet them..."

"There are ways, I imagine…"

"By asking."

Laughter.

"Asking…"

"It's not true, I'm joking."

"And when you go out with them, what do you do?"

"Hmm… Next question?"

"Next question? Okay. But you don't want to remarry for now?"

"There are too many children… No, I'm joking," Slim laughs.

"Well, it's just that I imagine the richest man in the world must have many candidates trying to snap him up, so to speak. When you go out with a woman, how do you distinguish between the one who wants you because of who you are and the one who is looking for something else, looking for money?"

"The same way you do."

"Yes. You can just tell."

"Well, more or less."

Money and success are a magnet for wheedlers and backslappers. Slim says he knows how to steer clear of that kind of greed, and that it's part of the human condition.

"A beautiful woman, or a sports player, or a rock star gets chased more than anyone," he says in the interview he gave me.

"How do you feel when you have to deal with that aspect of the human condition?" I ask.

"The truth is that there are lots of people and I am right next to them, on the street or wherever, and they are very friendly toward me. I would say that fortunately people are nice to me. They want to take a picture or something, and fine, you take it. On the street I don't get business proposals."

"How many business proposals do you get per day or week?"

"Well, I get lots of letters, but I don't read them."

"And at the other end there's fierce criticism."

"Sometimes it's the same people: they flatter you on the one side and criticize you on the other. Like some of the blokes you've interviewed, who've told you things…"

"But how do you handle fierce criticism internally?"

"It's written down, in the letter I wrote to young people."

Slim looks for it in his desk, finds the paragraph and starts reading to me:

"When you give, don't expect to receive anything back, because 'a bit of fragrance clings to the hand that gives flowers.' That's a Chinese proverb. And this is very important: do not allow negative feelings to dominate your mood. Emotional damage does not come from other people, it comes from within. It's as simple as that. When they're attacking you with negative things, you must not take them on board, you have to see your life from a positive point of view always; otherwise, you're screwed. And as my dad used to say: 'Firm and patient optimism.' That's in the group's principles."

"Do you have to be ambitious to be successful?"

"I don't know what you mean by ambitious. I already said that being successful does not mean having money. Success is more than that. Let's say: to prosper professionally, to work, more than ambition you need to have a defined vocation, to clearly define your path, what you want to do, and to make an effort to achieve it. So, it's a matter of work, talent, vocation, and your team, because in the end, if you don't have a team, you cannot do things properly. A good team that's on the same page and has the same objectives as you do. In other words, more than being ambitious, you need to create leadership. You need to be a leader who can organize people and you need to be able to make things happen. I think that's the difference between a businessman and a dreamer, a planner and even a politician. The businessman, to prosper, to develop what he's doing, needs to have a good team and make things happen. So if you're going to develop a program in such and such a situation, make sure it doesn't just stay on paper: it has to happen quickly and flexibly."

"You say it's a matter of vocation. You, for example, studied engineering, but your vocation is the world of business."

"But I've been doing business from the age of twelve!"

"The fact you don't have houses abroad is often commented on, why?" I ask.

"I don't have a house abroad, not for reasons of austerity... Well, we have real estate investments abroad."

"I know the mansion you own opposite the Met in New York."

"Well, people say that's my house and God knows what else, but we bought that one to sell it. Why would I want to live in a seven-story house!"

"And why not?"

"It's not that I'm overly interested in *not* having a house. What's more, we *should* have one, but when I travel I stay in a hotel: that's really just to be practical."

"What hotel do you stay in when you go to New York? At the Plaza?"

"I've been to several. Maybe the one I've been to the most is the New York Palace, because when I go to some offices that's the one within walking distance. I've been to several. I don't have one I always have to stay at."

"Why is that house opposite the Met abandoned?"

"We're selling it. The plan has always been to sell it. It's a nice location."

"Could you tell me about what you spend the money on that is directly to do with you? Tell me an eccentricity you have regarding money. It seems incredible that one of the richest men in the world does not have an eccentricity with their money..."

"An eccentricity? What's an eccentricity?"

"I don't know, something frivolous you spend money on, something you maybe regret buying. An extravagance."

"Oh, something I bought and regret? An extravagance... well, a car. My car. Then, from time to time, they last me ten years."

"But they are old cars..."

"But one day I'll replace them. I don't know. Something that I regret?"

"Yes, something frivolous."

"No, nothing."

"A yacht? A very big plane?"

"Oh, well, I bought those. We have those and that's it."

———

"The rich will always accumulate capital and income faster than the poor," says essayist John Lanchester. "It's a law as basic as that of gravity." In the logic of neoliberalism, this is not a problem because the economic growth of one person will supposedly contribute to that of the rest, even though as time goes on inequality will necessarily increase. But as Lanchester points out, "the increase in inequality isn't just some nasty accidental side-effect of neoliberalism, it's the motor driving the whole economic process."

According to Jacques Rogozinski, one of the key aspects that has been under-analyzed is the fact that Slim's rapid accumulation of capital—going from being a billionaire to one of the world's top 1 percenters—was more connected to a bankruptcy trial in the United States than to the existence of a monopoly in telecommunications. With his forthright style, Rogozinski describes the route of growth of Slim's fortune, which in 1991, according to *Forbes*, was $1.7 billion.

"Let's imagine for a second that this $1.7 billion is just Telmex and that Slim does not own Sanborns, the mining companies, the paper factories, nothing. Then let's do the following analysis: from 1991 to 2003, Slim's fortune increased from $1.7 to $7.4 billion. I said to my team: 'Calculate the return rate, over eleven years from 1.7 to 7.4, and it's thirteen. That means his fortune increased by 13 percent each year. But then I looked again and said: 'OK, just out of curiosity, let's imagine he has $1.7 million and he decides to move to Australia and he takes his $1.7 million and puts it in the Standard & Poor's' index.' Then I told my team: 'Look at what the Standard & Poor's rate in the United States was in '91 and tell me as well what it was in 2003 and do the same analysis. How much would he have had in 2003?' Well, turns out that instead of $7.4 billion he would have had $6.7 billion, and that's not such a massive difference, is it? This other guy went to sleep, went to hang out on the beach in Australia, and his fortune, on its own, was multiplied in Standard & Poor's. What happened, then, between 1990 and 2003? Telmex wasn't the reason Slim had those levels of earnings. In 2003, two bankruptcy judges in the United States assigned to Slim all the assets of two American companies that had gone bankrupt in Latin America. One was AT&T and the other was called MCI. Then Slim kept all their assets. The great Mexican monopolist keeps all the assets because they say he doesn't know how to compete! Well then, I still don't understand how it's possible: AT&T went bankrupt in Mexico the first time, but then don't come and tell me that it was Slim's monopoly that didn't allow it to grow, because if that was true, how did AT&T go bankrupt in the rest of Latin America? I mean, you've already convinced me that they couldn't grow AT&T or MCI or any other because of Slim, but why did they go bankrupt in other places where there *is* competition? Because they were a bunch of dudes who didn't know how to handle their investments in Latin America. These two American companies who came to Mexico couldn't handle Brazil, Chile, Argentina or Colombia either, and Slim enters a contest and keeps all the assets of these two companies, and that's how he gives a boost to América Móvil in Latin America and his fortune grows that much."

———

In 2011 I lived in New York. During my stay, a friend from Mexico City came to visit me and before taking him to see the Statue of Liberty or walk over the Brooklyn Bridge, I took him to see places in Manhattan that bear the Slim brand. We walked along Park Avenue to 38th Street, where we caught a whiff of marijuana, which, it must be said, is one of the typical aromas in the city's streets. From there we went to the 5th Avenue. At the crossing with 38th Street we started the Slimtour with an eleven-story building at whose main entrance there are two faded American flags. The building is nothing special. It is pretty anti-climactic for any admirer of extravagance to see that Slim's first purchase in the Big Apple is such a boring building. On the other hand, the doorman is one of the most entertaining people to be found on the whole island, and he told us about Slim's regular visits to the place.

Slim bought the building for just a little over $200 million and although the only thing he's done with it since then is collect from the tenants the same rent that the previous owner used to charge, there is a fanciful rumor that the two empty shops in the main part of the building, which were empty when I visited, will be turned into a Sanborns. We saw up close the gray-pink facade of the empty commercial spaces and my friend assured me, with all certainty, that it would become true: they will open a Sanborns there. I craved their classic green enchiladas.

The following stop on the tour was building 141 on Broadway and 39th Street. According to sources from Venture Capital, the real estate company that advises Slim on his property purchases in the city, Slim is interested in the area, which, unlike the one described above, is rather hip. At all hours of the day, suited men stride across the streets alongside men clad in sportswear as if on their way to the gym—all wearing headphones, more of a "must" than any other accessory for that New York look.

Then we made our way to 8th avenue, between 40th and 41st streets, to see a shiny skyscraper: the new premises of the *New York Times*, with which Slim began his rapport in 2009, when he gave them a loan of $250 million. Over time, he bought shares in the newspaper until he owned 16.8 percent, making Slim in 2015 the largest individual shareholder of the company headed by Arthur Sulzberger. Soon after establishing a relationship with Slim, Sulzberger wrote this brief biography for a *Time* op-ed in 2009, when the magnate was declared one of the personalities of the year:

I recently had the great pleasure of meeting Carlos Slim. He had decided to invest in the New York Times Co. and thought it would be a good idea to get to know me and my senior colleagues. It was obvious from the moment we met that he was a true *Times* loyalist. We had an enjoyable conversation about what was happening in this country and everywhere else in the world. Carlos, a very shrewd businessman with an appreciation for great brands, showed a deep understanding of the role that news, information and education play in our interconnected global society.

What also became apparent is that for Carlos, insight and understanding are catalysts for action and accomplishment. This speaks to why Carlos has funded extensive public-health education programs and why he's helped thousands of students throughout Latin America get their own laptops and learn more about digital technology.

Carlos, 69, believes that as people know more, they have a far better opportunity to change and improve their lives. As he spoke at our meeting, he conveyed the quiet but fierce confidence that has enabled him to have a profound and lasting effect on millions of individuals in Mexico and neighboring countries. Carlos knows very well how much one person with courage, determination and vision can achieve. And I am delighted that he brings those attributes to the New York Times Co., to Mexico and to the world.

This closeness between Slim and the most important newspaper in the world has aroused suspicion. The *Wall Street Journal* questioned it in 2013: "Slim is a case study on how the dysfunctional system in Mexico impacts on the United States. In 2009, Slim dipped into his deep pockets and rescued an emblematic institution, the *New York Times*, with a loan of $250 million, which has already been paid. He also started to increase his shares. Now Slim and his family are the largest shareholders of the company, which is no doubt the most influential news organization in the United States. Does Slim have an influence in how the newspaper reports on his fortune? A spokesperson for the newspaper says emphatically no: 'The *New York Times* maintains the highest standards in journalistic ethics.'"

Although the *Wall Street Journal*'s criticism could be considered biased by some, it is not the only place where questions have been raised. Independent critic Paul Roderick Gregory, researcher at the Hoover Institution at Stanford, published a 2013 article on the scarce coverage of the *New York Times* about Slim. A professor of economics at the University of Houston, Gregory looks at the attempts of Peña Nieto's government to regulate the Mexican telecommunications market, dominated by Slim, as well as the absence of articles on the subject published by the New York newspaper. He also questions why an OECD report, in which the companies of the magnate are harshly criticized, was not disseminated. Gregory culminates his article by highlighting:

> The ultrarich of the world have learned that PR companies cannot offer the protection from public criticism and the contempt of politicians and press. Carlos Slim prospered through the combination of business vision and political connections to become the richest man in the world in a relatively poor country. He did this through the transfer of money from the poor and middle class to himself—a

feat that is not usually popular among the educated classes. Slim earned the respect and silence of the renowned newspaper with the purchase of merely $155 million in shares in the *New York Times*, which earned him the title from editor Sulzberger of a "a true *Times* loyalist."

George Soros, the most visible speculator in the world (who is not loved in educated circles) acquired immunity by giving more than $1.5 billion to the left and to progressive causes. Soros paid three times more than Carlos Slim.

At the highest level, Warren Buffett donated $30 billion to worthy charitable organizations in 2012 alone, and fully supported President Obama's redistribution campaign. Buffett companies can fight against the IRS with fury to lower taxes without the slightest risk of controversy or accusation.

Of the three, Carlos Slim has the better deal.

In 2009, when Slim and the *New York Times* began their relationship, the then-correspondent of the newspaper in Mexico, Marc Lacey, wrote an article mentioning this fact and speaking clearly about Slim's style:

Carlos Slim Helú was clearly annoyed. He had invited dozens of foreign correspondents to lunch one day last fall and, after many questions about business trends, one journalist pressed him on how it felt to be worth so much in a country in which many people struggle to get by.

Mr. Slim cut off the questioner and defended his stewardship of a vast business empire. His curt tone made clear that he did not favor that line of questioning.

Mr. Slim, Mexico's richest man and now a major shareholder in and lender to the *New York Times*, has a complex relationship with the news media. He invests money in an array of television and newspaper companies and says he sees a bright future for those media companies that adapt.

But when the news media focus their spotlight on him, he sometimes gives the impression that he wants to be left alone to make more money in peace.

After Lacey's piece, though, Slim's critics in Mexico claim that the *New York Times* never again published another article questioning the magnate.

———

Our Slimtour in NYC looped back to 5th Avenue, but this time at the intersection with 54th Street, to see another of the buildings that Slim speculatively might buy at any moment. It's at number 693 and is currently a Forever 21 store. Although the premises are nothing too stunning, it's the most original construction in the area. Perhaps something a bit too extravagant for someone as sober as Slim.

A few meters ahead is the famous Hotel Plaza, which is our fifth stop on the Slimtour, because there, in the Great Hall, on the night of June 9, 2004, the richest Mexican in the world publicly praised Marcial Maciel, founder of the Legionaries of Christ. The tour ends on 5th Avenue at 82nd Street, opposite the Metropolitan Museum of New York, at Slim's most famous New York property. None of the seven bedrooms or the twenty-five reception rooms distributed over seven stories in the 1901 mansion are inhabited, but a sign informs us that if there is any emergency, Andrew Schuman can be contacted at 212 529 7415, or by email. If you are lucky, as we were, opposite the magnate's house in Manhattan you might find a noisy truck where you can buy diet yogurt at a very reasonable price. Slim bought the property for $40 million from a real estate agent called Tamir Sapir. In 2015, the Mexican magnate managed to sell it at double the price: his buyer paid $80 million.

In the end we didn't even set foot in Saks, because we wouldn't even have been able to afford a handkerchief.

The iconic 5th Avenue store was visited by other Mexicans in August 2012, although they were there to protest rather than shop. They were the members of an organization called Dos Países, Una Nación (Two Countries, One Nation), which accused Slim of monopolistic practices and a lack of philanthropic support of the Latino community in the United States. This group's protests grew over time and on May 9 of the following year, while Slim was giving a speech at the New York Public Library with Salma Khan, creator of the online mass education model, the protestors succeeded in sabotaging the event: peals of laughter from twenty of their members interrupted the speech. The situation seemed so absurd that even Slim had to laugh together with Khan and the moderator of the panel. As you can see in a YouTube video, one of the activists intervenes by saying: "I'll tell you what's funny: Carlos Slim's charity is laughable." On the way out, the protestors projected this phrase on the walls: "Monopolies are no laughing matter." Other protests also took place in California and Slim filed formal complaints through his subsidiaries. The magnate's PR team disseminated the version that businessman Ricardo Salinas Pliego, his rival in Mexico, was the brain behind those acts. However, the office of the owner of TV Azteca denied this in a statement.

Slim has not only faced protests in the United States. In the land of his ancestors, he was also interrupted while giving a speech about the new society of communication and technology in the main auditorium of the American University of Beirut, where a group of Lebanese sympathizers of the Zapatista National Liberation Army protested with placards that said: "For everyone everything, for us nothing," while at the same time they decried "capitalist terrorism." In that visit to the land of his father, Slim donated $50 million to boost the use of technology among young Lebanese people, as well as a plan to protect the work of poet Khalil Gibran.

"The Occupy Movement started out in New York against the 1 percent of people who hold the world's wealth, a percentage in which you are included. What's your opinion on this initiative and other similar ones, such as Yo Soy 132 in Mexico, Indignados in Spain and those other young global expressions of dissent?" I ask Slim.

"I think one of the problems we are seeing is that there is a lack of direction when driving change. The other main issue is that there are countries, let's call them 'societies,' that are still in a state of, how should I put it, backwardness, with an agricultural mentality, where the state has close ties with religious groups or religious groups have a tremendous influence over the state. They experience more problems for that reason, and one of the serious issues that is emerging in this new society is that technology has progressed so quickly and productivity has been advanced to such a degree that we are leaving many people behind without employment. So there's a rejection of the economic crisis and the lack of employment opportunities. That's why I've proposed they work twelve hour days, three days a week. Then you have to look for new solutions. For example, look at what López Obrador has said, that he'll go back to the Constitution of 1917... Well, I don't think we need to go back 100 years for a world that has seen massive transformations over [that time]. I think any politician who wants to be in government—unlike the politicians who just want to take part in the debate for the fun of it, forget about those—the politicians who truly want to be in government need to understand the future and see what's coming, not only what's happening now, but what is yet to come. Toeffler wrote that forty years ago, and now the Chinese are doing it very well. Anyone who wants to be in government needs to get with the times and understand what the new paradigms are for society—including participatory democracy, not just electoral. Civil society needs to be more participatory. Freedom, diversity, plurality: freedom becomes very important. Competition, autonomy, human rights, ecology, looking after the environment, these are paradigms that are radically different than what societies used to focus on. In the past, they used to have slaves, there was social immobility. That's why the edicts were read out, because not many people were literate. The press was not very effective, because people were illiterate until the nineteenth century."

That was how Slim summed up many of the issues facing the world today. One he failed to mention was that of inequality.

31

Favela

Seen from afar, the tiny houses look like multicolored heather spreading wildly over the hills. When you get near, the "pacified" favelas of Rio de Janeiro are electrifyingly unpredictable, although TV dishes—red for Embratel and blue for Dish—have become a homogenizing element in those neighborhoods. I visited several of the favelas; according to the government of Brazil, these were now under the control of the state, which had seized control from the drug gangs. It was April 2012, and the most visible dispute taking place in those towering, low-income neighborhoods between the companies offering their cable TV, broadband Internet and landline services to a sector of the population that had remained isolated for years. Embratel had an army of salespeople combing the newly pacified favelas on foot in search of clients for their Mexican boss: Carlos Slim.

The pacification of the favelas was a euphemism for the police occupation that began prior to the World Cup 2014 and the 2016 Olympic Games. The police invasion was quickly followed by an invasion of salespeople vying to win over new customers who, despite being favela residents, are in many cases emerging out of poverty and consider cable TV as one of their basic needs. Embratel offered one of the best deals around: 100 television channels for $16 per month.

In Brazil, Slim offers the Triple Play service in ninety-three cities located across fourteen federative units. He also has a network of over 47,000 kilometers connecting around 10 million houses, over

50 percent of the cable television market in Brazil. The favelas of Rio de Janeiro are an emerging market in dispute.

Favelas are riotously alive with Arab-style alleys, cables, nests, and wheelbarrows transporting construction materials: cement, breeze blocks, wires. Vehicles speed up narrow roads that wind up around stairs upon stairs echoing with the sound of children coming out of school. I stop for a drink at Bar Cristal, run by Antonio and Joana, who've been married thirty-three years. Suddenly a street peddler comes in, flogging original Nike T-shirts. A man who works next to the police station is wearing a medallion of San Jorge. Football team flags flap about windows across the rows of houses balanced precariously on top of each other. Engine noises drown out the discussions of men with scars who are out with their kids. Motorbike riders sporting Jamaican flags file past, their dreads wet with the sweat of the coast. Walk down Rúa Presidente Joao Goulat (you could write a whole sound piece about this street alone) until you meet Avenida Niemayer, where you find the only entrance to this favela. Here you are rewarded with a view of the Leblon beach. The best in the city. Better than Ipanema and Copacabana.

Over the next few days, I visit several other favelas. First I drop by La Providencia. Researchers from an employers' association conducted a socioeconomic study of the favelas and demonstrated that there were was also a hierarchy between them, with distinct social classes. The southern favelas, near the touristy part of town, were wealthier than those in the center. In La Providencia, the per capita income is $439; in others such as Babilonia, near the famous Copacabana area, it's $630. Here Slim's salespeople share the territory with flip-flop clad pressure cooker hawkers trudging uphill among multifamily homes sprouting blue or red antennas since the arrival of the pacifying police. At number 275, Ana Paula Barbams tells me she doesn't have a cell phone or Internet, but she does have Embratel cable. She's watching channel 60, which is broadcasting a Hollywood film at four in the afternoon. At the start of her contract, she paid R$39.90, and three months later the fee went up to R$50. "They always do that," she says. On Rúa Uruguai I conduct the following census by snooping around windows or open doors:

at number 275, a woman is watching Embratel TV, at number 269, a woman peers through and it seems her TV is switched on (Sky antenna) while she's doing something else, maybe ironing; at number 265 there's a church "Assamblea de Deus," a three-story building painted lime green, where there is neither Sky antenna nor Embratel. Stray dogs, motorbikes, and young shirtless men glide by. There's also an altar to Saint George, the Rio de Janeiro saint, who killed dragons—and for that reason, the Vatican recently decided to push him off their list of saints. But Rome is far away and here Saint George is all around. Following along Rúa Uruguai, number 151 is a house in ruins facing a group of builders in blue jumpsuits digging up scree from blockaded, serpentine roads; number 165 is Hotfruit & Mercearia, a corner store where a kid uses an old wooden fruit crate as a vehicle, dragged around by his mom. On the street there's a stray white cat that the neighbors call Paper because it was very thin when it arrived.

Another of the new territories where Slim finds clients is called Babilonia. A mototaxi charges me two reales to get there. Babilonia is an urban development that includes newly built football and volleyball courts. At the neighbors' association there is a SKY-VIP ad. I head over, passing food stalls and workshops, a car mechanic, a solderer, car body shops, a tailor's. I spot a girl with a chili tattooed on her shoulder. Ana Beatriz: athlete of the future. Beatriz has very large hands; her kit is sponsored by Embratel. Nearby there's another favela called Chapeú Mangueira. After my arrival I see a red Budweiser truck drive past with the slogan: "Great times are on their way." The street is called Ari Barroso, after a football commentator. A hotdog seller who works in Chapeu tells me she still doesn't feel that the economy in her neighborhood is changing, despite the occupation of the pacifying police. "The good thing is there is no drug violence and that kids no longer have weapons, but there is still trafficking." Then I visit Edson Vander in his two-bedroom home, with a living room, kitchen and bathroom, which he rents for $700 a month. He tells me he previously didn't have Sky or Embratel but Gatonet—as they call the illegal connections that used to be the norm here. Since the police have arrived in the area, every week Sky and Embratel employees offer special deals for the favela. Edson is fed up with it, but he has taken up the offer from Slim's company. Before we talked, he had been concerned, watching the news on his TV about Idi Amin, the last male gorilla in captivity in South America, who had died at age thirty-eight in the zoo in Belo Horizonte due to kidney failure.

This transformation of Rio de Janeiro's favelas represents, beyond drug cartel disputes, the creation of new markets for telecommunications companies. And Slim is among those who are winning.

To carry out his Latin American expansion through América Móvil, Slim took advantage of the growth of the captive cellular telephony market in Mexico, which went from 8.3 million users in 2000 to 96.2 million in 2012. One of his main targets was Brazil, whose telecommunications market he entered in 1999 when he purchased the companies ATL, Americel, Tess Celular and Claro Digital, which he fused in 2003 under the brand Claro. He purchased Embratel one year later while obtaining control of the company Telecom in South America. In purchasing Embratel, the Mexican magnate acquired the biggest system of long distance and satellite services in Brazil, as well as the largest submarine cable system.

Over time, Slim would consolidate his telecom empire in Latin America thanks to his investments in Brazil. Omar Rodrigo Escamilla Haro gave the title "Corporate constellations and power alliances: Analysis of the company América Móvil in the Brazilian telecommunications market" to his master's degree thesis in sociology at the State University of Campinas, Brazil. According to the Brazilian researcher, the way in which Slim became a multimillionaire over such a short period of time is no different than the path followed by some of his contemporaries, such as Eike Batista in Brazil, Alisher Usmanov in Russia or Mukesh Ambani in India. All of them took advantage of privatizations of state public assets between 1980 and 2000, the period during which the main purpose of neoliberalism was to create national economies based on the flexibility of productive processes (work, logistics and transports, salaries) that aligned with the needs of global value chains.

The researcher, who forms a part of the NGO PODER, narrates

the maneuvers that finally consolidated Slim's dominance in Brazil and the rest of Latin America:

> In 2010, the shining star of his empire, América Móvil, became the largest telecommunications corporation in Latin America, with a base of 259.3 million clients, made up of 211.3 million subscribers in cellular telephony, 27.4 million in landlines, 12 million in broadband access, 8.6 million in television services.
>
> The way in which América Móvil achieved these numbers was through $25 billion in financial restructuring, which allowed it to fuse its assets with those of other telecom companies owned by Slim, including the two main mobile and landline telephony companies in Brazil: Claro and Embratel. Immediately after, the number of América Móvil shares circulating on the stock market increased by $32.1 billion to $40.5 billion (including preferential shares). With this move, América Móvil not only became a more compact company, but also a better capitalized one thanks to the presence of its new international partners, represented by investment funds and foreign private banks that went on to control 25.1 percent of its assets.
>
> Having recharged his batteries, in October, Slim purchased an important proportion of the share package of the Brazilian company Net Servicios, that included a client base (Internet, fixed telephony and cable television) of 9 million users. This made América Móvil the largest cable television company in Latin America, with an optic fiber network of 290,000 kilometers; that also made it the largest telecommunications infrastructure corporation in the world, according to the *Financial Times*. This way, Slim managed to balance the Brazilian market forces faced with the wave of mergers carried out by their competitors Telecom Italia and Telefónica de España.

In Escamilla Haro's opinion, Slim has used Brazil as a base for his continental expansion, in order to control over 50 percent of cable television in the country and make América Móvil one of the largest corporations in the world, as well as the dominant company in mobile telephony and cable television services in Latin America.

One of Slim's allies in Brazil during those years was José Dirceu, who in Luiz Ignacio "Lula" da Silva's government held the powerful role of chief of staff to the president, until he was forced to resign following allegations of corruption. In 2012, he was finally sentenced by the Supreme Court of Brazil, which found that Lula's right-hand man had paid a monthly sum to legislators of different parties to approve several initiatives brought forward by the Brazilian president.

Before being sentenced to ten years in jail, in an interview with the prominent magazine in *Piauí*, Dirceu confirmed that his firm, JD Asesoría y Consultoría, had worked for Slim. However, he clarified that his consultancy work for Slim referred to other Latin American countries: "Don Carlos, not here. We can work together, but outside Brazil," Dirceu claims he said to the magnate, who purchased different companies in Brazil while Dirceu was the second most important man to Lula, a former socialist who, throughout his government, pushed for something known in certain sectors as "a more human capitalism"—which Slim used to continue strengthening his empire.

32

Libre Empresa

The idea that we need to heavily privatize public enterprises is not new in the world and much less in the vision of Carlos Slim. In 1984, some thirty years before launching his proposal for privatizing airports and highways, as well as reducing the working week, Slim was part of a project which from afar could sound like fiction, or the result of a Cold War conspiracy theory that still held sway in the 1980s. But it was not. This is the story of how a group of Mexican millionaires decided to band together to take hold of all of Mexico's state-owned companies. To this end, they created a company with the name of Libre Empresa, S.A. (LESA).

There is an official document with minutes of a meeting held on April 5, 1984, between a group of Mexican businessmen. At the foot of this document are the words: "Document I, which has been sent to and has been made known to Mr. President Miguel de la Madrid." According to the text, participants included Carlos Slim Helú, Emilio Azcárraga Milmo—father of the current proprietor of Televisa—as well as the Mexican businessmen Antonio del Valle, Adolfo del Valle, Juan Mata, Carlos González Zabalegui, Guillermo González Nava, Antonio Madero, Carlos Autrey, Abel Vázquez Raña, José Luis Ballesteros, Juan Diego Gutiérrez Cortina, José Serrano, Juan Gallardo, Jaime Alverde, Roberto Servitje and Antonio Cosío.

According to the written record and the statements of two participants in that meeting, Azcárraga explained to the other businessmen that the federal government needed their help to consolidate a new strategy that would make the PRI's project viable. For that purpose, at the end of Azcárraga's speech, they agreed to create a stock corporation to which each would contribute, initially, 25 million pesos, which would be collected by Alejandro Sada, director of Televisa. They also agreed that the following meeting would be on April 10 at Televisa San Ángel and that each one should bring another three businessmen along.

Slim did not attend the following meeting, but he sent a representative and his support for the initiative, according to the document delivered to President de la Madrid. Azcárraga Milmo lead the meeting and assured them that a few hours earlier he had spoken to the president, who had told him that in his view it seemed positive "that a group from the free enterprise sector should collaborate to support the state in economic restructuring and aim to achieve financial stabilization as soon as possible." Azcárraga Milmo announced that, once the agreement was settled between the members of the corporation, President de la Madrid would meet them at the official Los Pinos residence, together with the designated secretaries of state to study the transfer of state-owned businesses to the private initiative. During the discussions, the participants negotiated that, in addition to providing 25 million pesos to LESA as initial capital, each would deliver 1 percent of their net annual sales, "as this is a demonstration from Mexican businesspeople who wish to support the Executive in establishing a true mixed economy system."

No euphemisms were used to name what this group of businessmen linked to the PRI regime intended to do that year. Their intentions were clear in the official document:

a) The objective of the corporation will be to acquire from the State all the companies it operates, except those which are property of the nationalized bank, and thus aid it in its responsibility, both in the economic and the social arenas.

b) The companies brought together by the stock corporation will be transferred in the shortest time possible to other corporations interested in them.

c) Companies or corporations deemed unfit to achieve their goals may change the nature of their business or disappear, attempting in this case for the productive force to be substituted by another equal one of recent creation.

For LESA to begin operations, Azcárraga asked the businessmen to deliver the money at their earliest convenience, because once the funds were obtained he would meet with President de la Madrid to inform him of the progress. Other agreements highlighted in the minutes are: "To make public our enthusiasm, faith and trust in the country and its institutions," as well as the decision that LESA would be a variable capital corporation, with an administration board presided over by a partner, on monthly rotation in alphabetic order based on surname.

This group of businessmen close to the PRI regime created another document and sent it to the then-minister of finance, Jesús Silva-Herzog.

With the trust that the government inspires in us and our firm belief in a mixed economic regime, a group of Mexican businessmen decided to form a company whose purpose will be to negotiate the purchase of all the companies operated by the State, with the exception of the nationalized bank. The objective is to aid the State in the sale of said companies, and aid the businessmen in purchasing them, under the fairest terms possible.

This company has now been legally constituted and is called Libre Empresa, S.A. de C.V. (LESA de C.V.).

This group of businessmen aims to grow its members by inviting all those wishing to participate in revitalizing the Mexican form of mixed economy, in order to strengthen Libre Empresa, S.A. de C.V. "LESA," with a capital and income based on a percentage of the sales of each one of the participating companies.

This will help achieve the above objective, which, in addition to strengthening the principle of the mixed economy system, enables the State to reassign to other national priorities the resources currently committed to operating these companies.

Libre Empresa, S.A. de C.V., "LESA" will be a variable capital corporation, which will act only as an intermediary, and must therefore be liquidated as soon as it has achieved its mission, which is, on the one hand, to purchase from the State all the companies operated by the State, and, on the other, to sell these companies to the interested Mexican companies.

We propose the creation of a mixed working group, operating for as long as necessary, divided in as many branches of activity as required, in order to carry out the operations as swiftly as possible.

The State may participate with the percentage of shares deemed appropriate, in order to make possible the realization of this objective.

Regardless of the possible opinion that the specific weight of our sector will not notably increase due to the fact of purchasing companies that are already functioning, and, furthermore, when some of them are operating in red numbers, the favorable decision of the State would provide a totally different perspective to our sector, which would doubtless have significant repercussions in the entrepreneurs' trust and decision to reactivate our investments as soon as possible.

However, LESA failed as a model under the pressure from different sectors of the PRI regime itself. It was not until the following presidential term, under Salinas de Gortari, that the process of selling off state-owned companies occurred. Without LESA as an intermediary, many businessmen participating in that delirious project, like Slim, would finally gain control of the main national companies.

The process was planned (as López Obrador suggests in his book) so as to provide it with a certain air of legality and transparency. Businessmen participating in bids or bank auctions, after losing, would immediately win in the following round. In the struggle for power over Telmex, participants included Slim and banker Roberto Hernández (who, seven months after his defeat purchased Banamex, the largest bank in the country). During the bid for the latter, the second place went to Carlos Gómez y Gómez, who later received Banco Mexicano Somex. Bancomer was transferred to Eugenio Garza Lagüera, Ricardo Guajardo Touche and Mario Laborín, and in second place came Adrián Sada González,

Guillermo Ballesteros and Gastón Luken Aguilar, who were given, three months later, Banca Serfín. Banco Internacional was given to José Antonio del Valle Ruiz, Eduardo Berrondo Ávalos and Agustón Villarreal, and those who occupied the second place in the tender, Hugo S. Villa Manzo and Luis Felipe Cervantes, received Banco del Centro one week later. When Multibanco Mercantil de México was given to businessmen José Madariaga Lomelín and Eugenio Clariond Reyes, the second place went to Ángel Rodríguez Sáez, who was later given Aseguradora Mexicana (Asemex). Banpaís, another of the main national banks, was given to businessmen Julio C. Villarreal Guajardo, Policarpo Elizondo Gutiérrez and Fernando P. del Real Ibáñez, while second place in the bid went to Jorge Lankenau Rocha and Enrique García Gámez—who were later given Banca Confía. And the list goes on.

This is how Mexico made way for the creation of a new economic class that in the 1990s entered the *Forbes* lists like never before. And in 2007, Slim, one of the participants of that project called LESA, would become the richest man in the world.

"The thing with LESA," says Slim in an interview, "is that back then the government said there were no buyers for privatization. So what we did was get a group of investors together to tell the government: 'There *are* buyers.' That was it. We went to talk to Silva Herzog and de la Madrid."

"Wasn't it a thinly veiled scheme for privatizing public companies?"

"No, it was a way of saying: look, there was a serious crisis with López Portillo, because he nationalized all the banks, they went to shit. The foreigners took their investments elsewhere, but there are Mexican buyers here and we are up for this. It was basically about sending that message to the government. What we proposed to the government was: there are investors, because after '81 I was the only buyer in Mexico. We Mexicanized five or six companies. So we went and said: 'If you want to sell the state-owned companies, there *are* buyers.' And they started to sell. Then Don Fidel Velázquez [leader of the largest labor union for more than fifty years] said that workers should only buy factories such as Bicicletas Cóndor and they had a very rough time. You did know that, right?

Then the government of Miguel de la Madrid started to privatize companies. It wasn't about buying all the state-owned companies."

"You have a saying about money and the politicians that I've heard you say at many public events: 'A businessman can do with one dollar what a politician cannot do with two or more.'"

"It's a definition that is used in engineering: an engineer is someone who does with one peso what someone who is not an engineer does with two."

"I have heard you use it to speak specifically about politicians."

"We could extend the same analogy from businessmen and non-businesspeople to, for example, in your case, a journalist or writer: hey, you do one page in five minutes, and I take one hour to do it and I do it worse than you do. People have talents, experience, vocations and abilities to do some things or to do others. Obviously, when it comes to investing efficiently, the job is best left to those who are specialized in that area instead of those who aren't."

X

33

Retirement

If we were to add up the donations of the richest Mexican in the world we might get the impression that he is a champion of philanthropy. However, with an accumulated fortune of $75 billion, Slim's scale of generosity seems mediocre when compared to that of other multimillionaires. With that kind of capital, he could pay the foreign debt of Lebanon twice over, and he could finance all its health research with what he earns in three weeks. It took him one week to earn the money he has given to Bill Clinton; the donation that Shakira received, smiling, for her foundation did not even take him a full day of his time. It's as if the limits of his generosity only went as far as the number of digits on his desktop calculator.

However, Slim is a complex character who does not fit into the stereotype of a mere miser. The reason he does not give away money is that he aspires to have his money continue to produce more money, with him at the center. Diego Fonseca considers him to be a "son of the lost school: that of the CEPAL [Economic Commission for Latin America and the Caribbean]." When he completed his undergraduate studies in civil engineering, Slim traveled to Santiago de Chile to complete a postgraduate degree in industrial programming at the Latin American and Caribbean Institute for Economic and Social Planning, a body created by a special UN fund. During that time he discovered and studied the ideas of Raúl Prebisch, an Argentinian economist whose advice to future businessmen was: "Before thinking, observe." The magnate was studying something that even today sounds strange and has been under-analyzed in its particularities: Latin American capitalism.

Slim, explains Diego Fonseca, "can be inscribed in the developmentalist school in the broadest sense: a businessman who was intellectually educated in the '60s, when the belief was that large Latin American bourgeoisies could be built as an autonomous model of development from the capitalism of central nations." And fifty years later, that's what happened. The businessman has spearheaded a Latin American capitalism that in the 1960s seemed very remote.

The Chilean teachings that Slim received during that decade seem key to understanding his way of doing business now. Fonseca explains:

> What Slim did with the businessman who offered to make a photography book for Christmas is very typical of him: purchasing opportunity. He has the capital and the other has a debt (he did a job without checking the price first, and has commitments with the providers who did the work for him). Slim took advantage of the other's lack of preparation (not checking the price first) and submitted him to an education that could be called "current net value": either you get nothing, or at least you take this. It's harsh, it's tough, but the other guy should have done his homework. Maybe he was after some sort of patronage; but Slim was doing business.

In the midst of Carlos Slim's philanthropic vision, special cases appear, such as that of former president José López Portillo, a Mexican lawyer fascinated with Quetzalcóatl, the Aztec god represented by the plumed serpent, about which he set out to write a literary saga that never got beyond the first volume. In the mid-1970s, López Portillo had to abandon his literary ambitions and govern Mexico during the PRI regime, where the norm was for the president in power to name his successor and organize fictitious elections in which even the deceased voted for the official party. In the 1990s, when he was no longer in office and wandered like a soul in torment, in the exile to which fallen emperors of the PRI regime were condemned, López Portillo contacted Slim to ask for help: he wanted to write a book. He had divorced the concert pianist Carmen Romano, his wife of many years, to marry Sasha Montenegro, a vedette of Yugoslavian descent who left him in severe financial straits after a tumultuous divorce. The philanthropist Slim, together with his partner Juan Antonio Pérez Simón, gave him money each month so he could dedicate himself to writing. Feeling in debt, the former president, who in his glory days used to travel abroad with his wife's grand piano, hand-wrote thank you notes addressed to Slim or to Pérez Simón, such as this one, which he sent to him in the '90s:

> Once again and ahead of time I have received 50,000 new pesos that you agreed (with Don Carlos Slim and at your request) to give me monthly, which you have done very punctually. Nothing in exchange have I done or said. I have waited for the call willing to give my efforts in return and nothing. And although this amount has afforded me tranquility to write my "Dinámica política de México," I feel indebted to you. Remember that I am a lawyer and that I was not bad at my job, and I possess the ability to give an opinion on any matter, except fiscal, due to the deformation in my knowledge that the Ministry of Finance left in me, when I was its director. I can give talks, which I would not dare to call conferences, on multiple subjects, for any audience you choose and with the frequency that you deem useful. [Two illegible words] I feel (at my age, and in my condition!) like an intern of sorts! With a hug for you and Don Carlos and my respects to your families, reiterated by your grateful friend.

In another one of his letters, López Portillo says he is embarrassed to contaminate the friendship by asking for money to spend his last days. There are no stories about Slim taking the calculator out each time this ill and aging former president needed help to pay for his treatment in Cuban hospitals. The richest Mexican in the world did not haggle over López Portillo's book project, which was perhaps wilder than that of the businessman who, in the middle of a charity event, supposedly proposed to make a book to give away for Christmas and who forced Slim to pull out pen and paper to make calculations and haggle down to the last cent. It didn't seem to matter that the book that the former president of Mexico wrote under Slim's patronage was a terrible investment for him. Only Slim knows why he gave away money each month in exchange for such an uncertain project with which the former president justified the help of the magnate after his retirement. One afternoon I found the book by chance in a magazine shop in the airport next to other remaindered books. It cost me one dollar. It cost the richest Mexican in the world a great deal more. Or maybe it didn't.

I asked Slim what his main objective was as a businessman, after he had celebrated his seventy-fifth birthday in January 2015.

"My main objective is to develop human capital in the Carlos Slim Foundation, with health, education, culture, nutrition. To start the program with prenatal care for mothers onward... And to contribute our grain of salt to see an end to underdevelopment. Mexico and Latin America already have an income of around $10,000 per capita. What they need is more consistent growth and a better provision of income. The only way to combat poverty is to develop more human capital. That is, for people to have more education and training, not academic, but in general so they have more to offer to the labor market. That is, rather than being trained just in manual labor, that you are trained in two or three or five different activities. And, the better the training, the easier it is to find work and the better paid you are. To that end, it's very important that there's a lot of investment, that you generate economic activity, and for that economic activity to generate employment, allowing nations to work their way out of underdevelopment. Now, the whole thing about poverty in our countries is not only a social, ethical, moral problem—it's also an economic problem. The fact that people are in poverty without education, with bad health, and without employment, is bad for the economy. So, based on being able to educate everyone, train everyone, be better and generate sources of employment... The only way to get out of poverty is through employment. So, in the end, we are looking for economic activity."

"What you're describing can be fostered through your foundations and companies, although you also need political allies."

"Let's see... look: it's two different things. On the one hand, there's the role of the foundations: the foundations are not going to give employment. The foundations can help improve health, improve nutrition; to improve people's quality of life, to improve their education, to help people do more sport; all the activities we carry out in relation to social justice, scholarships... All that is very important, it's one of the necessary and convenient conditions, but it's not sufficient for us to be able to access development. The foundations' activities obviously don't happen in a void. We give scholarships to young people at all the universities, and in the health institutions, but the massive part is the use of technology for education and for work training, and in that arena we've made agreements with the Khan Academy, with Coursera. The Khan Academy is for elementary education, Coursera is for higher education, and we have created programs for professional training."

"Technical training like plumbing?"

"Yes, or information technology. It's twenty-minute courses and, well, in this digital village, I think we'll do the next one in July, because 258,000 people took this one (a Guinness world record). In reality it was a bit more than that. And there you will not only see or browse or learn to use the computer, but there are different classrooms or areas, or spaces where they are taught to use the Khan Academy or Coursera, or matters of business activity. That's where we launched courses for professional development. We have the platform and we develop the platforms.

"This is regarding the aspect of developing human capital. The other is to generate jobs. So, with me on the boards and in the new companies we are in, in which I am personally, working directly." ("Can you pass me a Pact of Chapultepec?" he says to an assistant.) "Do you know it? So, we've gotten into some activities that when we came in had not been sufficiently developed to generate employment."

In an article written by Slim that was published in the magazine *Contenido*, the magnate, in addition to highlighting the work scheme of his mining company, Frisco, he talks about another of his priorities at his seventy-five years of age: "In the case of telecommunications we continue to invest because we know that it is the nervous system of the new civilization and that if Telmex does not make those investments, nobody will—not foreigners, and not nationals. Without that infrastructure, Mexico is in bad shape: it's worse than not having highways."

In 2014, Frisco produced the equivalent of 12,000 kilograms of gold, 13 percent of the national production that year, which was sold to entities such as Bank of Nova Scotia, Dutch company Trafigura Beheer BV, Italian Metagri and Japanese Asahi Refining. But in the first months of 2015, Frisco lost 34 percent of its value.

When I asked Fructuoso Pérez García, Slim's friend, whether he believed that Telmex was the company in his portfolio to which Slim felt most attached, he replied that it wasn't and told me he believed that in reality it was the several companies created by the magnate to participate in the ongoing privatization of the Mexican oil industry.

"The building company Ideal was recently created. Swecomex is a company that he purchased and they want it for Pemex work right now, essentially, right?"

"How do you see the future for Slim? Will he get more involved in the businesses or start to take it easy?" I ask Fructuoso.

"Well, it's not that he gets more involved, it's that he already is involved. So he has a mindset of constant creativity and he keeps his eyes open. Imagine how many people must make business proposals and so many things that at any time might seem interesting to him… because of what he has, and what he could do. On the other hand, well, there are his children, they're qualified and things are going well for them. The day that Carlos wants to retire, he already has a very important family organization."

"Beyond his sons and sons-in-law, are other family members involved?"

"Carlos tells me that one of his sisters was extremely intelligent and that his nephew, Alfonso Salem Slim, is one of the people who is very involved with Carlos, in the area of construction; he's a civil engineer. And, well, Héctor Slim is the director of Telmex. Now Telmex was divided into Telmex International and national Telmex, and Héctor is national director of Telmex. Héctor is Julián's son. And Julián has another son, Beto Slim, who manages other things, among them the Calinda hotels."

"But those are in partnership with Ignacio Cobo, right?"

"Nacho is involved in that too, and I believe he is the president of the group, or something like that in Calinda, but Beto is also in a managerial position there with Nacho. Anyway, the family has always played an important part in business."

"Is that the Lebanese way, more or less?"

"Well, that I don't know, but I imagine so because the Lebanese people I know, that's what they're like, very family-oriented. I remember when we were at school sometimes Carlos said during the holidays, 'Does anyone feel like working? We can go to work with my dad at La Merced.' And he would go with his dad, to do whatever, carry boxes or whatever. So they're a very close family, around business and everything. They never stop working. I don't see Carlos retiring."

34

Sophia

At age seventy-five, Carlos Slim saw a slowdown in his incessant accumulation of capital. The amount he lost in the summer of 2015, $14.9 billion, is equivalent to the cost of seven Empire State Buildings in New York. According to the financial agency Bloomberg, this was due in part to the fact that América Móvil, Slim's main telecom company, had to change its prices and products ahead of the new entry of AT&T into the Mexican market, which occurred within the framework of the telecommunications reform. The other factor that caused the reduction of Slim's fortune was that Minera Frisco's value dropped 55.7 percent due to the fall in the price of gold internationally.

But the enthusiasm at the heart of Slim's consortium did not seem to wane and an emphasis was placed on diversifying the businesses in which he participates. An internal document, in which works of construction, innovation and investment are mentioned, highlighted that in recent years Grupo Carso has built more than 6 million square meters in commercial and real estate projects in different locations around Mexico. It also mentions the construction of Line 12 of the Metro in Mexico City; the administration, via concession, of 1,267,000 kilometers of highways and the treatment of 60 percent of the Valley of Mexico's wastewater at a plant in Hidalgo.

One of the most important works highlighted in the report is the construction of a 17,400-kilometer long submarine cable that follows the coast of the American continent through eleven points of contact: Jacksonville and Miami, United States; Cancun, Mexico; Puerto Barrios, Guatemala; Puerto Plata, Dominican Republic; San Juan, Puerto Rico; Barranquilla and Cartagena, Colombia; Fortaleza, El Salvador; and Rio de Janeiro, Brazil. This is along with Independencia I, Mexico's first self-elevating (jackup) oil rig, which is being used to drill several wells over nine kilometers deep in the Gulf of Mexico.

Another stand-out project is that of Bordo de Xochiaca, which for thirty years was a landfill site for around 20 million people who live in Mexico City and surrounding areas. The site was closed down in 2006 and Grupo Carso invested during the two following years in the construction of a community development of around 1,200,000 square meters, which includes a hospital, a shopping center, an Olympic stadium, a cycling track, two gyms and fifty-seven courts for practicing different kinds of sports.

Around 350,000 square meters of lawns were grown in the area, with which Slim turned an urban landfill into a development now called Ciudad Jardín (Garden City).

As for the revitalization projects, another one that stands out is that of a state in the south of Mexico. "In the state of Guerrero—the document explains—the governor invited Mr. Carlos Slim Helú to participate in a rescue plan for Acapulco, having seen the success of the project in the historical center of Mexico City, adapting this model for its application in this important and emblematic tourism destination."

The "traditional Acapulco restoration project" is the official name of this initiative launched by former governor Ángel Aguirre. It was through this project that Slim met Sophia Loren, one of the most important actors of the twentieth century, with whom the magnate developed a special and public relationship, in the midst of the economic turbulences that his empire has suffered in recent years. His friendship with Loren immediately captivated the press, which had previously speculated about his status as a billionaire widower, connecting him to the Mexican actress Blanca Guerra and Queen Noor of Jordan.

Aguirre, a PRI politician who switched to the center-left PRD and was elected governor of the state of Guerrero, decided to stimulate the regeneration of the famous port of Acapulco after several years of deterioration caused by drug cartel violence. Hosting an international film festival that would welcome internationally famous actors and directors became one his main objectives. The name of Sophia Loren was immediately mentioned and a special team of the governor's began long negotiations with representatives of the legendary Italian actor, who lives in Geneva, Switzerland. In addition to paying a seven-figure sum not yet officially disclosed, the governor's team had to charter a special flight so that Loren would not have a stopover in Mexico City and could arrive directly from Europe to Acapulco.

"Although she has the status of a diva, Sophia Loren behaved extremely professionally during her whole stay in Acapulco. She arrived on time to all the events and fulfilled all her agreements," says one of the people who coordinated the actor's visit to Guerrero. According to this source, the only awkward moment was during an interview with Adela Micha, one of the most important TV journalists in the country, who asked Loren some questions she did not approve of:

"You were so admired, so desired by all kinds of men, were you never tempted?" Micha asked at some point.

"You make me blush," Loren replied.

"Seriously? I don't think so! Are you shy, Sofía?"

"I'm so shy that I couldn't even begin to tell you how shy I am. This interview is making me feel embarrassed."

"Please don't say that. Why?"

"Because you're delving into my feelings, inside me, and sometimes it's difficult to reply naturally regarding things you've kept inside for a long time."

"What have you done to maintain your status as a great diva? Has that always been important to you?"

"I don't even know if I'm a great diva. I don't know."

"You know you are."

"No, I don't. I don't play with that sort of thing, ever."

The interview ended on a more cordial note, with Loren making a joke about the journalist's high heels. "Careful, don't fall. Your heels are like sky scrapers," she said.

It was the night of November 18, 2011, during the inaugural dinner of the Acapulco International Film Festival, when Slim finally met Loren, an actor he had admired since he was young. Governor Aguirre was in the center of the main table, flanked on one side by his wife and on the other by Loren. By orders of the governor, Slim was seated next to Loren, and he focused his attention on her, scarcely interacting with the other guests: the French actor Alain Delon, the Mexican actress Cecilia Suárez and his friend, business-man Miguel Alemán Velasco.

"There was a very interesting moment at that dinner party," says one of the event organizers. "Halfway through the meal on the beach, against all weather reports, it started raining and nobody knew what to do, but she [Sophia Loren], without looking away from her plate, put the napkin on her head and continued eating. The menu that was served included tamales with salsa verde, cucumber and jicama cold soup, and shrimp in tamarind and mango sauce. I think this gesture made a very deep impression on Slim."

At the end of the dinner, the businessman asked to be photo-graphed with Loren, and then they went on a stroll on the beach together and talked about *El Cid*, a film directed by Anthony Mann, in which Loren stars alongside Charlton Heston and Jon Fraser. According to what Loren said later, Slim told her that the film based on the life of the Spanish warrior Rodrigo Díaz de Vivar was one of his favorites. *El Cid* premiered in Mexico at the Diana cinema, in October 1963, the same year the magnate submitted his university thesis. While Slim was just graduating as a civil engineer, Loren was already an internationally acclaimed star.

Slim seemed to enjoy the Acapulco International Film Festival like few others. Over the following days he was seen next to Sylvester Stallone, with whom he was photographed simulating a boxing match.

However, his most meaningful encounter was the one he had with Loren. According to the governor's team, the Italian actress asked for Slim's phone number, but she did not call him for several weeks, until the businessman asked for her number to contact her. Then, one year later, Slim traveled to Geneva to see her. Their encoun-ter was made public, as they attended together a dinner in honor of Loren's late husband, film producer Carlo Ponti. Slim would later visit Geneva accompanied by some of his children, with the purpose of introducing his family to Loren and formally inviting her to celebrate her eightieth birthday in Mexico.

Our country is the scene of many tales from Loren's life: Carlo Ponti, her partner from age nineteen, was married and under Italian law at the time he could not get divorced, although he had the consent of his wife, Giuliana Fiastri. Ponti decided to take advantage of Mexican legal loopholes to get a fast-track divorce and marry Loren immediately in 1957.

According to the biography *Sofía: Vivir y amar* (*Sophia: Living and Loving*), by Aaron Edward Hotchner:

> Two Mexican lawyers had presented themselves before the court of Ciudad Juárez, and within 10 minutes had performed a couple of legal miracles: in the first place, they had secured a decree that, officially, divorced Carlo of his wife, and immediately afterwards, with a lawyer representing Loren and another Carlo, they had exchanged their wedding vows, in a proxy ceremony, held before the judge. A certificate had been issued. Now Sofía Scicolone (Loren's birth name), of Pozzuoli, was officially and finally married to Carlo Ponti, born in Milan. It was not the wedding Sophia Loren had dreamt of: "Two lawyers, more than a thousand kilometers away, pretending they were Carlo and me. But it was legal. That's what mattered."

The Italian actress accepted Slim's invitation. Loren arrived to Mexico on September 18, 2014, to participate in a series of events coordinated discreetly by Roberto Slim Seade, Slim's nephew. That day he gave a press conference and inaugurated an exhibition dedicated to her at the Museo Soumaya. Although it was speculated that the event might be attended by President Peña Nieto, instead the president of the Mexican arts council, Conaculta, Rafael Tovar y de Teresa, came on his behalf to cut the inaugural ribbon together with Slim, Loren and her children, Carlo and Edoardo.

The journalist Laura Manzo, who as well as knowing and following Slim's family very closely for several years, interviewed

Loren at that time and described their relationship thus in the magazine *Quién*:

> Carlos Slim reached out his hand and stroked Sophia's leg when she shed a tear during the press conference, the first day of her visit to Mexico. Slim held her arm the whole time, and looked after her like a gentleman. The affection and closeness between them was evident at all times. Glances, smiles, caresses, gestures and codes that only they could know and decipher. Sophia Loren, the woman of astonishing beauty, and Carlos Slim, the richest man in the world, have a special connection. And it makes sense.

The following day, Loren inaugurated a film festival in her honor at the Cineteca Nacional, where she was also awarded the Ariel de Oro, the most important award given by the Mexican Academy of Film Arts and Sciences. "I will take it with me to Switzerland," she said in her speech, "and I will put it in my library between my two Oscars because I consider it a very important award, given the love you are showing me. That way, every morning, when I wake up and I walk down the hallway to the library, I will think about you."

On September 20, Loren's eightieth birthday, Slim organized a red-carpet gala event at Museo Soumaya, with the presence of celebrities such as Andy García, Larry King, Forest Whitaker and Jon Voight. Edoardo Ponti, one of Loren's children, spoke during the event. He started his speech by saying: "I would like to take advantage of this opportunity to thank, on behalf of my brother and myself, Mr. Carlos Slim and his family. It is thanks to your great enthusiasm, your tireless energy and your close friendship with my mother that we are here tonight."

The actor also gave a short speech that night:

> When you're twenty years old, you never imagine that one day you'll be eighty. But when you are, you still can't believe it. This year in particular many people have reminded me of the legacy I have left in the world of cinema; but the truth is that my legacy does not compare with the indelible marks and memories left in my heart by all those who accompanied me in that journey.

One of the few advantages of growing old is that you realize what is truly important in life: the delicate simplicity of an act of tenderness, the strength that friends give you in your hour of need, and the value of love are the only things that bring you serenity and a true sense of triumph.

Fame and success, like fireworks, can temporarily overwhelm our vision but that satisfaction lasts only for a moment. It's the small and silent things that stay with you for the rest of your life and define who you are.

The quiet certainty of having built a solid family whose members love each other unconditionally.

The quiet certainty of knowing that I lived my life with honesty and integrity.

The quiet certainty that even now life brings us surprises and that each morning I get up with the desire to explore more, to learn, to share…

Here I am before you, my family and friends, honored and deeply moved to be able to share this unforgettable moment with all of you.

A moment that would not have come about without the tireless passion of a man with an inimitable dedication to the arts and commitment toward life, my dearest friend, Carlos Slim. Thank you, Carlos.

The next day, the head of the government of Mexico City, Miguel Mancera, named Loren the "distinguished guest" of the capital of the country and presented her with an award called "Alas de la Ciudad" ("Wings of the City"). Finally, the actor's celebrations concluded with a concert in her honor, directed by her son, conductor Carlo Ponti, who led the Orquesta Sinfónica de Minería.

"What do you value the most about your relationship with Slim?" the journalist Laura Manzo asked Loren during those days.

"He's a great man, very sensitive. He's a great friend and has very good manners. He's unlike anyone else, he's unique."

The last time I saw Slim, when I was saying goodbye, the businessman took out of his library a copy of *Sophia: Ayer, hoy y mañana* (*Sophia: Yesterday, Today, and Tomorrow*), Loren's memoirs published in a special edition promoted by Grupo Carso, signed by the actor. Unlike the explanations that accompanied the other books he gifted me, on this occasion, after giving me his friend's autobiography, the magnate simply smiled happily.

35

Failure

At the start of his government, on December 1, 2012, President Peña Nieto promised to lead a "modernizing" process under the slogan "Mover a México" which was translated for international marketing purposes as the "Mexican Moment." For many critics and citizens, the style of acting and communicating was inevitably reminiscent of the government of Carlos Salinas de Gortari. As in that presidential period, where controversial legislative reforms and ambitious infrastructure projects were carried out, Peña Nieto's administration succeeded, from the start, in persuading Congress to make fifty-four changes to the Constitution in a record period of one year. Educational and fiscal reforms were approved, along with an important energy reform that opened the exploration, production and commercialization of gas and oil to private investment —which Slim was preparing to participate in through his company Carso Energy.

In parallel, multimillion-dollar bids were also underway for infrastructure works, such as the Los Ramones gas pipeline, the new International Airport of Mexico City and the fast train to the capital.

However, the latter bidding process, for over $40 billion, was canceled at the end of 2014 after a scandal that exposed the influence of trafficking and corruption around the assignment of the contract. Juan Armando Hinojosa, an unknown Tamaulipas businessman who was a favorite of Peña Nieto's government, became, together with a brother-in-law of former president Salinas de

Gortari and a Chinese company, the beneficiary by direct adjudication of the works that would link Mexico City with the nearby burgeoning industrial city of Querétaro.

An investigation led by journalist Carmen Aristegui proved that Grupo Higa—the name of the Hinojosa Cantú's company—had given Angélica Rivera, wife of Peña Nieto, a mansion under an exceptional loan scheme. The revelation prompted the First Lady to issue a television statement in which she claimed that during her career as an actor in Televisa soap operas she had accumulated a fortune of over 100 million pesos, although she also announced that to avoid further criticism she would sell the property granted by Grupo Higa. Her claims prompted several Hollywood actors such as Rob Schneider to joke about moving to Mexico to work in TV dramas, since the pay there was far better. It also resulted in the radio station MVS firing Carmen Aristegui and her research team, whose members Daniel Lizárraga, Irving Huerta, Rafael Cabrera and Sebastián Barragán wrote the report.

This uncovering of influence peddling in the midst of the country's "modernizing" process took place precisely when the Peña Nieto administration was dealing, also erratically, with the disappearance of forty-three students from the Ayotzinapa Rural Teachers' College who were attacked and arrested by Guerrero police while preparing for a protest. Federal authorities made little effort to find the young men, who were born in one of the poorest regions in Mexico and were students at an educational institution with a long left-wing tradition, twelve days after their kidnapping by agents of the state. To date, only two of the forty-three students' remains have been found. Their forced disappearance attracted international attention to the human rights crisis that Mexico has been suffering since 2006, when it was demonstrated in different parts of the country that the political alternation achieved in 2000—the year in which a non-PRI presidential candidate was elected—did not necessarily imply the consolidation of a democratic transition. Authoritarianism, corruption and mafia connections in politics, which prevailed under the new rules of alternation, meant that between 2006 and 2014, more than 100,000 people were killed in acts of extreme violence, around 40,000 were forcibly disappeared, and thousands of cases of torture and illegal arrests, as well as other human rights violations, were never brought to justice.

A couple of years before the disappearance of their forty-three classmates, the students of Ayotzinapa had already been victims of this systematic repression. In December 2011, the governor of the state of Guerrero, Ángel Aguirre—with the support of the PRD, Convergencia, PT, PAN and the leader of the electoral left, Andrés Manuel López Obrador—ordered a police operation to repress a student protest. Two Ayotzinapa students were shot dead. Other protesters were threatened, jailed and also killed. In the aftermath, the governor dismissed a couple of police functionaries, who he later reinstated.

However, in March 2012, Aguirre received public support from Carlos Slim. The richest Mexican in the world was photographed, smiling, next to the governor.

Following in the steps of López Obrador, who made an alliance with Slim on the investment in the historical center of Mexico City during his period as governor of the Federal District, Aguirre secured a deal for the historical center of the port of Acapulco. In this way, Slim backed a repressive administration that turned a blind eye to the operations of mafia groups embedded in politics, which ultimately resulted in the disappearance of the forty-three students on September 26, 2014. The richest Mexican in the world has never made any statements or publicly condemned the tragedy. This was the prevailing political and social situation in Mexico and it intensified in January 2015, the month of Slim's seventy-fifth birthday.

How many new Mexican millionaires will emerge with the approved energy reforms that have put invaluable natural resources up for sale? Why should a small group of businessmen with good connections with the party in power be once again the main beneficiaries of the Mexican Moment, which, from the perspective of Ayotzinapa, was a far from glorious one? And for someone who has successfully amassed an enormous fortune, what is the moral responsibility toward a country wounded by corruption and a deadly war? These questions were perhaps on the minds of many during the birthday of the richest Mexican in the world. The success of a few should not be at the expense of the failure of an entire country.

"In August 2014, forty-three students from Ayotzinapa were forcibly disappeared. My question is not only what your opinion is on this event, but also why you have never made any public pronouncements on an issue that is so dramatic for the country," I say to Slim.

"Yes, this thing with the forty-three students is very dramatic, but what's even more dramatic is what's happening with thousands of others. Those forty-three are spoken about because they have names, but the others also deserve visibility. They are each people with a name and a surname."

"I'm trying to understand why a businessman as important as you makes no statement about these kinds of serious issues."

"Well, I can't keep making statements…"

"Businesspeople in other countries do when social upheavals such as this one occur."

"That is not the most serious part. The serious part is what is happening in the sense that it's thousands of people who are dying, not just forty-three, unfortunately. Then what we have to look for is for these things to be resolved with more intelligence and politics, and less violence."

"In Guerrero, in 2011, two Ayotzinapa students were killed at a protest and on that occasion governor Ángel Aguirre almost had to step down. He did not, but the Attorney General did and there was a political crisis; then suddenly the governor comes out with you at a public event and photographs are taken and distributed to the press."

"No, I think that's when we launched a digital classroom, wasn't it?"

"Yes, but it was precisely at a time when he was in the midst of a tremendous crisis, and appearing next to the richest man in the world helps—"

"We have to do what we have to do, regardless of what is going on around us. I don't know if I told you last time, and it has to do with Ayotzinapa and with everything that is going on: when Mexico is not united and when there's more conflict, there are more bad people. So what we need to do, and I hope this project contributes towards this, is to leave behind this lack of union and these violent confrontations, which are not going to lead the country to anything good. We spoke before about 1821 and José Iturriaga's book. So what we need to do is to avoid internal political and social confrontation. And above all avoid violence."

Acknowledgements

Over the years while writing this book, I received advice on complex subjects such as finance, telecommunications and politics. I want to point out one person in particular, who unfortunately passed away before this project was completed: journalist Miguel Ángel Granados Chapa, who provided information, suggestions and tricks of the trade. Another person who was fundamental in this process also passed away: Conrado Osorno, an uncle who used to give me books by Og Mandino when I was a teenager. My uncle Conrado was a fierce critic of Carlos Slim in the 90s, due to the way in which he acquired Telmex; however, like many Mexicans, in recent years he had changed his views on the magnate and even saw him as an exemplary Mexican in many ways. His incessant questioning and perceptions helped me not to forget this perspective with which Slim is now often viewed in Mexico.

Likewise, my thanks are due to Julio Villanueva Chang, editor of Peruvian magazine *Etiqueta Negra*, with whom I worked extensively on the profile of "The Mecaenas who uses a calculator," which served as the basis for this book, and to *Proceso* magazine for the International Journalism Award that was given to me in 2011 for my story on Julián Slim Helú, which is also a part of this book. The jurors were Jon Lee Anderson, Juan Villoro, Alma Guillermo Prieto, Vicente Leñero and Rafael Rodríguez Castañeda.

At age fifteen, I read *Los periodistas*, by Vicente Leñero, and *La guerra de galio*, by Héctor Aguilar Camín, two works of fiction about the government of Luis Echeverría's coup on the newspaper *Excélsior*, directed by a journalist called Julio Scherer, in the seventies.

In the same way as some teenagers, thanks to their earliest readings, are marked by classic heroes such as Tom Sawyer or Marco Polo, I was marked by the discovery of an excellent journalist who faced censorship during a time that is now legendary in the recent history of Mexico, when *Proceso* was created. I became a voracious reader of don Julio Scherer. There was nothing he wrote that I didn't read ipso facto. I devoured his books and even carried them around with me everywhere I went as an existential compass of sorts. In my first tasks as a reporter and to this day, when I'm faced with important dilemmas, I often ask myself inwardly what Scherer would do in that situation.

Something that always amazed me of don Julio—who I was lucky enough to meet in person—was the way he connected with the high centers of power, that Spartan determination with which the director of *Proceso* used to tell the truth to powerful figures. While working on this book, I thought a lot about this valuable aspect of his, because sometimes I became tired and felt I should abandon the project of writing about such a powerful man and focus instead on writing again about stories focusing on marginality. However, the legendary heroes we forge in our adolescence are destined to remain in our dreams. They remain as gods that accompany our pagan and quotidian life and, suddenly, manifest: that November in 2011 when I received from his hands the award on the thirty-fifth anniversary of *Proceso* was one of the happiest moments of my life, and it gave me the encouragement I needed to complete this book.

Thanks to Issa Goraieb, Raymundo Pérez Arellano and Adriana Esthela Flores, bastions during my trip to Beirut.

In New York, Francisco Goldman, Jon Lee Anderson, Rocío Cavazos, Michelle García and David Sullivan (RIP).

In Mexico City, Batsheva Faitelson, José Martínez, Alejandro Rodríguez, Federico Arreola, Guillermo Osorno, Jesús Rangel, Carolina Enríquez, Fabrizio Prada, Emiliano Monge, John Gibler, Fabrizio Mejía, Froylán Enciso and Juan Villoro. Also, for their fraternity and support, my friends Alicia Cárdenas, Alejandro Almazán, Alejandro Sánchez, Manuel Larios, Neldi Sanmartín, Juan Carlos Reyna y José Luis Valencia.

In Monterrey, César Cantú, Jessica Guerrero, Guillermo Martínez Berlanga, Karem Nerio and Abraham Nuncio.

For certain specific sections, I received help from Diego Fonseca, Elda Cantú, Emma Friedland, Ely Treviño, Fernando Montiel, Miguel Ángel Vargas, Gabriela Pollit and Gustavo Guzmán. At different times I also received special help from Melissa del Pozo, Lucía Paola Olivares, Ana Lucía Heredia, Jorge Hernández and Sarasuadi Vargas.

Special thanks are due to the editorial team composed by Cynthia Chávez, Aurora Higuera, Enrique Calderón, Cristóbal Pera and Andrés Ramírez.

Lastly, thanks, more than anyone, to my whole beloved family.